The Encyclopaedia of Guilty Pleasures

The Encyclopaedia of

Guilty
Pleasures

1,001 Things You Hate to Love

By Michael Moran, Tom Bromley, Simon Trewin,
Sam Stall, Lou Harry and Julia Spalding

JOHN MURRAY

© Michael Moran, Tom Bromley, Simon Trewin and Quirk Productions, Inc.

First published in the United States of America in 2004 by Quirk Books

First published in Great Britain in 2006 by John Murray (Publishers)
A division of Hodder Headline

The right of Michael Moran, Tom Bromley, Simon Trewin and
Quirk Productions, Inc. to be identified as the Authors of the Work has
been asserted by them in accordance with the Copyright, Designs and
Patents Act 1988.

1

A CIP catalogue record for this title is available from the British Library

ISBN-13 978-0-7195-6138-2
ISBN-10 0-7195-6138-8

Typeset by Palimpsest Book Production Ltd, Grangemouth, Stirlingshire

Printed and bound by Clays Ltd, St Ives plc

Illustrations by Kevin Sprouls

Hodder Headline policy is to use papers that are natural, renewable and
recyclable products and made from wood grown in sustainable forests.
The logging and manufacturing processes are expected to conform to the
environmental regulations of the country of origin.

John Murray (Publishers)
338 Euston Road
London NW1 3BH

Introduction

In 2003 the boy band Blue scored yet another of their huge chart hits with the aching ballad 'Guilty'. Co-written with Gary Barlow, the group turned in time-honoured fashion to the legal system for the song's metaphorical motif. 'If loving you is a crime,' sang one of the ones who isn't Duncan, 'then I'm guilty.'

We're not completely certain that Blue were singing about Pot Noodles, but for the purposes of this introduction, let's assume that they were. Pot Noodles, along with the other 1,000 entries that make up this book, are one of life's guilty pleasures – those guilt-edged activities for whom the fashion police have enforced their policy of zero tolerance. Things like *The Da Vinci Code*. Chicken Nuggets. Laurence Llewelyn-Bowen.

For too long now, people have felt unable to acknowledge their enjoyment of such activities in public. For too long has our culture of sneer kept our enjoyment behind closed doors. Well no longer. This book is the first step down the rocky road towards cultural rehabilitation. The 1,001 entries contained within are proof of what we all hoped was true. That there are people out there like us. That there are people with equally appalling lapses in taste and judgement. And maybe, just maybe, this knowledge will give us the confidence to step outside, to look people in the eye and paraphrase Blue's bugger-the-consequences statement of intent: if loving *Deal or No Deal* is a crime, then, god-damn it, we're guilty.

So good that they're bad. So bad that they're good. Pleasure seekers of the world unite: you have nothing to lose but your embarrassment . . .

Please share your guilt at www.1001guiltypleasures.com

A.O.R.

What does the 'A' stand for in A.O.R.? Is it Adult Oriented Rock, American Oriented Rock or Awful Oriented Rock? Recent research by the Musical Faculty of the Lower Californian Institute has suggested that it is in fact a mixture of all three. Ostensibly an excuse for middle-aged, middle-management Americans to wig out, A.O.R. is in fact one of the most intriguing sub-genres of modern music, built on a curious paradox of rock guitar shapes and soppy lyrics. Think Boston's 'More Than A Feeling' or Chicago's 'Hard Habit To Break'. The collected work of Toto, Foreigner and Journey. In recent years, a number of these artists have turned up under a new and somewhat disputable classification: classic rock. A Trade Descriptions Act case is still pending on this.

Aaronovitch, David

There was a time when David Aaronovitch used to write a column in the *Guardian* and the *Observer* that seemed singularly designed to make sandal-wearing beardies choke on their morning muesli. Aaronovitch's political position was the one stance that would really wind up the lefties: he was New Labour to the core, famously sticking his neck out over WMD and, when they weren't discovered, refusing to commit hari-kiri as he'd promised. Yet despite all this, and though we'd never admit it in public, Aaronovitch doesn't just make us aggravated, he also makes us think. The bastard.

ABBA

When a group called 'Björn & Benny, Agnetha & Anni-Frid' soldiered out of Sweden in 1974, it looked like just another phonetically challenged novelty act. But thanks in large part to music clips created by fellow Swede Lasse Hallström (who would go on to direct *The Cider House Rules* and *Chocolat*), the popularity of the quartet (sensibly renamed ABBA) endured long after it stopped performing 'Waterloo' and 'Dancing Queen' in 1982. Credit this to its two-tiered fan base. On one level were the proudly fanatical ABBAnatics; on the other, those who joyously bobbed their heads to 'Super Trouper' and 'Knowing Me, Knowing You' but wouldn't own up to it in public.

A resurgence began with the 1994 film *Muriel's Wedding*, which appropriated many of the group's greatest hits for its soundtrack. It climaxed with the all-ABBA musical *Mamma Mia!* (which had all the depth and insight of an episode of *You've Been Framed*). Nevertheless, it gave the group a longevity and a standing equalling, if not the Beatles, then at least the Bee Gees. See also **Disco (Dancing)**; *You've Been Framed*.

Abbott and Costello

Not as compulsively silly as the Three Stooges, as transcendent as the Marx Brothers, or as easy to parody as Martin and Lewis, Abbott (the unfunny one) and Costello (the fat one) nevertheless managed to make a string of semi-amusing films from 1940 (*One Night in the Tropics*) to 1956 (*Dance with Me, Henry* – now there's a money title). Their work, though far from genius, enjoyed a long afterlife as pre-Satellite only-alternative-to-live-bowls Sunday afternoon television fodder. See also **Lewis, Jerry**.

Advert Breaks (Making tea during)

Does anyone ever buy a thirty-second slot assuming that the entire TV audience is still watching? They'd be far better off putting an advert up in our toilet. Perhaps one by the kettle? Or on any other channel in the world apart from the one we're watching. A three-minute break is a three-minute license to flick. If you're like us, your instincts are so well honed that you know the exact moment to return – that split-second freeze-frame of the final advert. For added enjoyment, think about all the money that McDonald's and Tesco and HSBC and Persil have pissed away over the years while you've been off making a cup of tea. It might not be the profoundest way of getting one over on big business, but that doesn't stop it feeling good.

Advert Catchphrases (Quoting of)

There's a brief window of time in which it's acceptable to repeat an expression you heard in an ad. After that, as much as you want to say 'Calm down dear, it's only a commercial' or 'Wassup', and as much as a situation may call for it, sorry, but the parade has passed. This golden moment can range from days (for ads fronted by Peter Kay) to seconds (for, say, anything with Michael Winner).

Adverts (Debt Consolidation)

There's a special breed of television commercial that is targeted exclusively at people chucking a sickie from the office. The set-up is forever inviolate – an anonymous call centre somewhere, populated by homogeneously Caucasian and implausibly smiling drones, through which a vaguely-familiar actor wanders (sitting on a desk now and then to suggest a somewhat casual attitude) while burbling on about 'combining all your debts into one soul-destroying millstone'. The ads appear to be aimed at feck-less skip-dwellers who think that borrowing to pay off a loan makes some sort of financial sense. There is, however, a deeper message: 'Unless you get back to work right now, slacker, you could end up getting sacked and having to borrow money from a washed-up *Blue Peter* presenter too'.

Advice Columnists

Think of a major personal problem that can be condensed into four newspaper column inches. Now imagine an answer to that problem that could fit in the same space. Absurd? Of course. And yet we have a track record of seeing Dear Deirdre, Dr Miriam Stoppard, Clare Rayner, Anna Raeburn and dozens of regional rip-offs as life-changers. Rarely have we paused to ask how serious we really are about fixing a problem if we're willing to send it to a columnist who may take months to reply – if she replies at all. But that argument misses a fundamental point. We turn to these columns rather than to news and editorials because we're attracted to a world where titillation masquerades as advice; where it's not about the letter writer, it's about the reader. Who can resist 'sympathizing' with the woman who inadvertently had an affair with the plumber while her husband was on an oil rig, the man who wants advice on how to ask his wife to get her sister to join them in bed or the schoolgirl who wants to know if it's true that you can't get pregnant if you do it standing up?

'Agadoo' See **Black Lace (The Pop Duo)**.

Agutter, Jenny (In *Logan's Run*)

Jenny Agutter starred in an odd futuristic film in which people were killed when they hit the age of thirty. Which is ironic,

because without wishing to reduce her long and distinguished acting career to one solitary film, Agutter is very much immortalized for her role in the 1970 children's classic *The Railway Children*. Outshining even Bernard Cribbins, Jenny was all posh innocence personified, and several years too old for the part she was playing. Funny how Dads were always happy to sit with the kids while the film blasted out on Boxing Day morning.

Aha! See **Alan Partridge (Quoting)**.

Air Guitar

For the novice there is the Fender Tennis Racket; for the master, there is the limited edition 1962 Les Paul Invisible. Why spend years attempting to master the art of the six string when, with a winning combination of mime and an overactive imagination, you too can get Down Down with Status Quo? Air guitar is not recommended in public: when you reach for the Air Strat, it's normally the sign of too much to drink. But this isn't so much to do with the embarrassment of your air riffs, nor even the strange gurning look you're wearing on your face. No, the danger of public air guitaring is the way it reveals the worst excesses of your record collection. Think about it: when was the last time you saw someone air guitar along to Franz Ferdinand, or Bloc Party, or the Strokes? All we are saying is that when the Darkness appears on the pub jukebox, or Queen, or Rainbow, be careful. Keep your imaginary axe in its invisible air-guitar case, and rock out when you get home. See also **Status Quo**.

Airplane! See **Films that Parody Other Films**.

Alan Partridge (Quoting)
It's *Monty Python* for the Nineties, a semi-excusable form of trainspottery that should be resisted in most forms of civilized conversation. There are the latecomers who say things like 'Back of the net' or 'Jurassic Park'. There are the intermediates who mutter 'Let it go Lynn, you're never going to meet him,' and then there are the experts, the very knowing *Knowing Me* fans, who sprinkle the televisual gems ('No manners, but what a critic') with the quoter's holy grail: entire regurgitated scripts of the original radio show. What's Umberto Eco? What's your favourite coloured car? We're just one big happy family. Steve Coogan never quite managed to escape his most famous comic creation, and neither did we.

Album Cover Art
The generation that was raised on CDs will never know that fabled time when some people considered album covers an art form. Rockers loved to debate the symbolism of Led Zeppelin's *Houses of the Holy* children-on-the-rocks imagery (inspired by Arthur C. Clarke's sci-fi novel *Childhood's End*); Pink Floyd's *Dark Side of the Moon* pyramid prism; and *The Velvet Underground & Nico* with its Andy Warhol banana. Of course, yesterday's designers admittedly had more space to play with. In a CD world, the *White Album* would have been merely the *White Drink Coaster*.

Alcopops

Imagine a drink with a sugar content high enough to appeal to the immature teenage palate, but packing an alcoholic wallop big enough to render the most demanding underage drinker insensible within minutes. You've just imagined Alcopops. If you'd imagined them in 1994 you'd probably be worth over £100 million by now. It's enough to drive anyone to drink, isn't it? There are close to 200 types on the UK market at the moment, each a more lurid colour than the last, and sharing only a sickly-sweet taste and the word 'ice' in their name. They're ghastly of course, and as they're targeted so cynically at the disaffected-teenager market we'd be in favour of banning them completely – if only they didn't taste *so damn good*.

ALF

Mork & Mindy with a puppet.

Allen, Irwin

Had he only given us *The Towering Inferno* and *The Poseidon Adventure* – two flicks where the primary pleasure was guessing who among the star-studded casts would die – film producer Irwin Allen would have earned a place of honour in this book. But the Academy Award winner (for a 1953 oceanic documentary, not for *The Swarm*) just couldn't stop giving. Seemingly determined to destroy every conceivable human edifice in every conceivable way, the 'Master of Disaster' went on to produce such TV films as *Flood!* and *Fire!* and *Cave-In!* See also **Gimmicks, Film**; **Heston, Charlton**; **Rampaging Animals (Films About)**.

Allis, Peter

Golf, in many ways, has attempted to drag itself into the twenty-first century. There are things like Street Golf and Ian Poulter wearing funny trousers and doing silly things with his hair. BBC commentator Peter Allis, however, remains firmly, and brilliantly, old school. There's nothing more withering than Peter watching a chopped shot into a bunker and murmuring 'Dear oh dear'. There's nothing more comical than the golf overrunning and Peter suggesting we tell 'the wife' to keep the dinner warm as we're not going to be torn away from the TV. The thinking man's Murray Walker, in our book.

Almond, Marc See **Urban Myths**.

Alphabetti Spaghetti
Few foods are as nutritious or as educational as Alphabetti Spaghetti. Heinz had been making the nation's favourite spag-in-a-can for decades before they hit on the idea of shaping the pasta into letters. Once they had crossed that Rubicon, however, all hell broke loose: Super Mario Brothers, Pokémon, and SpongeBob, all were grist to the Heinz shaped-pasta mill. We know it's for the kids, but is it so wrong if we spell out something offensive on our toast while we summon up the energy to cook something decent? See also **SpongeBob SquarePants**.

amazon (Buying Things on Without Thinking About the Cost)
amazon used to be just books and CDs but now it's everything from nose clippers to garden furniture, clothing to capuccino-milk frothers and all-you-can-watch DVDs for £6.99 a month. The evil geniuses in Seattle have found the holy grail: making shopping as appealing to guys as girls by inventing a feature called 'one-click shopping' – if you switch it on then you can literally browse, click and purchase before your conscience has kicked in. Two days later it arrives on your doorstep. Is it working? Well, put it like this, in 2005 they grossed $2.98 billion of sales. Sorry, must dash – there's a man at the door. See also **eBay**.

amazon (Reviews)
Was this review helpful to you? No, not very much at all as it happens. Everyone's a critic these days, and thanks to the joys of the Interweb, other people's badly-drawn thoughts

and ill-founded opinions can now be used on the pages of amazon to influence your purchasing decisions. Who hasn't seen a glowing four-star rave by Chuck123 from Arizona, and thought, 'Great, that's my Christmas shopping sorted for this year'? Who hasn't witnessed a half-page, zero-star diatribe by Jenny H from Basingstoke and thought, 'Maybe the Beatles aren't so great after all'? Let's face it, if the review is a hatchet job, it's written by someone with an axe to grind. If it's glowing, you know it's by someone who knows the author. Apart from those posted for *The Encyclopaedia of Guilty Pleasures*, of course. Those are all genuine. Honest.

American Pie See **Teenage Boys Losing Their Virginity (Films About)**.

American Tourists (Misdirecting)

You are standing on a street corner and accosted by cartoon-character American tourists wearing Hawaiian shirts in a way likely to cause a breach of the peace, asking you loudly for directions to 'Lie-sester Square' or to 'Edin-burgg Cassal', then you can either take your time to give them clear and concise instructions that will deliver them quickly and safely to their destination . . . or you . . . er . . . don't. We always find the best route from Trafalgar Square to the Houses of Parliament involves walking to Marble Arch (three miles), taking the Central line to Bank, changing onto the Docklands Light Railway to Canada Water where a riverboat to Westminster Pier (via the Thames Barrier), a brisk walk to Embankment Tube where the Northern Line (Mill Hill East branch) tube to Hampstead, followed by a taxi via the unmissable Hendon Police Training College does the trick every time. Thank y'all.

Americans (Losing at Anything)

It doesn't really matter what the sport is; it doesn't really matter who they are playing; our instinct for the underdog remains undimmed. So when the US faced Iran in the 1998 World Cup, who could resist a cheer when the Islamic fundamentalists defeated the leaders of the free world? Perhaps it is their just desserts for having a national baseball championship and calling it the 'world series'. When the 'world' are allowed to take part, it's a different story: the Olympic champions are another US favourite, Cuba. An American businessman buying Manchester United? It all seems rather apt. See also **Manchester United (Losing)**.

Americans (Watching Them Complain)

'Whaddya mean you're out of Waldorfs? What kind of god-damn dump is this place?' This phrase, spoken by a guest of a certain nationality in *Fawlty Towers*, could never have been spoken by a Brit. Never. We simply don't know how to complain – it is not in our nature. We put it down to potty-training and a throwback to Victorian manners. Mary Poppins would not approve. The fact that we can't do it doesn't mean, of course, that we can't derive enormous pleasure from watching others do it. A lot of Americans still arrive in Britain labouring under the misapprehension that we still live in an *Upstairs Downstairs* culture where everyone has 'staff' and that a fistful of dollars will ensure a five-star reception wherever they go. As a result they enjoy nothing more than leaping forth with vitriol to shame waiters for late orders, hotel reception staff for unavailability of rooms and taxi drivers for not wanting to take them from London to Edinburgh. We think their rudeness is unacceptable and we have half a mind to tackle them about it but actually, on second thoughts we don't want to cause a fuss so maybe the best course of action, all things considered, is to write a stiff letter to *The Times*. Well actually let's sleep on it and see how we feel in the morning – it might be better to let the whole thing blow over. Sorry.

Anderson, Pamela

In 2003 Pamela Anderson started voicing a grown-up cartoon called Stripperella, about an exotic dancer who fights crime. The job was perfect, because the woman was already a caricature of sorts. Famous for her larger-than-life attributes (both of them), this native of Canada gained fame by starring on *Baywatch* as C.J. – a lifeguard in a tiny red bathing suit who excelled at running up and down the beach. If you tell someone you're a Pamela Anderson fan, please don't push your luck by saying you think she's a great actress – just admit you've watched her more, er, 'candid' co-starring appearance with ex-husband Tommy Lee so many times that your modem crashed. See also *Baywatch*; **Masturbation; Movies (Pornographic); Naked Celebrities (Photographs of)**.

Anderson, Richard Dean See *MacGyver*.

Angels (As Plot Devices) See *It's a Wonderful Life*.

Animal House
Raise a twenty-one-beer salute to the film that made it cool to screw up in college. Filmed in 1977 with a budget of $2.7 million and a cast composed mostly of nobodies, *Animal House* became the second-biggest film of 1978 (after *Grease*). It holds the distinction of being the best film starring a *Saturday Night Live* alumnus (John Belushi) ever made; forms an indispensable link in the Six Degrees of Kevin Bacon game (yes, he was in there, as were Donald Sutherland and Tim Matheson); and inspired a short-lived TV series called *Delta House*, which introduced a very young Michelle Pfeiffer to the world. See you at the toga party.

Animal Magic
The fun of this long-running nature show wasn't for the various discoveries we made about the world of nature. No, it was all down to host Johnny Morris, and his hilarious animal impressions. No creature was safe from Johnny sidling up, saying, 'Ooh look, it's Mr Parrott' and for 'Mr Parrott' to 'reply', 'Hello Johnny, how are you?' His elephant voice was a particular favourite. An entire generation of children know nothing about animals but everything about doing silly voices. See also *Crocodile Hunter, The*.

Ann Summers (Parties)
When you think of an Ann Summers party, you probably think of nylon lingerie and low-comedy sex aids being sold in a Lambrini-fuelled hen party atmosphere. That's exactly what you should think, because that's exactly what they are. Still, there's

an undeniable appeal in buying such items in a less judgemental environment than the snooty confines of Agent Provocateur or Coco de Mer. And besides, if something's likely to be torn off in the heat of passion, wouldn't you feel more relaxed knowing that it cost less than a round of Babychams?

Ant and Dec
Which is which? Who knows? Do they? Who cares?

Antiques Roadshow, The
Antiques Roadshow draws viewers by playing on wishful thinking. To wit: what if that old doll/old book/old painting collecting dust in the attic is really an antique that's worth a fortune? Bow-tied experts with rare-roast-beef complexions and fruity voices set up shop in well-to-do county towns, try not to look disdainful as they 'appraise' piles of tat brought in by thousands of locals and every now and again hit paydirt. The most entertaining part is watching people trying to look nonchalant as they find out that, say, that old teddy bear is in fact a Steiff cinnamon bear worth £4,000 or that Granny's old snuff-box actually belonged to Napoleon and is worth six figures 'for insurance purposes'. We feel there is untapped mileage here – why not set up shop in a badly-lit pub car park in Toxteth and get 'local characters' to bring along 'family heirlooms' from sacks marked 'Swag'. 'Has this been in the family long, sir?' 'About thirty minutes.'

Aquariums
The dolphin shows are fascinating. The sea lions are hilarious. And you are a bastard. That's the unsettling feeling a visitor to an aquarium gets when they see so many intelligent, energetic sea creatures penned up and performing for the amusement of a bunch of holiday makers. You don't have to be a card-carrying Greenpeace member to realize that dolphins probably could think of better ways to amuse themselves than by leaping out of the water after a mackerel. And yet, there *you* are, paying the admission money necessary to keep them there.

Arcades See Computer Games.

Archer, Jeffrey (Reading the Books of)

There is something curious at work here: no one has ever admitted to buying his novels, but he is still one of the best-selling authors of all time. How so? Well next time you are in a holiday home and faced with the choice between *Knitwear: A Celebration*, a pile of mouldy *Reader's Digest* condensed books and one of Archer's early novels such as *Not A Penny More, Not A Penny Less, Kane and Abel* or *Shall We Tell The President?*, we guarantee that you will begrudgingly pick up one of these glossy books – and within minutes be caught in his web. Soon you will be feigning a jippy tummy so that you can sneak off and read on and on and on in the smallest room in the house. As the novel sweeps you along through cliffhanger and plot twist to a thrilling set-piece denouement, you will (almost) forget that the book you are holding put money in the pocket of that great humanitarian. Almost.

Archers, The

This everyday tale of old rural professionals was originally intended as an educational tool to remind country folk of their old pre-war skills after the dark days of the Second World War, when farming types were far too busy exploiting evacuees and making assignations with airmen to worry about spile-troshing and the like. Since then it has evolved into a kind of anti-soap that seems to revel in the possibilities of the non-event. No bodies under the patio here. The show's appeal to jaded urban-ites is largely a product of its scheduling: the daily 7 p.m. episodes fall within the daily commuting hour for most office drones but the almost interminable omnibus edition of Sunday mornings provides the ideal excuse to stay in bed at least until the beginning of *Desert Island Discs*.

Argos (Shopping at)

It's a damp afternoon in Bromley and you decide to wander in to Argos and have a bit of a laugh at the over-laminated chained-to-the-desk catalogues, the hundreds of mini biros and the dole office seating and then something happens. Before you know it you start to leaf through the catalogue, find yourself unable to turn down the too-good-to-be-true offers and then you are filling in your seven digit code number on the form, queuing up to pay and then waiting for that exciting moment when your customer number flashes up on the screen and your item cascades down a big chute. You leave feeling like you've won a prize.

Army-Navy Surplus Shops
These little shops of wonders sprang up after World War II, when there was, well, a lot of surplus Army and Navy stuff lying around. Loaded with everything from mess kits to camouflage fatigues to gas masks, they are the perfect places to gear up for camping, fishing, or hunting expeditions. Fashionistas of every political stripe have long prowled the olive-green sales racks, seeking to achieve that smart military look without having to march around in the hot sun, and maybe even take a bullet, to earn it.

As Seen on TV Products See **Ronco, K-Tel and JML; Innovations Catalogues; Iceland; Chat Lines (Advertised on TV)**.

A-Team, The See **Mr T**.

Australian Pink Floyd Show, The
Too young to have seen the Pink Floyd in their pomp? Too sensible to have seen the later, corporate rock manifestation of what was arguably the world's leading (and indeed only) twenty-fifth-century acid blues combo? Us too. There's only one rational response: go and see a band so slavishly accurate in their imitation of the glory years Floyd that they probably use the right kind of cables. All right, they don't look all that much like the original performers, but then again you probably couldn't pick Nick Mason out of a police line-up anyway. Go and see the Australian Pink Floyd show. Tell them we sent you. Just don't expect anyone to respect you in the morning. Especially not us.

Autographs
Big-time celebrity signatures can be worth a pretty penny. Recently a President Nixon-autographed yo-yo sold for more

than $16,000, and one of Elvis Presley's cancelled cheques brought in over $10,000. But while legendary recluse J.D. Salinger is worth having, those of most second-string luminaries will never be worth more than the paper they're scrawled on. So what accounts for the hundreds of otherwise-normal people who line-up for signed photos of, say, the guy who wears the R2-D2 costume or someone who used to present *Blue Peter* and is now opening his local fête? Here's a reality check: that celebrity doesn't remember signing your copy of her autobiography (let alone writing it), the pop star doesn't recall scribbling his name on your concert T-shirt and that porn star has absolutely no memory of signing your, well, you get the idea.

Autopsies (Television)

We've come a long way since *Quincy, M.E.* These days every police procedural worth its salt showing streetwise detectives loitering near the Big Metal Table while the pathologist (usually in mid-slice) nonchalantly says, 'See these cuts on the forearms? They're what's called "defence wounds". She didn't die easy.' The path to today's graphic autopsies was pioneered by *The X-Files*. Towards the end of that programme's run, no episode seemed complete without Scully cracking open the chest of at least one desiccated/mutilated/flame-broiled corpse. Later, the bone saw was passed to shows like *Silent Witness* and *Waking the Dead*, where on-camera dissection was raised to an art form. You wanted to look away but . . . okay, maybe you didn't want to look away.

Avon

What Seventies housewife didn't have Avon's Dutch Maid decanter displayed on a nice lace doily somewhere in her house? What man didn't splash on aftershave from a bottle shaped like a stagecoach? What little girl wouldn't have *sold her soul* for that miniature pink ice cream cone with a waxy shaft of strawberry lipgloss hidden under its plastic soft-serve cap? Sadly, that golden era of naïve toiletries is gone. Still, Avon (founded in 1886 as the California Perfume Company, but renamed in 1939 after the river in Shakespeare's birthplace) reminds us of a gentler era of consumerism, when an immaculately coiffured Avon

Lady showed up on your doorstep every two weeks with her case of garish lipstick samples and then floated into your living room on a cloud of Sweet Honesty. See also **Cheap Perfume (From the Chemist's)**.

Award Ceremonies (Pointless)

The National Soap Awards, the National Television Awards, the *Elle* Style Awards . . . Need we go on? Basically deeply manufactured opportunities for us to sit back with a box of tissues and share the highs and lows of the on-best-behaviour tabloid fodder as they whoop, holler and punch the air as they win 'Best Celebrity Hairstyle', 'Best On-Screen Tears' or 'Most Ironic On-Screen Storyline Given What You've Been Up To In Your Private Life'. We love seeing the faux-collegiate smile on the losers' faces, and best of all the next morning you can revel in the 'Soap Stars In Trophy Punch-Up', 'TV Bitch Fight' and 'Drunken TV Star's Coke Shame' headlines that tell the real story of the night.

Award Shows See Award Ceremonies (Pointless); MTV Video Music Awards, The; Oscar Acceptance Speeches (Embarrassing).

Awful Records (Pretending to Like in an Ironic Way)

See also **A.O.R.**; **ABBA**; **Air Guitar**; **Australian Pink Floyd Show, The**; **Bee Gees, The**; *Can't Stop the Music*; **'Cat's in the Cradle'**; **Cassidy, David**; **Darkness, The**; **Denver, John**; **Electric Light Orchestra, The**; **'Escape (The Pina Colada Song)'**; **Everett, Kenny**; **G, Kenny**; **Karaoke**; **KC and the Sunshine Band**; **Radio 2**; **Ringo**; **Village People, The**; **YMCA**.

Baby Wet Wipes

They're supposed to make the nappy-changing experience a more gentle one for the baby in your life. Yet many a parent has realized that a moistened wet wipe across the face (a new one, of course) can be a refreshing pick-me-up in the middle of a stressful day.

Back of the Net See Alan Partridge (Quoting).

Bacon Sandwich

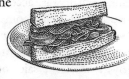

We're not God, but if we'd made the earth in six days, then on the seventh we'd have got up, put the kettle on and invented the bacon sandwich. It's such a brilliantly simple concept: two slices of toast, three crispy rashers (let's not be stingy now) and a healthy (ahem) dollop of sauce. Some people think you can tell a lot about a person from whether they put ketchup or brown sauce on the sandwich. We think you can tell whether they like ketchup or brown sauce. For added pleasure, why not make a bacon sandwich when you've got a vegetarian to stay? Watch their nose twinge as the smell wafts across the kitchen. Enjoy their mouth salivating as you munch in and they can't. It's cruel, yes, but it's their choice, the lentil-eating lemons.

Baileys Irish Cream

The true meaning of Christmas: a nauseating concoction of cheap spirits and stale milk which against all good sense leads to a glow of *bonhomie* in even the flintiest of hearts. Feed Baileys to your local Scrooge and watch in wonder as they soften and melt like an inexpertly-prepared Baked Alaska. You might even try some yourself. Don't drink it at any other time of year though – that's not a guilty pleasure, it's just plain wrong.

Banana Splits, The

Almost no one knew what the hell Bingo, Fleagle, Drooper and Snorky, the Muppet-like stars of the *Banana Splits Adventure Hour*, were supposed to be. And as the plot of this programme? There wasn't any plot. The four costumed freaks simply cavorted around the set, providing the glue between several short, serialized adventures such as the *Arabian Knights*, *The Three Musketeers* and a live-action cliffhanger called *Danger Island* (starring Jan-Michael Vincent). Side note: Daws Butler, who voiced Bingo, also did the honours for Elroy Jetson and Yogi Bear. Now *that's* a CV. See also *Muppet Show, The*; *Teletubbies*.

Barbeau, Adrienne

This woman was, according to her CV, an actress. She was in a couple of US sitcoms and then graduated to films such as *The Fog* and *Escape from New York* (both directed by her then-husband, John Carpenter). We have no idea what roles she played, what she said, or whether she was any good. Because, sadly, we couldn't stop staring at her *awesome and majestic breasts*. In every generation, it seems, a woman appears with cleavage that stands at the pinnacle of aesthetic perfection. In the 1970s (and into the Eighties, before Pamela Anderson took up the mantle) this was Barbeau. Not looking at her chest (revealed in all its shirtless glory in 1982's *Swamp Thing*) was like visiting America and not going to Disneyland. See also **Anderson, Pamela**; *Halloween* **(The Movie Series)**; **Parton, Dolly**; **Masturbation**.

Bardot, Brigitte

The idea of a model trying to make it in the acting world is nothing new. Take, for example, yesteryear bombshell Brigitte Bardot. After appearing in the pages of *Elle* magazine at the age of fifteen, she jumped to the screen a few years later in the French film *Le Trou Normand*. Her sex kitten persona was defined by 1956's *And God Created Woman*, about a free spirit, the two men who love her, and the town that lusts after her. At eighteen she married the film's director, Roger Vadim (who would go on to marry Jane Fonda and Marie-Christine Barrault, a hottie Triple Crown that has yet to be equalled in the player record books). Never much of an actress, Bardot bailed on the business in 1973 to devote herself to animal rights activities. If only Kathy Ireland had been so clever. See also **Fonda, Jane**.

Barenaked Ladies, The

As with their clothes-free namesakes, Canadian band the Barenaked Ladies are not a liking best admitted to in public. We can't pin it on their being Canadian (Neil Young is too, and he's great) but more to do with their (excuse for a) funny bone: the BNL attempt that most horrific of musical compositions – the humorous song. The result is, even when they're writing gorgeous pop hooks – and there are bundles on their albums – all anyone ever remembers is their two parts wacky, one part wack hit 'One Week'. Chickity China the Chinese Chicken? File under . . . the stairs.

Bashir, Martin (Interview Specials by)

Suffice it to say that Martin Bashir is unlikely to be receiving a Christmas card from Michael Jackson this year, nor be invited to a Buckingham Place garden party . . . erm . . . ever. Twenty-seven million people tuned in to watch his 2003 *Living With Michael Jackson* and by the end of the ninety minutes, in which Bashir's multi-million dollar question, 'Is it really appropriate for a forty-four-year-old man to share a bedroom with a child that is not related to him at all?' was answered naïvely with a simple, 'That's a beautiful thing.' Jacko was reaching for his lawyers and the police force were reaching for search warrants. Eight years earlier, in a slightly more touchy-feely (and very scripted) double-act with Diana, Princess of Wales, we heard, amongst other things, such choice Diana-isms as the Camilla-classic 'There were three of us in this marriage, so it was a bit crowded'; the paranoid '. . . that again was a huge move to discredit me, and very nearly did me in' and the Hewitt-inspired 'Yes, I adored him. Yes, I was in love with him. But I was very let down.' We weren't – we lapped up her every doe-eyes-through-fringe gaze and coquettish giggle.

Bathroom Cabinets (Looking in Other People's)

 Let's face it – everyone does it, and it's a chance to play detective at every dinner party you attend. It might be stating the obvious, but lock the bathroom door before you snoop into your hosts' dark, dirty secrets. Then turn the taps on and smartly click open the bathroom cabinet . . . Now, what do we have here? Some Dentufix ('I knew those teeth weren't real'), Anusol ('Ouch'), hair dye matching your host's natural locks ('Thought so!'), Viagra ('Hell-oo!') and KY Jelly ('Too much sharing'). After the investigation, splash your face for a dewy-eyed look, or slash your lips with fresh, bright gloss – good detectives always cover their tracks. Return to the table, and see the whole scene (and in particular, your formidable hostess) afresh.

Batman (The TV Show)

From the moment this series premièred in 1966, absolutely no one thought the tilted sets, the Bam!s and Boom!s that appeared during fight scenes, or even Adam West's codpiece were to be taken seriously (except, perhaps, for West himself). Still, even after all these years, it's fun to watch the likes of Victor Buono (King Tut), Eartha Kitt and Julie Newmar (both as Catwoman), and Otto Preminger (Mr Freeze) act all menacing and stuff. See also **Superheroes**.

Battleships (The Board Game)

There are a few children's games that even seasoned adults would like to take one more crack at. Take Battleships, in which each player positions an aircraft carrier battle group on a grid his opponent can't see. Then they take turns calling out Bingo-like coordinates (B-7, I-10, etc.), seeing who can 'hit' the other's fleet. Nowhere outside of a Tom Clancy novel can one take so much satisfaction in sinking a submarine. See also **Clancy, Tom**.

Battlestar Galactica

What was lamer than being a *Star Wars* nerd? Being a fan of this short-lived ABC series. Raced out in 1978 to cash in on the success of Luke, Han, and the rest of the gang, it featured a massive budget (for TV), elaborate sets, a filling-loosening orchestral score, and state-of-the-art special effects. Everything but a reasonable premise and decent scripts. Referred to by incensed critics as *Battlestar Galaxative*, the show folded after only twenty-four episodes. See also **Disco (Dancing)**; **Disco (Fashions)**; *Star Wars*.

Baywatch

Arguably the most unlikely international sensation since Zamfir, Master of the Pan Flute, this show began life as a quickly cancelled 1989 NBC series starring post-*Knight Rider* David Hasselhoff and post-*Hardy Boys* Parker Stevenson. After NBC bowed out, the programme's creators, perceiving a huge pent-up demand for a programme about Californian lifeguards who perform rescues and deal with their complicated personal lives while running around mostly naked, took the project into syndication. Budgets were cut, as was Parker Stevenson, and expensive action sequences were dropped in favour of music-video-like montages of the actors (especially the female actors) running in slow motion. The changes created a media juggernaut seen in some 140 countries worldwide. It also made David Hasselhoff, for some reason, a huge international star, and ignited the careers of Pamela Anderson and Carmen Electra. Ironically, sixty-five per cent of the show's fans were female. See also **Anderson, Pamela** and **Hasselhoff, David**.

Beach Volleyball (Watching)

Boxing is a magnificent spectacle of endurance that needs no explanation. The purpose of a marathon is also self-evident. As for beach volleyball, a firm grasp of the game is not needed to appreciate hardbodied men and women wearing skintight outfits and bouncing up and down in pursuit of a ball. Who cares about the rules?

Beaches See **Chick Flicks (In Which Someone Dies)**.

Beano, The
The *Beano* is the best comic on the planet, simply because it 'gets' how children think. In a more PC world, the comic's lead character would never be a 'menace' who spent his life terrorizing the 'softy' with glasses. But the playground is never the most PC of places, and so a cartoon celebration of Specky Four Eyes being twatted is welcomed by children everywhere. The magazine's biggest stroke of genius was perhaps the Dennis the Menace fanclub, for which one got both a Dennis the Menace badge and a furry Gnasher. It doesn't matter that you've grown-up. They're still effortlessly cool.

Beans and Sausages
No matter how careful you are about what you eat, sooner or later you will encounter one of those evenings when the preparation of a healthy, balanced meal seems a little too much bother. Enter the humble tin of beans: its unprepossessing exterior contains representatives of all the major food groups: vegetable, in the form of a tasty tomato sauce, pulses, in the form of the beans themselves and . . . well that's it. A tin of beans is nutritious but can be a trifle dull. Which is where the sausages come in. Fortifying the basic bean/sauce combo with meaty goodness of unknown provenance, their smooth texture bespeaks hours of care from the finest meat reclamation and processing machinery devised by the mind of man. Ooh pardon me!

Beauty and the Beast (The TV Series)
Fans of this late-Eighties television programme, which updated the fairy tale to contemporary New York, gush over its inspired storyline. But anyone who followed the tale of Catherine Chandler (Linda Hamilton) and

her very special relationship with the sexy man-beast Vincent (Ron Perlman) knows its cult following was mostly interested in the duo's slow dance around the topic of Getting It On. When Hamilton left the production after the second season to have a baby, attempts to write her out of the show didn't fly with viewers. A dozen episodes into Season Three, the writers tied up some loose ends and closed shop. See also *Star Trek*.

Beauty Contests

Credit the Greeks. Or at least, the mythological Greeks. It was Zeus, after all, who ordered Paris to judge whether Hera, Athena, or Aphrodite was the most beautiful of goddesses. Aphrodite won. (History leaves no record of the first runner-up, who would have filled in for the winner had she been unable to complete her duties.) These days, beauty contest fallout is limited to couch potato arguments over the merits of Miss Birmingham vs. Miss West Midlands and an occasional 'whoops-I-forgot-to-mention-the-*Loaded*-shoot' scandal. Package holidays and feminism dealt the beauty contest a crippling blow by poisoning its roots in the holiday camps and its fullest flowering in the televised Miss World competition. Modern organizers tend to put a lot of focus on intangible qualities like 'personality', and stress that the bathing suit competition is really about 'fitness'. That sort of denial is a sign that it's not just the people at home who feel a tinge of guilt about their participation in such an antiquated, yet fun, form of ogling.

Beavis and Butt-head

A pair of music-video-critiquing teens next to whom even the characters of *Wayne's World* seem intellectual. Mocking both teen losers and pretentious critics (B & B's standard line of criticism: 'This blows'), the show faced frequent attacks for the boys' dubious behaviour. One Season Two episode came complete with the disclaimer, 'Breathing paint thinner will damage your brain . . . look what it's done to Beavis and Butt-head'. Another: 'WARNING: If you're not a cartoon, swallowing a rubber full of drugs can kill you'. See also **Humperdinck, Engelbert; MTV**.

Bee Gees, The

Of course Maurice, Robin and Barry had a career prior to the film and its blockbuster soundtrack (including the 1975 hit 'Nights on Broadway' which we haven't heard of either) and they stayed in the charts afterwards (remember 'Too Much Heaven'? Er . . . no). However, it's the *Saturday Night Fever* disc and the Beatles defilement known as the movie *Sgt Pepper's Lonely Hearts Club Band* that are the trio's cultural touchstones. Each is in its own lovable way a guilty pleasure – the first for reminding us that disco was vapid but fun, the latter for being the worst film ever made (but disturbingly watchable). They weren't of course always called the Bee Gees – in a memorable appearance with Clive Anderson they famously reminded the nation that they had at one point called themselves Les Tosseurs – allowing Clive to rejoinder 'Well you'll always be tossers to me,' before they stormed off. See also **Disco (Dancing)**; **Disco (Fashions)**; *Saturday Night Fever*.

Before and After Photos

There's something disturbing yet fascinating about seeing a hideous 'before' picture juxtaposed next to a look-how-much-weight-I-lost or a look-how-good-I-look-when-fashionistas-get-hold-of-me 'after' shot. Never mind that the subject is grim in shot No. 1 and hap-hap-happy in shot No. 2. Never mind that the first pic looks like it was developed in mud, while the second was handled by Mario Testino. Just mitigate your jealousy of the second figure with the rationale that you would *never* let yourself go like Mr or Ms Before.

Benny Hill Show, The

Even though silent comedy supposedly died with the advent of sound, no one seemed to have told Benny Hill. Think of Benny Hill (real name Alfred Hawthorn Hill) and the likely image is of 'our Benny' and his cohorts chasing women across open fields to the sounds of Boots Randolph's 'Yakety Sax'. His secret? Never underestimate the comic potential of pairing fat men with buxom women. That short bald man was pretty funny, too. Especially when he got his head smacked.

Beverly Hillbillies, The

If mainstream America was so strait-laced in the mid-Sixties what accounts for that era's proliferation of bizarre sitcoms? Originally titled *The Hillbillies of Beverly Hills*, *The Beverly Hillbillies* followed a pack of poor mountain folk who got rich and moved to 'Californy'. Of course there's no need to explain how this happened: the theme song (which is undoubtedly playing in your head right now) says it all . . . Even today it sustains a fan base that includes Stephen King, Dan Akroyd and Billy Bob Thornton. (Okay, maybe Billy Bob isn't that big of a surprise.) See also **King, Stephen**.

Beverly Hills 90210

High school kids played by way-too-old-for-high-school actors is part of a grand tradition. *BH90210* more than upheld that ancient policy. When it first aired in 1990, it told the story of twins adjusting to life at their new, rather swish, school. To populate this cauldron of teen angst, executive producer Aaron Spelling rounded up twenty-four-year-old Luke Perry (whose permanent squint gave him the appearance of premature crow's-feet, or at least of having a fag on); twenty-six-year-old Ian Ziering, and the grandma of the group, twenty-nine-year-old Gabrielle Carteris. Plus there was Spelling's seventeen-year-old daughter Tori, a guilty pleasure in and of herself. But at least she was the right age. See also **Spelling, Aaron**; **Spelling, Tori**.

Bian, Liz See **Crank Phone Calls**.

Biblical Epics

There's something really twisted about the pleasure we get from big-budget Hollywood films based on the Testaments, Old and New. Cecil B. DeMille realised the trick was to lure audiences with sin and then deliver salvation. Hence the presence of hot-as-hell Anne Baxter in *The Ten Commandments*. The violent action in these films is also a bit overboard, but in a good way. What do you remember more clearly about

Ben-Hur, the religious message or the kick-ass chariot race? See also **Heston, Charlton**.

Bid TV

One of the many freeview channels whose existence is purely to fleece stupid people of their hard-earned cash. The concept is simple: they've got 200 sets of satin sheets (plus four, that's four, matching pillows) to sell; the price ticks down and everyone who has bid pays the lowest price. Whether these channels don't have enough viewers, or whether no one actually wants a set of satin sheets (plus four, that's four, matching pillows) we're not sure. But the result is your host stuck in presenting purgatory, trying to sound jolly for ten, twenty, thirty minutes about satin sheets. Never are they allowed to say, 'oh, no one's buying this, let's move on'. They have to stick it out; and so do you.

Big Log (Dropping a)

We don't want to lower the tone here, but this wouldn't be a complete chronicle of guilty pleasures without a reference to the delights contained within the smallest room in the house. We're talking about what *Roger's Profanisaurus* would describe as a 'dead otter', 'depth charge' or 'dreadnought': an eminently satisfying clean drop that in a less inhibited society would find you inviting friends round to share your glory.

Big Mac

Two all-beef patties special sauce lettuce cheese pickles onions on a sesame seed bun. Or so litanized the famed McDonald's advert. What wasn't mentioned? The 33 grams of fat. The 85 milligrams of cholesterol. The 1,050 milligrams of sodium. Okay, it does have 3 grams of dietary fibre. That's *something*, isn't it? See also **McRib**; **Chicken Nuggets**.

Big Mouth Billy Bass

This mounted, singing fish was the must-have 'ironic' gift of the early days of the twenty-first century and a mainstay of car-boot sales ever since. Basically a plastic fish glued to a 'mahogany' effect plaque, it used a clever combination of lights and . . . er . . . batteries to produce a tinny thirty-second burst of 'Take Me to the River' or 'Don't Worry (Be Happy)' that caused instant hilarity for one and all. Oh, how we laughed. Created by Texas-based Gemmy Industries and based (in look, not voice) on a fish acquired from a Texas taxidermist, Billy started out as a big fish in a relatively small pond. But after an overwhelmingly successful market test in a limited number of American shops, Billymania exploded and hit the UK like a wet fish in the face. Soon came not just spin-offs, but so many rip-offs that Billy was on the verge of being pushed off the shelves by singing pike, trout, turkeys, and pretty much every other imaginable game species.

Bill and Ted / Dude, Where's My Car? / Wayne's World
Three film franchises united by one thought: it's fun to laugh at stupid people. More accurately, it's fun to laugh at stupid American people that have curiously infectious catchphrases. No matter how amusing these winningly surreal celebrations of Californian stoner 'culture' may seem though, there's absolutely no excuse for using the word 'dude' anywhere in the British Isles. Before you ask, that goes totally double for Cornwall.

Bionic Woman, The See *Six Million Dollar Man, The*.

Black and White Minstrels, The
Twenty Papa Lazarous pushing a lady in a big hat on a swing. And singing. What's not to love?

Black Lace (Erotic Fiction)
Started in the early Nineties by the suitably chaste-but-curious Virgin Books, this range of legitimized one-hand clit-lit has taken the world by storm, selling over 4 million copies. Curiously they never appear on the best-seller list but we suspect they aren't always bought through, how shall we put this, 'traditional' bookshops. With titles like *Switching Hand* and *Bedding the Burglar* ('Maggie Quinton is a savvy, sexy architect

involved in a building project on a remote island off the Florida panhandle. One day, a gorgeous hunk breaks into the house she's staying in . . .') there is nothing to be ashamed of – this is 'literature'.

Black Lace (The Pop Duo)

Every mobile DJ has a box marked 'To be opened in case of emergency' containing 'YMCA', 'The Birdie Song', and at least one, normally two, Black Lace singles. 'Agadoo' is an absolute essential, and it is permissible to deploy 'El Vino Collapso' in special cases. Of course every self-respecting music lover will decry such shameless dumbing-down, but these songs have a power to move the most reluctant of feet.

Blackberry (Checking Email Constantly on Your)

What's there to feel guilty about here? An opportunity to read and respond to your email surreptitiously 24/7 wherever you are, whatever you are doing and to kid your clients that you are in the office attending to their needs? Magic! They are the ultimate boy-toy with a QWERTY keyboard, proper Internet access for high-speed Web-browsing and a palm-sized weird shape that comes in blue – once you have your 'Crackberry' you need never have a life again. The only drawback is that the trackwheel makes a slightly creaky clicking noise so that when you are idly checking your email in the middle of the night there is a danger that your partner may wake up and wonder what you are up to – especially if it's set to 'vibrate'.

Blair, Linda

The pea-soup spewing little girl in *The Exorcist* has put together possibly the most hilariously misguided film career of all time. Blair appeared not just in bad films, but in projects that marked the low points of their genres. Most famously, she starred in what some call the worst sequel of all time, *Exorcist II: The Heretic*. She also did the unforgettable (but not in a good way) made-for-TV film *Born Innocent*, which spotlighted the problem of young girls who are sent to reform school and then raped with a broom handle by their fellow inmates. These days she's deeply involved in animal rights – but not so deeply that she can't add such efforts as *Gang Boys* and *Double Blast* to her bizarre CV. See also **Coreys, The (Feldman and Haim)**; **Demonic Children (Films About)**; **Prison Films Featuring Women**.

Blake, Quentin

Roald Dahl was great, but he was so much greater because he had Quentin Blake doing his drawings for him. His scratchy cartoony, comic style brought to life so many of those books that, even now, we still feel a soft 'aw' when we see one of his drawings. Maybe J. K. Rowling should give him a bell.

Blankety Blank

The kick of watching *Blankety Blank* during its heyday was the strong sense that the two-tiered panel was truly having a good time. The game was simple: host Terry Wogan read a sentence or two that included a strategically spaced blank (e.g. 'The caveman said, "I just went to a very unusual wedding. A dinosaur *blanked* my bride."'). Six celebs wrote down possible blank-fillers and the people-on-the-street contestants tried to match their answers. It felt like innocent 'adult' fun, spiced with the inevitable sexual innuendos insinuated either by the loaded questions or by the smart-mouthed stars, which usually consisted of a subset of any of the following: Kenny Everett, Barbara Windsor, Sandra Dickinson, Gareth Hunt, Keith Chegwin, Lionel Blair, Bonnie Langford and Angela Rippon. See also **Game Shows**.

Blaxploitation Films

At its best, this Seventies genre was all about African Americans making movies for other African Americans. It all began in 1971 when Melvin Van Peebles wrote, starred in, and produced *Sweet Sweetback's Baad-asssss Song*. A long line of ghetto fabulous hits followed, including *Shaft*, *Blacula*, and *Foxy Brown*. Unfortunately, the movies soon began to exploit the community they were supposed to elevate, emphasizing violence and the thug life over reality. For white viewers, the creepy tinge of guilt comes when characters start talking about

The Man – and you realize they mean *you*. See also **Grier, Pam**.

Blazing Saddles See **Films that Parody Other Films**.

Blind Date

Dating is one of life's most awkward, stressful experiences, so when lovely Cilla and the gorgeous 'Our Graham' came along and packaged this nightmare ritual as prime-time television, we lapped it up. We loved the (heavily scripted) spontaneous banter between the contestants. ('My question to Number 1: If you were a pizza what flavour would you be?' 'Steve, I'd be Pepperoni with extra chilli – because I'm spicy with extra bite'); the badly concealed expressions of self-loathing as the most gorgeous contestants were inadvertently rejected only to see a fat girl from Barnsley or a computer salesman from Truro with overbite and a loud shirt step out from behind the screen. Off they went on their fabulous date and she turned out to be a mardy cow who only had eyes for the waiter and he turned out to have a grating sense of humour, a laugh like a hyena on smack and a spotty back. Back in the studio Cilla tried to paper over the cracks as the couple relived their arguments over behaviour in the hot tub and what was said on the last night after too much tequila. Cilla rarely had to get her hat out.

Blue Lagoon, The

An adolescent love story secretly adored by adolescents everywhere, who turned on in the hope that the blue in the title didn't refer to the colour of the water. Brooke Shields and Christopher Atkins were the shipwrecked children washed up on a desert island, who proceeded to shed both inhibitions and clothes in a Bounty-Taste-Of-Paradise type snogfest. It was all a bit ropey to be honest but in a feat of almost exceptional ingenuity, the producers managed to dig out a sequel, *Return to the Blue Lagoon* out of exactly the same plot.

Blue Peter (Vandals)

It wasn't big. It wasn't clever. But in the mid-1980s, the jolly-hockey-sticks TV world of *Blue Peter* was rudely interrupted by the arrival of a group of teenage louts – including a future England football international – who jumped over the wall and trashed the *Blue Peter* garden. We don't remember anything particularly heinous – no Goldie strung up by the paws or 'Simon Groom is a ******'** graffitied on the *Blue Peter* tortoise, just a few plant pots being upturned – but the over-reaction was as if someone had been brutally murdered. One presenter was clearly struggling to avoid using words such as 'string', 'up', 'birch' and 'borstal'. Which just made it funnier for the rest of us.

Bluewater Shopping Centre

Less a load of shops under one roof and more a temple to interest-free credit. Containing 330 'of the finest stores and restaurants' it thinks of itself as 'the most innovative and exciting shopping and leisure destination in Europe today'. Its philosophy is simple: to make shopping an enjoyable, stress-free experience; but they are really missing a trick here. To truly live up to that claim they need to have all couples banned from attending together. Men should be allowed to attend only to act as chauffeurs and cashpoint machines; under no circumstances should they be allowed to sit outside dressing rooms, avoiding each other's eyes as their womenfolk come out in the fifth of nine potential black skirts, asking their opinion. Never.

Blume, Judy

What Shakespeare did for romantic love in *Romeo and Juliet*, Judy Blume did for puberty.

Board Games (Junior Versions of)

Scrabble. Cluedo. Monopoly. As a child, such games are a thing of adult wonder, a glimpse at a future life of fun and sophistication. Well wait no more little ones, now that you can enjoy the high life of 'junior' versions of these grown-up games. Actually, we should have put the inverted commas around 'enjoy' rather than 'junior', because let's face it, enjoyment and junior games don't exactly go hand in hand. Have you ever played Junior Scrabble? The words are already written out on the board – all you have to do is plug the gaps with your letters. Where's the skill in that? Where's the training for furious adult arguments about whether 'xo' is a legitimate two-letter word? There is, of course, a challenge for an adult in a junior game: trying not to win. But let's be honest, where's the fun in that?

Bond Films (On TV)

The trouble with modern Bond films is that they pay far too much lip service to current political realities. The idea that Britain is a comparatively insignificant player on the world stage, and that our crack special forces operatives are too busy avoiding American airstrikes to concentrate on taking down international terror masterminds rather takes the fun out of things. Now the proper Bond films, the old ones they show on the telly, have no time for all that; theirs is a world where British craftsmen not only still make cars, but find the time to pimp them out with rocket launchers, ejector seats, and little whirly disc thingummies that puncture other peoples' tyres. So put your feet up, dunk a ginger-nut in your tea, and enjoy the satisfaction of international law being applied in the most violent manner possible, without any reference to due process or chance of appeal. That's entertainment. See also **Bond Films Featuring Roger Moore**; **Bond Girls (Suggestively Named)**.

Bond Films Featuring Roger Moore

Tell a group of friends you want to have a get-together to watch *Goldfinger*. Now, watch their reactions when you tell those same friends you've changed your mind and plan to screen *Moonraker* instead. Roger Moore actually made a handful of decent non-Bond movies, but his tenure as 007 is not exactly seen as the high point of the series – not that we don't still watch when they turn up on TV. See also **Bond Girls (Suggestively Named)**; **Emmanuelle (Movies Featuring the Character of)**; **Bond Films (On TV)**.

Bond Girls (Suggestively Named)

Fans of James Bond films like their women sexy, submissive, and saddled with ridiculous names. Who could top such 'triumphs' as Honey Ryder (Ursula Andress in *Dr No*), Holly Goodhead (Lois Chiles in *Moonraker*), and the never-to-be-improved-upon Pussy Galore (Honor Blackman in *Goldfinger*)? The addition of Pierce Brosnan as Bond in 1995's *Goldeneye* spawned an attempt to bring the franchise's views on women into the Nineties. But that didn't stop the writers from offering up a female assassin named Xenia Onatop. See also **Bond Films Featuring Roger Moore; Bond Films (On TV)**.

Boob Tubes

If ever there was an article of clothing designed *for* a woman *by* a man, the boob tube is it. Consisting of a band of rib-knit fabric hovering around the bosom, these strapless, one-size-fits-all garments neither lift nor support, leaving breasts with no other option but to hang in limbo with public exposure just inches away. No wonder they've been the bane of official dress codes since the moment they appeared on the fashion scene in the 1950s, stylishly paired with matching shorts and skirts for the beach. Always a hit on a snowy midwinter's night in Sunderland, boob tubes are the perennial wardrobe choice for women who want to get noticed at any cost and girls who want to get sent home from school early.

Book Clubs

This is, of course, a wonderful book and you would scarcely believe your luck if you were offered a copy for 99p. Credulity would then be stretched to its very limits if two other, almost as impressive volumes were thrown in to sweeten the deal. All you would have to do to secure this (as it turns out, Faustian) bargain is to endure a year or so of increasingly stern letters from the Mildly Amusing Paperback Club of Great Britain or, their agents in this matter, Deadly Bert's Mutual Loan and Wounding. Every Sunday after lunch at least one person you know signs up to one of the Byzantine contracts outlined on the back of one of the supplements. You will easily be able to identify the Book Club member; it will be the person with three enormous unread hardbacks about the Pyramids, and a somewhat haunted expression.

Booker Cash and Carry

Is there anything more delightful in life than a friend with a Booker Cash and Carry card, and the opportunity to buy ridiculous amounts of food and drink at wholesale prices? This is shopping writ large: boxes containing enough tampons to insulate your attic; side-by-side gallons of fruit drink shackled together like Tony Curtis and Sidney Poitier in *The Defiant Ones*; and enough sweets to have some to spare even if the trick-or-treaters line up to the end of your street.

'Born to be Wild'

Once the anthem of every moped rider in the western world, 'Born to Be Wild' was popularized in 1969's damn-near-unwatchable hit *Easy Rider*. The song had been released a year earlier as part of the band Steppenwolf's self-titled debut album (a disc completed in four days on a $9,000 budget). Unfortunately, this tune isn't nearly as cool as it once was. It's now the theme song of millions of balding, desperate, middle-aged men who still want to think they're bad.

Bowling (Ten Pin)

Bowling is a sport in much the same way as pork scratchings are health food. Very few people ever practise bowling, except perhaps for an illicit hour the weekend before a friend's birthday. You can easily identify a serious bowler, as he (and it will be a he) will have his own ball, a bizarre glove/plaster-cast contraption, and a loose shirt that does much to conceal his burgeoning beer-belly. The rest of us will continue to bowl once a year, rejoicing if our score enters triple figures and regretting that impulsive hot dog which will be repeating on us long after the glow of imagined exercise has faded.

Box Sets

You like music. You like collecting music. What could be better than owning a multi-box set of CDs of all your favourite hits of the Seventies, and then some? Welcome to the world of CD Box Sets, so big that they take up an entire advert break to get their completeness across. And then comes the clincher: this wonderful collection isn't available in any shop . . . Why not, voiceover man? We don't know much about retail, but might you not shift a few copies if you got your produce into HMV? Just a thought. And actually, here's another one. If you're enough of a music fan to buy this many discs, wouldn't you already have most of these songs in your collection? See also **Greatest Hits Albums**; **Time-Life Books**.

Boy Bands

Boy bands encompass a range of musicians from the Four Freshmen to Frankie Valli and the Four Seasons but the term most commonly refers to those who rise to teen-magazine-cover success on the wings of bubblegum pop (think the Osmonds, New Kids on the Block, Take That, and Westlife). Fortunately most disappear as soon as their fan base grows old enough to know better. But sometimes they come back for good.

Branson, Richard

As a package, Branson works annoyingly well: beards, jumpers and tombstone teeth have never been a good look, but on him they just work. We would probably throw money at him if he prefixed *anything* with the word Virgin. It is the perfect brand – we know that it is a huge worldwide beast, but Branson's hands-on presence kids us into thinking he is actually running a charity and we are lucky to be given the chance to invest in it. We all know the story – how at the age of twenty young Richard founded Virgin as a mail-order company, opened a record shop, then a record company, released Mike Oldfield's *Tubular Bells*, which sold 5 million copies, signed the Sex Pistols and the Rolling Stones, sold Virgin Records to EMI for a cool billion dollars, diversified into Virgin Atlantic Airways, Virgin Publishing, Virgin Cola, Virgin Cinemas, Virgin Trains, Virgin Brides, etc. etc. and is still working to make Virgin as well known around the world as Coca-Cola. For fun he flies around the world in balloons trying to break world records. Annoyingly he seems irrepressibly nice, straightforward and decent, like an early-model Tony Blair. Were this the US he would run for President and were we Americans we would probably vote for him.

Bread (Mopping up Sauce with)
Sometimes, at the end of a meal, one finds oneself in the awkward situation of having some sauce left over on one's plate. But fear not, for further enjoyment can be yours thanks to a brilliant new invention: bread. Simply fold your slice of bread in two, sweep it round the plate and enjoy all the extra bits of goo that other diners leave behind. And don't worry about the occasional look of disgust on other people's faces. They're just jealous, that's all.

Breakfast Club, The
The Breakfast Club is to John Hughes what *The Caretaker* is to Harold Pinter – the artistic summary of everything its creator is about. Although it's a film for teenagers, many an adult has secretly seen themselves in Emilio Estevez's misunderstood jock, Molly Ringwald's misunderstood prude, Anthony Michael Hall's misunderstood geek, Judd Nelson's misunderstood thing, and Ally Sheedy's misunderstood freak. See also **Weird Science**; **Hughes, John (The Films of)**.

Breasts (Artificial Augmentation Of) See Wonderbra, The.

Breasts (Ogling) See Anderson, Pamela; Barbeau, Adrienne; Bardot, Brigitte; Baywatch; Boob Tubes; Farrah Fawcett Poster, The; Freeman's Catalogue, The; Parton, Dolly; Wonderbra, The.

Bridal Magazines
No wife-to-be is 100 per cent immune to bride-mag fever. The symptoms are mild at first: a harmless perusing of *Wedding and Bride* on the magazine rack at WHSmith; and maybe a few sudden, unexplained references to fondant icing or canapés and confetti. Then comes an obsessive-compulsive hoarding of *Hello!* magazines, the regular viewings of *Four Weddings and a Funeral* and finally an uncontrollable urge to set up a wedding list at PJ's or Conran. With a multi-million-pound wedding industry

pushing everything from bridesmaid dresses to personalized wedding balloons, it's hard for a woman not to fantasize about how she and her groom would look in some of those happy photo shoots – even if you know inevitably that the wedding reception is likely to end up with the joyous combination of pub car park, the police and Michelle and Carol tanked up on 'breezers' smacking the shit out of each other.

Britain (Hollywood's Version of)

Hollywood's take on the UK has always been a little – how can we put this? – approximate. The 'hilarious' fudging of historical fact in films like *Braveheart* and *U571* is to be expected – and indeed Mel Gibson's willingness to insult British filmgoers or Kevin Costner's afternoon stroll from the White Cliffs to Sherwood Forest is as much a part of the culture of cinema as Aramaic subtitles and Kia-Ora. Any American film director researching a UK-set film is given a (colourised) copy of *Passport to Pimlico* and told to get on with it. Hence the incredible frequency of red double-decker buses which always seem to turn up exactly where they are needed in films – even in the postapocalyptic London depicted in *Sid and Nancy*. But the cab rides that always take in a couple of goes past Buckingham Palace, that's different: that really does happen to Yanks every time they come over here. Our cabbies have got to get their laughs somehow.

Broadband

In the eighteenth century of the Internet (i.e. three years ago) when a 56K dial-up connection was the Porsche 911 of the Internet Super Highway, we got excited when a picture only took three minutes to download, line by line, and a tiny video clip was ready for viewing before a beard was grown. But then someone invented Broadband. Now it's on tap 24/7 and Internet Explorer can autocomplete the URL you are entering; it practically reads your mind and gets you where it knows you want to go without asking you first. Hell, you can even get WiFi Broadband on trains and there are plans to send up three satellites which will cover the entire surface of the globe with Broadband access. Broadband is now bigger than Jesus and there ain't nothing you can do about it . . . except log on, tune in and get turned on.

Bronson, Charles See *Death Wish*.

Brown, Derren
Calling Derren Brown the British answer to David Blaine is a lazy comparison, even if they do share the same initials. Still, the British answer to David Blaine is everything we want from a magician: forget pulling rabbits out of hats – this guy wants to mess with your head, and in the case of one notorious bout of Russian roulette, his. Exploitative? Perhaps. Great TV? Definitely.

Bubble Bath
'Take a bath with Mr Bubble. He'll get you so clean your mother won't know you,' boasted a commercial from the 1960s. Hmm. Long-lasting bubble fun takes on a different meaning when you're thirty-seven than it did when you were seven, though you're never too old for the delights of giving yourself a Father Christmas-style beard. See also **Shops That Sell Smelly Things for Your Bathing Pleasure**.

Bubble Wrap (Popping)
If you get a kick out of the crafty finger/thumb popping action then do not worry – you are not alone. In 1957 Alfred W. Fielding and Swedish engineer Marc Chavannes were messing around in a garage in Hawthorne, New Jersey, trying to invent a plastic wallpaper with a paper backing. Mercifully, they failed and in a eureka moment realized that they had instead invented the solution to all packaging problems, which they named Bubble Wrap. Their Sealed Air Corporation grosses over $3 billion annually – that's a lot of popping. Who hasn't had a surreptitious pop on the sly? Hell, there's even a Bubble Wrap Appreciation Day on 26 January and a stupidly addictive Web site for virtual popping at www.virtual-bubblewrap.com. Don't try it unless you have the rest of the day free. As the bumper sticker says, 'Therapy is expensive, poppin' bubble wrap is cheap!'

Bubble Yum

All forms of bubble gum are guilty pleasures. But when you make a variety that's chunky, soft, comes in bizarre colours, and even has a silly name, you've got a chew that no self-respecting adult will admit to buying, let alone masticating. Roughly 1.3 billion chunks are sold each year – enough since the brand's inception to circle the equator seven times. Not that you'd want to do that. It's hard enough getting just *one* piece off your shoe.

Budweiser

 First brewed in 1876, the self-anointed 'King of Beers' is made from only five ingredients: barley malt, hops, yeast, water, and, of all things, *rice* (which apparently helps improve the clarity of the finished product). But the truly creepy thing is that every batch in the world, whether brewed near the Anheuser-Busch headquarters in St Louis or in Japan, tastes almost exactly the same as every other batch. This is both a technical achievement of the highest order and a source of horror to aficionados, who think each vat of fermented grain should be as distinctive as a fingerprint. Which is fine if you're at a tasting party. But sometimes, all you really need is something cheap and inoffensive to fill up the beer bong.

Building Implosions

There's something primal – and pleasurable – about watching things explode on-screen. And there's fun, too, in watching things deliberately imploded in real life. Since 1773, when 150 pounds of gunpowder were used to bring down the Holy Trinity Cathedral in Waterford, Ireland (more of an explosion than an implosion, but still an industry landmark), the curious have lined up to watch as firepower, maths, and luck have their way with supposedly immovable objects.

Bumper Stickers

Traffic-calming plans such as congestion zones, red routes and gyratory systems don't work – luckily. For there is a big plus to this gridlock: it gives you an opportunity for a crafty snigger at the literary masterpieces that are bumper stickers. Originally an American invention used by truckers to show off about where they had trucked, who they had trucked with and what they enjoyed doing whilst they weren't trucking, the craze swiftly overtook the rest of the world. Among our favourites are 'My Other Car's A Porsche'; 'Passion Wagon – Don't Laugh, Your Daughter's Inside'; 'How Do I Set A Laser Printer To Stun?'; 'The Proctologist Called . . . They Found Your Head'; 'Save Your Breath . . . You'll Need It To Blow Up Your Date' and 'Don't Like My Driving? Call 0800-FUCK-YOU'. Right.

Bunton, Emma

Baby Spice, one sometimes feels, was in The Spice Girls for the dads. The acceptable face of paedo-pop, she pulled the whole range of coquettish and Lolita-like poses while Ginger shouted 'Girl Power!' and Scary practised her kick-boxing. It wasn't wise to admit she was your favourite in public. And that's even more so the case now, as Baby's solo career slowly ebbs away. Which is a shame, because although her sub-Sixties sound isn't up to much, her Bardot-like look remains both rather fetching and, a few years on, slightly less dodgy.

Bus Stops (Drenching People at)

Picture the scene: it is pissing down and there is a dejected looking crowd of about nine people near the bus stop, made up of old ladies with tartan shopping trolleys and Yorkshire terriers, and young mothers with small children in overladen buggies. They are gazing longingly into the distance, looking for that elusive No. 37 bus when you heave into view. By the bus stop there is a small lake masquerading as a puddle. The puddle is probably twenty-five feet long and some six feet wide and there may even be some leaves floating on it. You are keeping an even course but steering slightly to the right to avoid it when something inexplicably makes you speed up and steer left, as near to the curb as you can without mounting the pavement. The combined sharp left steer and the speed and the narrowness of the gap between you and the curb creates a wave of Biblical proportions which drenches the queue both from the left in a full-on spray and then from above, crashing over them as they dash for refuge in the inadequate bus shelter. Do remember to test your brakes afterwards.

Buscaglia, Leo
The cuddliest of the self-help gurus – assuming you're into cuddling self-help gurus. See also **Inspirational Books**.

Buying Presents (For Your Other Half Knowing that They Are Actually for You)
It can be difficult to get your other half to really indulge you with presents you want, so the best way out of this cul-de-sac is to buy yourself as much as possible on your wish-list, but legitimize the expense by cleverly 'giving' them to your other half. Hey presto – on Christmas morning the fragrant girlfriend gets a new socket set ('you'll be so much more independent if anything ever goes wrong with the car') or a new roof rack ('it'll be great for when we go to visit your mother') and the rugged boyfriend gets a selection of aromatherapy oils and a new set of Egyptian cotton bed linen.

C

Caddyshack

At the time of its cinema release, this raunchy farce set at a fancy country club was considered a flop. But a funny thing happened on the way to the video shop. Out of nowhere, fans started reciting 'immortal' dialogue from cast members Bill Murray ('It's in the hole!'), Rodney Dangerfield ('So let's dance!'), and Chevy Chase ('Do you take drugs, Danny?'). In the pantheon of films that men watch when there are no women present, it rates just behind porn (any porn) on the desirability scale. See also *Animal House*; **Chase, Chevy**.

Caffeine (Excessive Use Of In Drinks) See Red Bull.

Call Centres (Listening to Soul-Destroying Music while on Hold With) See Interactive Telephone Menus as your enquiry is important to us.

Calling for the Bill (Making That Annoying Writing-On-Air Gesture When)

A close second behind Clicking Your Fingers to Attract The Waiter's Attention. Enough said. Garçon!

Cameron, David

No one ever admits to voting Tory, but we're pretty sure someone's been doing it. The principal reason why the

Conservatives have failed to make a decent showing in recent elections is their apparent inability to find a candidate with more hair than Blair. Bald men are by far the most electorally disadvantaged minority in Britain and no one, no matter how liberal, will ever give one a chance. Now though, with a well-thatched minor aristocrat at the helm, the party of unapologetic selfishness can look forward to a purple patch which is likely to grow as steadily as Tony Blair's bald one. Already the man some wags (well, just us really) are referring to as 'the Jimmy Carr of politics' is setting housewives' hearts a-flutter across the Home Counties. Even when he's Prime Minister though, we bet no one will own up to having voted for Dave the Chameleon.

Can't Stop the Music See Village People, The.

Candy Floss

Candy Floss (originally called fairy floss) is nothing but raw sugar that's melted, spun into gossamer filaments, and then collected on a stick. Ironically, one of the four men who developed the process in the early twentieth century was a dentist named Josef Delarose Lascaux.

Captain Pugwash (Invented Stories About)

Of course there were never characters called Seaman Stains or Master Bates or indeed Roger the Cabin Boy, and Gang Bang Gordon the Shag-Happy Second Mate was one we made up just now. But that didn't stop this urban myth of sub-playground quality becoming a 'did you know?' fact. And despite the best efforts of the Pugwash creators to dispel this blatant untruth, the story lingers on for one very simple reason: it's funny. See also *Magic Roundabout, The* (Theories About); Urban Myths.

Car-Boot Sales

Harrods shoppers wouldn't be caught dead at the car boot sale. Or, at least, they wouldn't admit it. Yet the thrill of the hunt attracts folks from across the economic spectrum to car parks, school playgrounds and run-down stately homes in search of those elusive collectibles that somehow didn't make it to Sotheby's, *The Antiques Roadshow*, or eBay.

Carpenters, The

Seemingly existing, like *The Boy in the Plastic Bubble*, inside some sort of rarified place that no thundering guitar solo could ever reach, Karen and Richard Carpenter crafted such ultra easy listening hits as '(They Long to Be) Close to You', 'Rainy Days and Mondays', and 'We've Only Just Begun'. It was only after Karen's death from complications of anorexia in 1983 that critics reconsidered. The fact is, the tunes (one of which is undoubtedly going through your head right now) were quite catchy.

Cars (Pretentious) See **Corvettes**; **4x4s**; **Limousines**; **Sat Nav**; *Top Gear*.

Carrey, Jim

Mr Carrey is a double guilty pleasure. You feel embarrassed when you watch him do fart jokes as a Rhode Island state trooper in *Me, Myself & Irene*. Then you feel even more embarrassed when you sit through his more highbrow offerings, *wishing* he would do a fart joke. See also ***Dumb & Dumber***.

Carrie See **King, Stephen**.

Carrott, Jasper

Everything Ben Elton did, Jasper Carrott did about a decade earlier. The 'being funny at the beginning of their career' bit? Tick. The 'mainstream and not quite as funny' TV show? Tick. The 'should know better' sitcom (*The Thin Blue Line, All About Me*)? Tick. The execrable Queen musical? That, you see, is where Jasper remains a step ahead. His sole foray into music was his 1975 hit 'Funky Moped', which everyone bought for the *Magic Roundabout* sketch on the B-side. Carrott played to his strengths, and his strengths can be very strong – as anyone with a tape of his 1970s shows hidden in the back of a drawer can testify. See also ***Magic Roundabout, The*** (**Theories About**).

Carry On Films

Most reliable authorities agree that there are only six genuinely good *Carry On* films: *Cleo, Screaming, Up the Khyber, Matron, Camping*, and that French Revolution one. In fact over thirty were made, plus a few ancillary ones that feel like *Carry Ons*, have more or less the same players, and are shown on similarly dull Sunday afternoons. Although he is generally seen as the figurehead of *Carry On*, Sid James only appeared in about two thirds of the films. Virtually all of them however, irrespective of the setting, feel as if they feature lovable Wookie Bernard Bresslaw dressing up as a nurse: in the *Carry On* universe, it's a given that a 6'5" man will fit comfortably into a petite nurse's uniform as long as he has an amusingly high trumpety voice. The central philosophy of *Carry On*, that all humanity divides into around a dozen stereotypes each with their own catchphrase or signature laugh, has been debated for years, but irrespective of the outcome of this dispute we will continue to take comfort from this curiously British genre of cinema whenever a major summer sporting event is rained off. Ooh Matron!

Cars with Human Qualities See Hasselhoff, David; King, Stephen.

Cartland, Barbara

The women in Barbara Cartland's novels are typically wide-eyed, demure virgins with names ending in 'a'. The men are invariably dark, square-jawed and fully clothed (preferably in a uniform). By the time they finally get together, somewhere around page 118, it is with such breathlessly anticipated passion that when he 'kisses her until she [is] no longer herself but his' you can practically taste the salt on his lips. But wait . . . *gasp, gasp* . . . *we mustn't*! On the subject of her notoriously chaste sex scenes, Cartland once pointed out that 'You can't get more naked than naked, can you? And then where do you go from there?'

Cartoons (Adult Interest in)

It's okay for adults to watch *The Simpsons*. But getting caught enjoying, say, *The Powerpuff Girls* or *Ren and Stimpy* is tantamount to being caught playing Snakes and Ladders. Grown-up cartoon nuts challenged by unsympathetic friends/flatmates/spouses shouldn't make things worse by defensively asserting that while the slapstick action is geared to the pre-school crowd, the plots and dialogue are meant for adults. Instead, they should just smile sheepishly, change the channel, wait for their persecutor to leave – and then change back. See also *Flintstones, The*; **Hanna-Barbera Cartoons**; **Saturday Morning TV**; **Scooby-Doo**; **SpongeBob SquarePants**.

Casinos

These days it's not just about flying to Vegas to watch Elton or Celine in concert followed by a hard night at the roulette table with George Clooney, Julia Roberts and Brad Pitt. Oh no. The UK is catching up fast and trying to shed that Ronnie and Reggie Kray image of back-rooms, dodgy geezers and 'hostesses'. Nowadays, UK gambling dens are designed to satisfy the fantasies of players of all classes but the only fantasy they won't satisfy is the wish to go home a winner. See also **Las Vegas**; **Liberace**; **Fruit Machines in Pubs**.

Cassidy, David

Back in the early Seventies David Cassidy was the hottest thing in tight, fringed trousers. The star of the sitcom *The Partridge Family* from 1970 to 1974, he transformed his role as the front man for a pretend rock group into a real career as a pop idol. Of course once he reached the summit of fame, there was nothing to do but take the inevitable donkey ride down to Has-been Valley. Today he knocks around Las Vegas, headlining casino shows and, perhaps inevitably, singing old Rat Pack anthems.

Cat (Making To Look Like An Alien)

Difficult to resist. Just pin your faithful cat's little ears back (not with actual pins you understand but just with your fingers of course) and hey presto your mini-beast has become a laugh-out-loud alien wannabee with scary eyes and fangs. Try not to laugh AT your cat while they are in the room though, as they are terribly sensitive.

'Cat's in the Cradle'

Getting emotional the first time you hear a song is okay. (Perhaps, for example, you really weren't expecting there to be 100 yellow ribbons 'round the old oak tree.) But when a song – and the song we're talking about is Harry Chapin's weepy 1974 hit – climbs the charts on the backs of people who listen to it over and over again, even though they *know* that the dad who doesn't pay attention to his son is destined to wind up a lonely old man, we're not talking about guilty pleasure any more. We're talking about masochism. See also **Death Songs**.

Catchphrase

One of those televisual treats that makes you worry for the nation. The concept is simple: a picture is revealed to show a well-known catchphrase (a large number of cooks, a pan of broth going wrong). The contestants are even simpler: 'Is it "Have your cake and eat it", Roy?' It would have been great if just once, host Roy Walker (the cheese gratin to this particular dish) had said, 'Jesus! There's a lot of cooks there, there's a pan with the word "broth" on the side. What's with the "cake" shit, numbskull?' But like the true professional Roy is, he'd smile politely and say 'It's good, but it's not right.'

Cats

It's the most-mocked musical since . . . actually, we can't think of any others. But though critics have skinned this cat in almost every conceivable way, that didn't stop it from running for a quarter of a century in the West End. Admitting that you witnessed the antics of these felines as they try to make it to the  'Heaviside layer' is embarrassing even to people who thought Andrew Lloyd Webber's *Evita* was deep and his *Phantom of the Opera* was actually opera. See also **Webber, Andrew Lloyd**.

CD Covermounts

You've got enough CDs. Really, you have. And yet once every couple of months you'll find yourself tempted by a magazine you probably won't read just because there's a 'free' CD stuck to the cover. Stuck, indeed, with a tiny glob of artificial snot that defies all attempts at disposal. These CDs generally follow a set format: there's generally one track, performed by a band you like, that wasn't good enough to release commercially. That's known as *the hook*. The rest of the disc is padded out with fourteen tracks by bands that you've read about once or twice but made a mental note never to listen to. Computer magazines play a more dangerous game, cramming an entire CD-Rom full of needless software odds and ends that you definitely don't need and will probably make your PC incredibly unstable. The genius here is that the following month, the magazine will run a feature on how to clear all the unnecessary odds and ends off your computer to make it more stable. It's easy, then, to see why magazine publishers like to attach this landfill to the covers of their journals, but what's in it for you? The pleasure of sitting in your favourite armchair, rolling a piece of artificial snot absent-mindedly between your fingers, listening to music you don't like all that much, for *free*.

Celebrities (Break-ups)

In our egalitarian age, anyone can be famous. It's no longer necessary to be royal, or talented, or clever, or even interesting – as Jade, Jordan or Chantelle will happily tell you. Nevertheless, even the most well-adjusted reader will occasionally fall prey to the feeling that these people we read about in *Heat* are in some indefinable way a little bit *better* than the rest of us. The very fact of their ubiquity leads us to assume that they must be at the very least more sexually desirable than the average person. Consequently, when these celebrated individuals suffer some setback, especially in the field of romance, we are suffused with the consoling sensation that, whether or not they have feet of clay, they can from time to time step in the same mess as the rest of us. Wearing sandals. The Germans have a word for it. We just call it a 'guilty pleasure'.

Celebrities (Doing Ridiculous Things)

Proper celebrities, of course, throw a strop at the slightest unreasonable request: Mariah Carey once famously declared that she 'didn't do stairs'. Lesser celebrities, on the other less talented hand, are far more amenable. You remember the bit in *Fame* where the teach bangs her stick and talks about paying in sweat? These days, the celebrity 'studes' are shelling out something far more sticky. Hence the glorious televisual spectacle of Rebecca Loos, famous for being given a serious texting by David Beckham, appearing on Channel 5's reality TV show *The Farm* and being asked to, let's not be coy here, wank off a pig. What are the chances of getting Mariah Carey to follow suit? Let's be honest – what are the chances of getting Mariah within fifty miles of a farm? She doesn't 'do' pigs.

Celebrities (Excessive Interest in the Lives of)

See Anderson, Pamela; Autographs; Bashir, Martin; Footballers' Indiscretions; *Heat* Magazine; Hilton, Paris; Leslie, John; Naked Celebrities; Tabloids, 3am Girls; Titmuss, Abi; *Weekly World News*; www.imdb.com.

Celebrities (Impersonators)

The back pages of the entertainment industry's trade newspaper, *The Stage*, is full of some of the funniest advertisements you are ever likely to read. If you can't afford to book Robbie Williams for your hen night then why not choose between 'Andy McGowan as Robbie Williams' or 'Paul Reason as Robbie Williams'? Tricky choice. Alternatively, if you need Dame Shirley Bassey to open your local leisure centre but for some reason she is unavailable, you could always book 'Surely Bassey' instead. There is something inately fascinating about people who make their lives pretending to be celebrities and, for a moment or two, getting a buzz out of being treated like one by a pissed-up group of sales reps in the Doncaster Holiday Inn. They must know deep down that we are laughing at them, not with them, but every now and again, when the light catches them at the right angle and their voice hits the high notes then the audience forgets the deception and gets a glimpse through the glitter curtain of fame. But then of course the lights come up and

'Frankly Sinatra' looks a bit like that man who used to hang around at the bus stop after school, and you feel dirty and a bit sad.

Celebrity Love Island

Once, not so long ago, the term 'celebrity' implied that the person or thing being described was in some way celebrated by society at large. Now the word has come to mean: 'person who has by some happenstance come to our attention and is desperate to remain in the public eye no matter what the cost'. *Celebrity Love Island* is the apotheosis of this *Weltanschauung* – a rag-tag bunch of the accidentally famous, or nearly famous, are herded together into a kind of penal colony for the needy and encouraged to paw each other for our amusement. Somehow, despite our natural revulsion, we find ourselves drawn to the show much as our forebears were simultaneously revolted and amused as they toured the corridors of Bedlam. It's a tragic indictment of the kind of society in which we now live, where a night out with a former reality show contestant infects you with a transitory kind of celebrity of your own. It's also absolutely hilarious. More please!

Celebrity Squares

Take nine slebs. Make sure at least one of them was Willie Rushton. Stack 'em up in a box that goes one storey higher than the University Challenge imaginary boffin-stack. Ask them stupid questions. Get yourself an über-presenter like Bob Monkhouse and add a mildly irreverent voiceover from Kenny Everett. You've got TV perfection. What could you add to improve this inimitable mix? Nothing! Except maybe Frank Carson. Still showing on a cable channel near you.

Celebrity-Owned Restaurants See Theme Restaurants.

Center Parcs

An open-prison theme park for the middle-classes. On arrival you drive through a Guantanamo Bay-type security zone, present your papers and then drive clockwise round the Tarmac road with thousands of other 4x4 vehicles to your allocated

Barrett Home-in-a-forest, where squirrels cavort outside your patio and the décor is Ikea meets University of Kent study-bedrooms. And here's the clever bit: you then drive back to the car park and hire bicycles which, for the rest of the week, are the only legal form of transport. All of a sudden you can pretend you are in Holland, leave the cares of urban living behind and spend the week cycling to and from the 'central plaza' with the 'huge aquatic pleasuredome'. By Day Two you forget there is an outside world (until you come across the huge barbed-wire topped security fence deep in the woods) and happily spend hundreds of pounds in the on-site supermarket and in the 'Food Village', where a nightly ritual of 'Huckleberry's or Rock Legends, La Sapinière or Rajinda Pradesh?' soon becomes the only decision you need to make.

Centrefolds See *Penthouse Forum; Playboy; Playgirl*; Smith, Anna Nicole.

Chair-o-Plane See **Outdated Fair Rides**.

Chan, Jackie See **Kung Fu Films**.

Chap Stick (Flavoured)
Anyone can appreciate the fresh-as-a-first-kiss taste of cherry-flavoured Chap Stick and its strawberry cousin. But considering the little containers' universal tendency to go missing (and be replaced again and again by fresh tubes purchased impulsively at the checkout), the slogan might as well be 'There's a Chap Stick for every handbag, medicine cabinet, junk drawer, glove compartment, tumble-dryer, public-toilet floor, and space between the sofa cushions'. Sounds a bit rude, actually.

Charlie (The Perfume) See **Cheap Perfumes (From the Chemist's)**.

Charlie's Angels
'Jill, you're going undercover in a massage parlour. Kelly, I want you to crack a safe while wearing a bikini. Sabrina, you'll put on a white lab coat and impersonate a chemical engineer

until further notice.' You never knew what boundaries of practical gumshoeing would be broken when the three employees of the Charles Townsend Detective Agency gathered around Bosley's speakerphone to receive a new assignment. All you knew was that millions of people would gather around their TVs to find out. As the enigmatic Charlie would say, 'Good work, Angels.' See also **Farrah Fawcett Poster, The; Spelling, Aaron**.

Chase, Chevy

A Chevy Chase film is a bit like your favourite armchair. It's not flash, it's never going to win an award, but it's a pleasingly familiar and comfortable place to spend a couple of hours. Lacking the edge of fellow Saturday Night Livers John Belushi, Bill Murray and Dan Ackroyd, Chevy waded through a selection of action comedies (*Spies Like Us*, *Fletch*) but found his spiritual home as Clark Griswold in the National Lampoon's assorted *Vacation* films – the well-meaning father for whom every attempt to give his family a great holiday goes pear-shaped. See also *Caddyshack*.

Chat Lines (Advertised on TV)

You'd never call one of those things. You've got a life. And if there's no life to be had for an hour or two, you read books. Like this one. Good isn't it? Chatline adverts have a special fascination though. They try *so* hard to convey the impression that these things are populated almost entirely by attractive and sexually voracious young women (except the gay lines, we'll come to those in a minute) whereas even the simplest intellect is aware that the only people who would actually call these things are congenitally unattractive losers with oozing acne of a severity hitherto only seen in excessively CGI'd horror movies. Gay chatlines always seem to offer as their selling point that there are some absolutely *terrible* dancers on the line right now. You could ring them and jeer at their moves. For some of us it might be the only chance we will ever get to do that. Not that *we're* terrible dancers. Besides, we'd never call one of those things. We've got a life.

Chat Rooms

Imagine a singles bar where everyone is hot, horny – and blind. That, in a nutshell, is the attraction of Internet chat rooms. Participants can ditch real-world names such as Malcolm and Helen in favour of monikers like 2coolguy and sexxxyladi. And they can change their age, their sex, and pretty much any other detail of their personality and vital statistics as well, with no one the wiser. This takes lying to an entirely new level, in a venue where you can never be held accountable for your actions. How could it *not* be a guilty pleasure?

Chavs (feeling superior to)

Since records began, or at least shortly after, the privileged few have enjoyed mocking the great unwashed. It was an established amusement in Shakespeare's day, and creative lions such as Dickens and Mike Leigh have forged entire careers by inviting us to chuckle at our poorly-educated inferiors. Mindful of this, the finest political minds in the realm have sought to facilitate and maximize this simple pleasure by the clever expedient of degrading educational standards to the point where an emotionally incontinent, grammatically crippled clown clad in a pile of market-stall designer knock-offs can be found on even the most gentrified street, leading to widespread hilarity amongst us, the great and the good.

Cheap Perfume (From the Chemist's)

You can find them parked together on one neglected stretch of shelf, like some sort of olfactory scrapbook: Tabu, Charlie, Emeraude, Jean Naté, Love's Baby Soft, Wind Song, Skin Musk, and Jovan Musk. Some smell more like furniture polish than perfumes. Others remain as cloyingly sweet and floral as when your big sister fogged her bedroom with them to mask the equally fragrant bouquet of her best friend, Mary J. Uana. But though cheap and cheap-smelling, they nevertheless retain a pungent place in the toiletries section of our hearts. See also **Impostor Perfumes**; **Marijuana**.

Cheech and Chong
The bitter truth, man, is that this pair are only funny if you're stoned. See also **Marijuana**.

Cheese See **Fondue**; **Nachos**; **Cheese (Straightening the)**.

Cheese (Straightening the)
We like to be helpful round the house. We like eating cheese. So when a meal has reached its conclusion and it's time to clear away, we feel duty bound to contribute by 'straightening the cheese'. After all, there's nothing worse than putting a piece of stilton away that has been cut at various angles. It's just, well, ungainly. Fortunately, with the use of a knife (and a mouth to dispose of those straightening slices) the cheese can be made good for next time. Straightening the cheese is a tricky manoeuvre to master, and indeed, it may take two or three slices to get it straight to your satisfaction. But we can't help it if we're perfectionists.

Cher (With Sonny)
Cher was sixteen when she met record producer Sonny Bono. Soon the duo were in nightclubs singing 'I Got You Babe' and joking between acts (she got the punch lines, he played straight man). They made a bizarre pair, like a counterculture fusion of Burns & Allen and the Krankies. But the act struck a chord, due in part to their hippie-dippy chemistry and obvious affection for each other. Soon they were hosting their own variety series which, for one season, included then-unknown Steve Martin as a regular. The show ran from 1971 until 1974, when the couple divorced. See also **Cher (Without Sonny)**.

Cher (Without Sonny)
A singer of earnest novelty songs ('Gypsys, Tramps, and Thieves', 'Half-Breed'), an Academy-Award-winning actress (*Moonstruck*), a dance-music diva ('Believe') and a popular drag show archetype, Cher has proven that her hit-making time with Sonny was just an opening act. Her appeal springs from our fascination with seeing how many comebacks one entertainer can possibly make. See also **Cher (With Sonny)**.

Cherry Garcia

Although not the most familiar name in the Ben & Jerry's flavour canon (the editors of this volume preferring Phish Food and/or Chunky Monkey), this is certainly the funniest, and as an ice cream dedicated to the late frontman of hippie perennials the Grateful Dead is proof that all a so-so flavour needs to become a winner is a great name. After all, when was the last time you saw anyone buy plain old cherry chocolate at your local supermarket?

Chick Flicks (Cinderella Fantasies)

Feminist sensibilities melt like butter-flavoured topping under the heat of a good old-fashioned Cinderella story, one in which the geeky girl takes off her glasses and gets the boy; the ugly girl has a makeover and gets the boy; the low-income girl inherits a fortune and gets the boy; or the gawky girl learns to dance and gets the boy. Leading ladies from Audrey Hepburn (*Sabrina*) to Sandra Bullock (*Miss Congeniality*) to repeat offender Renée Zellweger (*Jerry Maguire*, *Bridget Jones's Diary*, *Nurse Betty*) have endlessly reprised the Ugly Duckling role, upgrading their existences by landing a great big Richard Gere/Harrison Ford/Tom Cruise trophy hunk. It's not something women like to talk about outside the anonymous rows of the cinema, but deep down we'd give anything to be Sandy in the final funhouse scene of *Grease*. See also **Dirty Dancing**.

Chick Flicks (Female Bonding)

No man in the history of moviegoing has ever 'got' such gender-specific film moments as, say, the naming ceremony in *Divine Secrets of the Ya-Ya Sisterhood*, or Kathy Bates's car-bashing episode in *Fried Green Tomatoes*. And frankly, that's not a problem. There's no shortage of female fans waiting to savour such high-five-worthy Girl Power scenes, the kind that cause grown women to wave their fists in the air and leave the cinema shouting a new battle cry such as '*Ya-Ya!*' or '*Towanda!*' Be very afraid. See also **Charlie's Angels**; **Chick Flicks (In which Someone Dies)**; **Croft, Lara**; **Film Soundtracks**; **Romy and Michele's High School Reunion**; **Schwarzenegger, Arnold**.

Chick Flicks (In which Someone Dies)

Death, one of cinema's favourite money shots, can strike quickly, catching us unprepared (*Beaches*). Or it can ride into town on a slow train that we can see coming for the entire 118 minutes (*Dying Young*, *My Life*, *Steel Magnolias*). Either way is fine. As any woman who snotted up with Debra Winger in *Terms of Endearment* will tell you, a movie-induced crying jag is a delicious form of masochistic escapism. Bring us ailing mothers, lost loves, and children gone too soon. When the house lights come up, we will look around at the sea of mascara-smeared faces and know that something wonderful just happened. See also **Chick Flicks (Female Bonding)** and *Love Story*.

Chicken Nuggets

Along with the Turkey Twizzler (as demonized by Jamie Oliver) the nugget is possibly the most insidiously unhealthy food since the hot dog, both a fast-food staple and an easy, no-brainer meal for parents. It's appropriate for neither role. Composed in most cases of a ground-up slurry of white and dark meat with an artery-clogging infusion of chopped skin, it's bound together with oils and then encased in batter. To get an idea of what this does to the nuggets' nutritional value, consider that a serving of only five chicken nuggets packs 270 calories and 17 grams of fat (compared to just 10 grams of fat in a plain McDonald's hamburger). And yet, this convenience food is hugely popular with young children – or rather, with the parents of young children who can't be bothered to read the ingredients of the things they feed their progeny.

Chicken Skin

Some types of skin are good for you: fish skin for its oil; baked potato skins for fibre. Chicken skin is just good. We think God invented chickens so he'd have something to roast for lunch on the seventh day. What we don't know is whether or not, like us, the task of carving the meat involved the stuffing as much chicken skin in His mouth as He could get away with. It's a perk of the job, the chef's prerogative. Only dirty people ask for some on their plate.

Children's Books (Reading Aloud from)

Having children does have many drawbacks (a total loss of both social and sex life, to name but two) but it does give you the opportunity to rediscover the delights of all those books from your youth: Jean de Brunhoff's wonderful story of the elephant King Babar and Queen Celeste, with those exquisite Laurent De Brunhoff drawings, Dr Seuss's cool feline dude the Cat in the Hat, Helen Nicoll and Jan Pienkowski's slightly rubbish and hippy witch Meg and her cat Mog, the classic Beatrix Potter oeuvre including Jeremy Fisher and Peter Rabbit and the magical *The Wind in the Willows*. Long after your infant has gone to sleep you drone on and on, reading aloud and regressing until you almost long for someone to tuck you in and make sure the bugs don't bite, and that all the monsters are far, far away. Night now.

Chip Butty

We'll say this for the Earl of Sandwich: he had his food groups sorted out when he invented his eponymous snack; carbohydrate, protein, carbohydrate. The same can't be said for his lesser known chum, Lord Butty, who came to the conclusion that the only thing to be stuffed between two slices of carbohydrate was yet more carbohydrate, deep-fried. There's little nutritional value (unless you argue that ketchup is one of your five-a-day servings of fruit and veg) but that's why this anti-Atkins treat tastes so good.

Chocolate (Breakfast Cereals Featuring)

Part of a balanced breakfast? Not a chance. Part of an I'm-single-and-I-can-eat-whatever-I-want dinnertime travesty? Absolutely. In the 1960s, breakfast cereal was transformed by an onslaught of sugar-heavy monstrosities – some of which had the hubris to include chocolate in the mix. Coco Pops are so chocolatey, so the advert has it, they even make the milk go brown. Yes, kids. And also your teeth.

Christmas (Day)

It is impossible not to get misty-eyed when the Ghost of Christmas Past comes back to haunt you with memories of staying up late to listen for Santa, early morning stockings, a snow-filled garden, endless present opening, a huge slap-up feed, crackers, chocolate, fizzy drinks and game-playing, all topped off with the Morecambe and Wise Christmas special. Shame of course that Christmas day, once you are an adult, is more likely to see you up at 5 a.m. with a hairdryer and a hot tap trying to defrost the turkey, forgetting to put the veg on until it's too late, receiving presents from your drunken relatives that you gave them last year and being so exhausted that when lunch is cleared away, you fall asleep on the sofa and wake up to disapproving looks from your mother-in-law, and the realization that the best thing on the telly is . . . guess what . . . a repeat of the Morecambe and Wise Christmas special.

Christmas (Songs)

1973, the apotheosis of Glam, perhaps the most Christmas-compliant of all music trends. That December, two of the greatest Christmas songs ever written slugged it out for the Number One position: Wizard's anthemic 'I Wish it Could Be Christmas Every Day' somehow stalled at No. 4, but Slade's inimitable 'Merry Christmas, Everybody' ruled the charts for a well-deserved five months. There must have been some bizarre festive alchemy at work in the West Midlands that previous summer. It's often forgotten that down in the Home Counties bespectacled, bewigged, behave-yourself Elton John also had a stab at the Christmas No.1 spot with 'Step into Christmas' that same winter: any other year he'd have owned the charts, but with those two titans to contend with, there was no chance. In the same way that the iconography of Christmas is somehow permanently imprinted with the late Victorian era, so the sound of Christmas will always be 1973. And that's just as it should be . . .

Christmas (TV Specials)

Most rational people gave up on shows like *Only Fools and Horses* sometime during the John Major era. Indeed, most of us had partially forgotten that *Last of the Summer Wine* or *One*

Foot in the Grave even existed, only to be ambushed by an inescapable feature-length special when we're incarcerated in our parents' lounge on Boxing Day. The paradox is that television programmes that would merit, at best, a haughty sneer in high summer represent a rare lacuna in the hiss of low-level antagonism that results from a group of incompatible adults cooped up together in cold weather with no obvious escape route and a steady drip of alcohol. The real joy of a Christmas special isn't the pleasure of seeing a well-loved family favourite extended for a double-length episode, probably featuring a guest appearance from Patrick Mower; it's the sheer relief of not having to talk for sixty minutes.

Christmas Decorations (Excessive, Tasteless Use of)

What is it about the birth of Christ that makes people lose all sense of aesthetic perspective? Decking the halls can be fun, but placing too many options in the hands of aesthetically challenged individuals can produce horrifying results. Who hasn't, while driving to their nan's house to deliver some holiday cheer, slowed down to laugh at a lawn featuring a life-sized nativity scene, or blithely stared at a living room filled with motion-activated, snoring and/or dancing Santas, miniature Christmas villages, and a nutcracker army big enough to pacify Afghanistan? Let such wretched excess be a lesson: when it comes to boughs of holly, a little goes a long way.

Christmas Gift Books (Panic Buying)

It's 6 p.m. on Christmas Eve and you have been shopping non-stop since 9 a.m., your bags are overflowing with gifts which have become less and less appropriate and more and more expensively desperate as the day has progressed. But still you are not done yet. In total despair you run into a bookshop and are overwhelmed by shelves of books as far as the eye can see. You need help. You need guidance. And then you see it: a pile of books by the till marked 'Christmas Gift Suggestions'. You push forward and survey the selected titles. They look 'gifty' (i.e. nice size and a nice shape), they look keenly priced with welcome money-off stickers, they have unintimidating covers and witty titles which mean nothing, sound wry and amusing and have a reassuring familiarity about them. Your quest over, you grab copies of *Oats, Slices and Loaves – A Humorous Breadcellany, Is it just me or is everyone really a giant lizard?, Unlocking the DVLA bloodline – the secrets behind the Highway Code* and *Being Brian Blessed*. Perfecto. You know that how-ever little effort you put into buying these books a little less went into writing them. The only mercy is they will definitely be forgotten by Boxing Day. That's our promise to you.

Christmas Lights (Activation of by Naff Celebrities)
Whereas most lights can be switched on and off by normal members of the public, Christmas lights are a special exception which only work when a particularly Zzz list celebrity presses the button. Being the start of a festive season, the ceremony normally occurs in mid-October, where a gaggle of particularly gullible chavs congregate at the local Arndale, hyped into a frenzy by the local radio station talking up the appearance of a mystery celebrity, which to their angel delight turns out to be Jade from *Big Brother*.

Christmas Presents (Recyling)
Don't dismay if you receive a pile of terrible presents on your birthday or at Christmas – smile sweetly and be effusive in your praise for both the appositeness of the gift and the gen-erosity of spirit. When you get home, crank up www.eBay.co.uk and turn them all into ready cash or, in the rare event that you have something that even the world's largest online mar-ketplace would baulk at, simply rewrap them and give them to somebody else next year. In some families there are floral-arrangement paperweights and bottles of plum wine that have been doing the rounds for so many years that their origins are cloaked in the mists of time.

Chuckle Brothers, The
They found their hairstyles and terrible terrible *terrible* mous-taches in a time capsule buried under the Oakwell centre spot in the early Eighties, they found their routines in a box of old Laurel and Hardy out-takes and they may well have lifted their 'To me, to you' catchphrase from the PG Tips chimps. They're

still the funniest men on British television, and if you don't understand why you're probably the kind of person that pays their student loan back. Shame on you.

Church, Charlotte

 Ms Church first came to our notice as a singer appealing principally to the elderly. Of late, however, the singing has taken a back seat to the more entertaining business of appearing in the tabloids. Charlotte has, despite her tender years, quickly mastered the basic celebrity skills of getting drunk and falling out of her dress, topless sunbathing, and feuding with relatives. Of course, the tabloids wouldn't be half so interested in the teenage millionairess had she not blossomed into a veritable vision of callipygian pulchritude. Wales's very own Paris Hilton naturally has her very own sex video scandal, except that it isn't a video, it's a picture on a mobile phone. This *is* Britain after all. We're on a budget.

Cider

Seemingly in defiance of a Brobdingnagian marketing spend, cider retains its image as the official cold beverage of peace convoys and village idiots. And rightly so. Secretly though, despite nary a dreadlock nor a smock between us, we think it can be fairly tasty. Between consenting adults and in private, of course.

Cigarettes

Cigarettes were once a guilty pleasure because your parents didn't want you to smoke them. Then they became an even bigger guilty pleasure because you knew they were bad for you. The thrill was further compounded when prices for coffin nails skyrocketed, leaving you to ruminate about the other things you could have spent your smoking money on. Then came reports on the dangers of second-hand smoke and stories of the shameful practices of the tobacco companies. Then everything from offices to football stadiums to military barracks were made smoke-free environments. Of course smoking is still a guilty pleasure – perhaps the guiltiest of all, considering the repercussions. But things were certainly easier, albeit unhealthier, back when it wasn't *quite* so guilty.

Cinema Food

Popcorn served in a dustbin. Cola in a bucket. Sweets you can't eat quietly. Nachos with a perfect-for-the-dark wobbly tray of goo. We may be wrong but one gets the sense that whoever invented cinema food wasn't someone who goes to the cinema. And yet despite all this, a pricing system that appears to take a number from the real world and triple it, and the knowledge that you'll wolf the whole lot down before the end of the trailers and feel thoroughly queasy for the duration of the film, joining the queue in the confectionary stand is all but obligatory. It's part of the experience, isn't it?

Clancy, Tom

Clancy, a former insurance salesman, has been the patron saint of war groupies ever since his first novel, *The Hunt for Red October*, became an international best-seller in 1984. His follow-up tomes, each of them around two inches thick and filled with enough technical jargon to befuddle a general, likewise sold millions. But Clancy's chief attraction isn't his terrorist-, war-, and intrigue-infested plots; it's the fact that he's living the life that millions of closet battle nerds fantasize about. The U.S. military loves him, apparently, which means he can hitch a ride on pretty much any piece of cool hardware that catches his eye, be it a tank, jet fighter, or nuclear-powered attack submarine. Let Dan Brown try *that*.

Classic FM

Edgy modern popular music is all very well, but have you ever tried to settle down for a nice quiet read with Hard-Fi or Franz Ferdinand on the radio? Luckily some clever Germans identified this issue and as a result invented classical music. Unfortunately, in a typically German oversight, real, undiluted classical music is too much like hard work for normal people and nowadays is only to be heard on Radio 3 – where it exists as a sort of catalogue for anyone that's appearing on *Desert Island Discs* soon and wants us all to think they're brainy. For the rest of us, a team of experts has winnowed out all the unpleasant Teutonic racket, leaving us with a restful background hum which can be ignored at will should you encounter a long and complex sentence in your book, which contains multiple subclauses, incomprehensibly long words . . . excess punctuation; (or parentheses); and requires you to concentrate on the actual wordage. The rare speaking interludes are handled by comfortingly familiar individuals like Simon Bates (chosen we think for his reassuring warnings at the beginning of old videotapes), John Suchet (always a safe pair of hands when conveying bad news like 'here comes some Wagner'), or David Mellor (who was unexpectedly available). Classic FM has been scientifically proven to be more restful than actual silence. Think of it as a screensaver for your radio.

Classified Football Results (Read by James Alexander Gordon)

We know that you can get the football scores on your mobile phone these days, with text messages telling you your team has scored before Peter Crouch gets all robotic, but there's only one way to properly receive the results, and that's at five o'clock, on the radio, read by James Alexander Gordon. It's the way his cadence alters depending on the result that makes it so special. So if it's Manchester United One (voice going up), you know that whoever they're playing, it's going to be Nil. If it's Manchester United One (voice down), then it's whoever they're playing, Two. It must be tempting for James to shit a few people up by mixing it up, but he never does. We would.

Clichés And Meaningless Corporate Waffle

At the end of the day, taking everything into consideration, weighing up the pros and the cons, looking at both sides of the coin and looking at the balance of probabilities this is one of those ideas that one needs to run up the flagpole and see if anyone salutes. Clichés are as old as the hills and filling up a boring internal report with as many as possible without actually saying anything is a great thing to do on a slow Friday afternoon. However, a variation of this has now appeared as a game that three or four people can play together in a crowded meeting without anyone else being the wiser: simply agree a list of 'wank words' in advance and you score two points for any you vocalize in the meeting – the first person to get to ten wins. Obviously it is a game of two halves and although you may feel sick as a parrot, you can always workshop the results, facilitate a focus group and 'action' some synergizing feedback. In fact, let's agendarize some facetime soon – we'll get our people to talk to your people. You think this entry is all over? It is now . . .

Clifford, Max

Name any tabloid scandal of the last decade – whether it be Rebecca Loos, Neil and Christine Hamilton, David Mellor or John Leslie – and Max has been behind the acres of tabloid coverage that none of us ever read because it is a bit tacky and unseemly. He has the demeanour of an undertaker who has won the lottery, which makes sense when you remember he knows where all the skeletons are buried. Come to think of it, he probably knows where *our* skeletons are buried too . . . Max, you know we're only joking with you, don't you? We love you really.

Cliffs Notes

Has anyone actually read *Moby Dick*? *Don Quixote*? *Tristram Shandy*? Well, they certainly don't have to. Credit this series of guidebooks, available since 1958, for allowing generations of students to booze all weekend but still get a C for their English Lit essay. The most popular pamphlet in the English-speaking world, year in, year out, is for *The Scarlet Letter*. Which means that *The Scarlet Letter* could well be the world's most-loathed book.

Clinique Pore Minimizer Make-up

We'll never know how many smooth-skinned beauties owe their complexions to this miracle product. Even if your boat is pocked with pores the size of plugholes, this Clinique product can provide a complexion that's as smooth as satin. Though few women would admit to owning such a high-maintenance product (or that their pores, of all things, have begun to fail them), you can bet that most of them do.

Clinton Cards

For those of you who have yet to experience the pleasure that is the range of greetings cards currently stocked by this high street giant, then your life is truly lacking in many departments. Have you seriously never beheld the joys of seeing a 'Get Well Soon' card featuring a watercolour painting of a kitten climbing out of a hobnailed boot, or a 'Happy 21st Birthday' card with a beautiful pastel-effect horse-drawn carriage on a cobbled street? Or had the opportunity to purchase a hilariously funny card featuring a saucy slogan for a colleague's retirement? Shame on you. See also **Greetings Cards (Dirty)**.

Cocktail

During that brief, shining moment when Tom Cruise was a star but wasn't yet an actor (post-*Top Gun*, pre-*Rain Man*), he headlined this fluffy flick about a superstar barman – yes, a superstar barman. Saddled with perhaps the worst ad line in the history of the movies ('When he pours, he reigns'), *Cocktail* featured endless scenes of Cruise tossing bottles in the air while women looked on admiringly. In addition to a lame story and even lamer dialogue, the film also featured a hard-to-avoid-in-the-summer-of-'88 soundtrack that unleashed both the Beach Boys' 'Kokomo' and Bobby McFerrin's 'Don't Worry Be Happy' on an unsuspecting world. See also *Top Gun*.

Cocktails (Tooth-Endangeringly Sugary Drinks Posing as) See also **Alcopops**; **Baileys Irish Cream**; **Lambrusco**; **Red Bull**.

Coffee-mate

This used to be the generic white powder one sprinkled in Styrofoam cups of office coffee in order to cut the metallic taste. Now, however, Coffee-mate comes in an assortment of flavours ranging from Amaretto to French Vanilla to Hazelnut – all the better to sprinkle in Styrofoam cups of office coffee in order to cut the metallic taste. By the way, they aren't kidding about this being a 'non-dairy' creamer. The top two ingredients are sugar and vegetable oil. See also **Flavoured Coffees**.

Cold Calls

'Hello sir, can we just ascertain that you are the owner of this property? You are? Well, fantastic news. Your postcode has been selected for the possibility of receiving a free fitted kitchen.' 'Yeah right', we hear you shout, but before you slam the phone down, hold on. We say, make them put the phone down on you. 'Possibility of a free kitchen? That sounds like the probability of a paid-for kitchen.' 'Oh no, sir, what happens is that we'll come and measure up your kitchen at no cost to yourself. You then have the chance to buy one of our kitchens at a heavily discounted price.' 'Right . . . and the free bit is where?' 'Well, if we include a photo of the kitchen in our trade magazine, then you get it for free.' 'Wow, that sounds so great. You do know that I keep a pet octopus in my kitchen?' 'An octopus?' 'Yes – do you think my kitchen can be designed to give him a bit more space?' Click, brrr.

Collins, Jackie

The 1980s are alive and well in the coke-snorting, free-loving, zebra print-adorned world of Jackie Collins, the naughty novelist who brought us *Hollywood Wives*, *Hollywood Husbands*, and *Hollywood Wives: The New Generation*. The younger sister of actress Joan Collins refuses to name names (wink, wink), but if you do your Internet homework, you might notice some parallels between a few select celebrities and Collins's vaguely familiar 'character composites'. Of course, not everyone's a fan of her raunchy prose. Barbara Cartland (no Tolstoy herself) described Collins's first book, *The World Is Full of Married Men*, as 'a nasty book, filthy and disgusting'. As if those were bad things. See also **Cartland, Barbara**; **Collins, Joan**.

Collins, Joan

Most actors trained at the Royal Academy of Dramatic Art would shy away from projects with titles such as *The Stud* and *The Bitch*. But Joan Collins has a knack for turning seemingly bad career moves into strokes of PR genius. As the conniving, one-dimensional Alexis Carrington in Aaron Spelling's diamond-studded soap opera *Dynasty*, Collins delivered eight years of corny lines with so much glamorous, mouth-twitching venom that some are moved to call her the original Shannen Doherty. See also **Collins, Jackie**; *Dynasty*; **Spelling, Aaron**.

Colonic Irrigation

Anything that involves some lubricant, a large quantity of rubber hosing, pillow biting and some very securely locked doors has to be at the very least guilty, if not pleasurable. There may even be some health benefits to pumping up to seven litres of warm water up your fundament but whether that is what the inventors (Greek, inevitably) were hoping to achieve has not been recorded in history. Princess Diana did it every Thursday and even real celebrities have done it on television, so it must be demonstrably beneficial. If you want to lie there on the practioner's couch paying £75 for the privilege of watching the contents of your colon float past you in a *Generation Game*-style experience ('and on the conveyor belt tonight: a tin of sweetcorn, some undigested animal fat and some beansprouts') then this is for you. See also *You Are What You Eat*.

'Comedy' Presents

By definition, comedy presents are those that get a laugh – okay, maybe just a smile – when opened. From that point on they're pretty much useless. In other words, if the person whose name you drew in the office Secret Santa exchange actually *displays* his Big Mouth Billy Bass, then you've both got problems. So why do we keep giving them? Perhaps it's to avoid the risk of buying something sincere but unappreciated, or of missing the mark in a profoundly embarrassing way. Or maybe, just maybe, all we want to do is give someone (even if it's just us) a moment of silly pleasure. See also **Big Mouth Billy Bass**.

Commando Picture Library, The

Commando Picture Library comics, although concerning themselves exclusively with the Second World War, were first published in 1961 in the darkest years of the Cold War (and incidentally, the high point of the Baby Boom). They were the entry-level gun porn for three entire generations of British men. Once hooked, impressionable youths with lives deficient in action and danger were led on, in turn, to sterner stuff like Sven Hassel paperbacks and eventually the *Band of Brothers* DVD box set. Generally focusing on a lone fighter ace or commando who is considered to be a coward by his peers until he vindicates his reputation by slaughtering several dozen young Germans, the stories are repetitive in nature, though this in itself gives the comics the comforting quality which is the root of their abiding appeal. Psychologists call things like comics read in adulthood a 'transitional object'. We just call them a guilty pleasure.

Computer Games

Technically, this high-tech waste of time was born in 1971 when a game called Computer Space, which included its own thirteen-inch black-and-white monitor, appeared. The problem was that the few people who could understand it weren't terribly interested. But a year later, Pong arrived with its simple paddle control and any-moron-could-understand-it rules, and an industry was born. Soon, thanks to such early hits as Space Invaders, Galaga and Asteroids, pinball machines were relegated to the nether regions of arcades and computer games were given the space in the window. Unlike pinball – where skill and luck could win you free games – video games were essentially nihilistic. Eventually, you died. No way around it.

The games didn't just hoover up coins out of the pockets of children. Adults, too, found themselves guiding Pac-Man on his fruit-gulping quest and playing Double Dragon until their fingers ached. The games came home, courtesy of Atari and its imitators, and the rest is mind-melting, money-eating, time-wasting, 'Shit, it's four o'clock in the morning' history.

Computers (Wasting Time on) See also **Doom**; **eBay**; **Emails (Offers of Free Money From Dodgy Nigerian Business**

Ventures); Emails (Pretending to be Someone Else When Sending); Google (Wasting Time Searching for Dirty Images on); Internet Message Boards (Spreading False Information On); Internet, The (Downloading American TV Shows From); Internet, The (Downloading Music From); Jokes (Emailed).

Concert T-Shirts

You know beyond all doubt that the black T-shirt hawked by the vendor outside the concert venue isn't worth £25. You could probably get a better-quality one at the nearest Matalan for half the price. But you plunk down the money anyway because the music rocks and you've just *got* to prove to the world that you – and 30,000 other iconoclasts – were there.

'Confidential' and 'Babylon' (Book Titles that Include the Words)

Find either of these two words on the spine of a book and you are almost guaranteed a fun, trashy read that you'll hate yourself for in the morning. The genre's touchstone is Kenneth Anger's 1975 tome *Hollywood Babylon*, which read like an entire series of *Eurotrash* transported to California, with all the ad breaks removed. Dragging to the surface scandals ranging from Fatty Arbuckle's wild parties to the Sharon Tate murder, it paved the way for a parade of volumes reminding us that screen idols are all too human. It also spawned a series of imitators including *Nashville Babylon*, *Hollywood Confidential* and the more recent bestseller *Kitchen Confidential*. See also *Eurotrash*.

Conspiracy Theories

The truth is that astronauts really did land on the moon in 1969, and Princess Diana died in a meaningless car accident. Of course that truth isn't nearly as interesting as the tens of thousands of convoluted conspiracy theories that have sprung up to 'explain' those two (and dozens of other) high-profile events. Why are so many people willing to listen? Perhaps, experts theorize, because buying into off-the-wall conspiracies is less frightening than facing the simple truth: life is a box of chocolates, and the fate of nations and individuals can hinge on random fortune – or the actions of a random loon. See also **Dianamania**; **Urban Myths**.

Cooking Programmes

While legions of TV viewers like to watch these programmes, most never get around to preparing any of the recipes they see. But that's okay, because shows such as *Can't Cook, Won't Cook*, *Hell's Kitchen* and *Masterchef* aren't for home cooks; they're for voyeurs. Anyone who has ever gasped out loud as Jamie gets Naked, Gordon Ramsay wields his big chopper or Nigella toys with a sausage whilst coquettishly licking her lips, knows what we mean. Cooking programmes are really about crumpet of the non-edible variety and bear as much relation to what you eat at home as 'specialist movies' do to the activities of the average marital bed. Today's food groupies can partake of a never-ending video smorgasbord on satellite telly and for a true guilty pleasure, try watching these shows while dining on a Pot Noodle or a bag of microwave popcorn.

Copper Coins (Hoarding)

Money is dreadful stuff. Imagine the grime it accrues as it's passed from hand to unwashed hand. Although the percentage of bank-notes bearing traces of cocaine is well known, few are aware of the exact figure for residual urine and fæces. It's 102 per cent. We could explain why, but it would take ages. This unsanitary state of affairs is a necessary evil when it comes to banknotes and the larger denomination coins, but for that funny brown money that collects in your pocket there is no excuse at all. The only reason that the 1p coin exists at all is because shopkeepers still believe that we, the great British public, think that £4.99 is a lot less than a fiver. We don't, and someone needs to tell them. For the 2p there is no justification whatsoever – unless you've bought *two* of those £4.99 things, in which case more fool you. A rational society would dispense with these dirty and unnecessary tokens forthwith. We certainly don't like carrying them around, but it's still *money*, so it doesn't seem right to throw it away. Enter the giant-sized pickle jar. Once the last of 1987's pickled onions has finally been eaten, the container is rinsed and begins to fill with the change we can't quite bin, but could never bring ourselves to spend. One day that jar will be completely full of the ghastly stuff, but then it'll be too heavy to carry to the bank. There really is no sense in continuing, but still we do it. The honest truth is that when we're emptying our pockets after a long night in the pub, that jar is a few steps nearer to us than the bin.

COPS

Nothing's more fun than examining (from a safe distance) the seamy side of life, which is why *COPS* has been a cultural phenomenon in the US since its first showing in 1989. It's no surprise that more than one satellite channel has licensed the show or one of its legion of imitators. The premise (cameramen follow real-life beat cops on their appointed rounds) has inspired parodies on everything from *Saturday Night Live* to the film *There's Something About Mary*. It also introduced Sky TV subscribers to the 'wife beater' T-shirt (as seen on an endless parade of usually drunk, always disorderly rednecks) and wised us up to the fact that winos can't seem to keep their trousers up. Given what the uniformed 'stars' of the series have to contend with, it's a wonder police officers don't shoot more people just on general principle. See also **Reality TV**.

Coreys, The (Feldman and Haim)

During the Eighties Corey Feldman and Corey Haim each enjoyed an all too brief moment of respectability. For Feldman, the ugly one, it was *Stand by Me*. For Haim, the other one, it was *The Lost Boys*. But then the two pushed each other's self-destruct buttons by appearing together in 'go directly to video, do not collect £200' comedies *License to Drive* and *Dream a Little Dream*. (They also reunited for a sequel to the latter. Yes, there was a sequel to *Dream a Little Dream*. No, we don't understand Hollywood either.) Part of the kick of watching the Coreys' 'career arc' is savouring the sheer volume of schlock work they've done. Even if, as a regular Blockbuster patron, you've noticed, say, *Meatballs 4* (Feldman), *Demolition High* (Haim), *She's Too Tall* (Feldman), and *Snowboard Academy* (Haim) languishing on the lower shelves, you still might have missed *The Stepmonster* (Feldman), *Prayer of the Rollerboys* (Haim), or *My Life as a Troll* (Feldman).

Corman, Roger

No one feels particularly proud watching films with titles such as *A Bucket of Blood, Teenage Caveman*, or *Slumber Party Massacre III*. But at least the mastermind behind those flicks (and dozens of other lurid, straight-to-video projects) delivers what he promises. Producer/director Roger Corman got his start in the 1950s, when he began a lifetime's obsession with retaining creative control of his projects – even if that meant filming them on a shoestring, recycling sets from other, bigger productions, and filling everything from the lead roles to the director's chair with no-names who worked for peanuts. Fortunately for Corman, those no-names included Francis Ford Coppola, Jack Nicholson, Robert De Niro, Peter Bogdanovich, and Dennis Hopper. The result was a handful of genuinely innovative films (a groundbreaking drug flick called *The Trip*, several well-received adaptations of Edgar Allan Poe stories, and the original, non-musical *Little Shop of Horrors*) to go with the kitsch. See also *Death Race 2000*.

Corporate Hospitality

What's better than food and drink? Nothing! Except perhaps free food and drink, made more guilt-free by the fact that no matter how afflicted you might be by middle-age spread, looking around it's clear that there will always be at least one other suit under more pressure from within than yours.

Corvettes

America's most pretentious sports car began life in 1953 as a nimble, surprisingly cool-looking roadster. Despite the virtual impossibility of obtaining parts or service here in the UK, a *certain* type of gentleman found them attractive from the very start, and as their counterparts in America traded up to newer models their cast-offs began to appear on British forecourts with increasing regularity. Over the decades the Corvette got bigger, faster and more bizarre looking but a few things haven't changed: the 'vette's ludicrous lack of space for passengers, tiny storage area, and its undying appeal to men in the throes of midlife crises.

Cosmo Questionnaires

No matter what the title of the quiz may be, the key question is inevitably 'How many orgasms do you fake a month?' For the love of God, tick your answers *in pencil*.

Costner, Kevin

Was it a dream? Did we really fork out to watch nearly three hours of Kevin Costner and a dreary load of rubbish about Red Indians? I know, it seems crazy now, doesn't it? It seems even crazier to think that at the end of the Eighties, this most wooden of leading men was the new Harrison Ford. Here's the rule of thumb with Kev: when sport is involved (*Bull Durham*, *Field of Dreams*, *Tin Cup*), his films are fine; when it isn't, watch out. *Robin Hood: Prince of Thieves*? He found himself Rickmanned. *The Bodyguard*? Houston, we have a problem. You think *Waterworld* was his nadir? Try *The Postman*. If only he hadn't appeared in that Madonna film.

Costumed Mascots

It went something like this: first, humans painted animals on cave walls to bring luck. Then they took it a step further and started dressing up like animals. Then humans started playing sport. Then they started dressing up like animals so that people in the crowd would have something to watch when either nothing was happening (in other words, if it was a Nationwide Conference match) or if the home team was getting slaughtered (in other words, if it was a Norwich game). Yet in a world where players are transferred from club to club, even from country to country, and every year brings another crop of Eastern Bloc mercenaries, it's sometimes difficult to drum up hometown loyalty. In that context, sporting mascots fulfill a very important role: offering an on-field, comforting constant in an ever-changing world.

Cotton Knickers (Enormous)

The lingerie industry has invented a number of euphemistic product names for underpants that could double as pillow-cases. Most commonly known as granny pants, these reliable unmentionables work because they don't expect much from the poor, put-upon derrière. In fact, while other styles push, pull, and ride up, enormous cotton panties do nothing but give, give, give. You'd be hard-pressed to find a woman who doesn't have at least one pair at the bottom of her drawer. See also **Thongs**.

Country Music See **Parton, Dolly**.

Cover Versions (Novelty)
Cover versions at their worst are karaoke for pop stars. Does the world really need Westlife's bad facsimile of 'Uptown Girl'? Actually, does the world really need Westlife? – but we're digressing here. Good cover versions, however, particularly when they're off the wall, are rather fabulous. We blame Travis, for their acoustic and wonderfully creepy reading of Britney Spears' 'Hit Me Baby One More Time'. After that, it was cool to go weird. Hear the Beautiful South do 'Don't Stop Moving'; Elbow do 'Independent Woman'; The Scissor Sisters do 'Comfortably Numb'; William Shatner do 'Common People'. OK, so maybe not the last one.

Crank Phone Calls
What was once the domain of bored teenagers calling Jesus College, Cambridge every Christmas ('Is that Jesus?' 'Yes.' 'Happy Birthday!' Etc.) has in recent years become a cottage industry. Not only do DJs like Steve Penk specialize in making crank calls on the radio, but the pranks have become so successful that they're now collected on CD. A well-constructed phone prank is like *Candid Camera* without the camera. Shh – it's ringing.

Crazy Golf
No golfer ever became famous by hitting a ball through a wind-mill or into a clown's nose. Yet for many – especially the many who holiday in tourist towns – a round of crazy golf is the only chance to experience the thrill of a hole-in-one or a sub-par round. Created in the early 1900s, crazy golf, or garden golf, was played with a swung putter on much longer courses than today's incarnation. It became so popular during the 1930s that Hollywood actors were discouraged from participating, because

studio moguls feared the sport would pull customers away from cinemas. Of course, it's been a long time since a movie star had to be talked out of playing crazy golf. These days the courses are filled with sunburned tourists, most of whom know that if they were really any good, they'd be out on the full-sized links.

'Crazy Horses'

The Osmonds, for those of you lucky enough not to remember, were a kind of proto-Westlife outfit made up of five clean-cut Mormon boys who specialized in sickly-sweet harmony singing. It's all the more delicious, then, that they were responsible for one of the fattest rock anthems ever to enter the UK top three. 'Crazy Horses' is founded on a flawlessly stupid ostinato which improves on the Kinks' heavy metal template 'You Really Got Me' by the simple expedient of replacing all the gaps with *more noise*. The youngest member of the band, Donny Osmond – yes *that* Donny Osmond – ups the ante with some endangered-synthesizer squeal horror. If that wasn't enough to convince you that the Osmond brothers were more than just a sappy ballad act, one of the older, chubbier brothers weighs in with a gruff shouty vocal which gives you the impression that he's fairly ticked off about cars, or smoking, or whatever it's about. Factor in an unforgettable horn arrangement by the perfectly named Jim Horn and you've got one of the most perfect pop-metal 45s ever. What a shame it's by the Osmonds. Well, that's why you've got some headphones – no one need ever know.

Crichton, Michael

Though he's penned plenty of other books (including *The Andromeda Strain*, *Terminal Man*, *Congo*, and the original screenplay for the TV series *ER*), Crichton is best known for creating a series of films and novels besmirching the theme park industry. It all began in 1973 when he wrote and directed *Westworld*, in which robots in a futuristic entertainment centre go berserk and kill the guests. He followed it up in the early Nineties with the blockbuster novel *Jurassic Park*, in which dinosaurs in a futuristic park go berserk and kill the guests. His most recent instalment is *Timeline*, in which the denizens of a theme park based on time travel go berserk and . . . well, let's just say they don't serve the visitors tea and biscuits. It's mindless fun, but one has to wonder if Mr Crichton is working through a traumatic childhood Disneyland experience. See also **Pre-*Star Wars* Seventies Sci-Fi Films**; **Theme Parks (Not Owned By Disney)**.

Crimewatch

Until the advent of reality TV, *Crimewatch* was the only way most of us could ever hope to appear on television. Every week, between the little playlets depicting reasonably well-executed crimes, there would be some fuzzy CCTV footage of a dimwit in a tracksuit waving a shotgun or chair-leg (it really is very hard to tell the difference) at a sub-postmaster. In sink estates all over Britain the proud cry would go up, 'That's our Darren!' In a world where the dullest lives are now accorded wall-to-wall TV coverage, *Crimewatch* has lost some of its USP, but the pride of seeing someone you know actually trying to better themselves, rather than just swapping pets with Laurence Llewelyn-Bowen or something, still takes some beating. Don't have nightmares.

Crisps (Barbecue Flavoured)

What's more addictive than a big bag of crisps? How about crisps coated in tomato powder, paprika, dehydrated onions and garlic, MSG, and other fun stuff? OK, so, the concept of barbecued potatoes makes absolutely no sense, but is it any less bonkers (or delicious) than Prawn Cocktail?

Crocodile Hunter, The

Back in the days of *Animal Magic*, we never saw our wildlife hosts venture into the danger zone, putting their lives on the line. Then came Steve Irwin, a.k.a. the Crocodile Hunter. The brave-bordering-on-suicidal Aussie specializes in capturing crocs all by his lonesome. What makes him so telegenic is his obsession with doing it his way, using ropes, sticks, and his own two hands. Much more fun before the show became a phenomenon, *Crocodile Hunter* has been on the air since 1996 and even spawned a dud film in 2002. See also ***Animal Magic***.

Croft, Lara

She's fit, she's sexy, and she comes with a set of controls so you can make her do whatever you want. A media darling even before her official debut in 1996 (she's appeared on nongaming magazine covers and even does product endorsements), Lara Croft is famous for racing around in form-fitting outfits, armed with a pair of 44s – and a gun, too. What more could a man want? Especially if that man is a PlayStation freak living in his parents' basement. See also **Computer Games**.

Cruises

At one time cruising was all about uncompromising luxury: fine dining, the Captain's table, elegant dress, and of course, only enough lifeboats for the first-class passengers. But the era of leisurely oceanic crossings vanished with the arrival of the passenger jet. Today, cruising is a distinctly more proletarian affair as indicated by the unmissable reality TV show *The Cruise* where it is all Eat-Your-Weight buffets, ballroom dancing demonstrations by couples from the Midlands called Barry and Jayne, 'International Cabaret' shows up to West End (of Blackpool) standard featuring entertainers and 'hosts' who wouldn't get gainful employment on dry land. Instead of crossing the Atlantic, ships bum around the Caribbean or Mexico's Pacific shores, or dodge icebergs off the coast of Alaska. Instead of formal dinners and masked balls, passengers tackle dodgy plumbing, floating shopping 'malls', casinos, and rock-climbing walls. Still, this sort of holiday has its advantages, particularly for the traditional parochial tourist. Closet xenophobes who book passage on one of these floating hotels (most are double or even triple the size of the 40,000-ton *Titanic*) can visit a rustic foreign land, then retreat to the ship's air-conditioning and 'with chips' menu if things get too rustic and foreign.

Cujo See **King, Stephen**; **Rampaging Animals (Films About)**.

Curry, Tim See *Rocky Horror Picture Show, The*.

D

Da Vinci Code, The

Less a book than a religion. If you haven't read or seen this then you feel like you have – Dan Brown's mammoth block-buster story about the Church suppressing the 'truth' that Jesus had a child with Mary Magdalene has probably been more widely read, discussed and bought than, well, the Bible . . . It is omnipotent, omnipresent and omniverous. Its clever mix of modern thriller and historical codes, ancient societies and con-spiracy theories has convinced many fans but has also angered the Vatican – though their indignation is, of course, all in vain. Dan Brown could probably run for Pope and get elected. As our Latin teacher once said, 'Jesus Flevit.'

Daily Mail (Getting Annoyed at)

Foreigners. Foreign women. Foreign women who are single mothers. Foreign women who are single mothers, claiming bene-fit and vote Labour. Why, one can almost see the headline now: 'Is This The Most Evil Person in Britain Today?' It's difficult to resist a copy of the *Daily Mail* if one is lying there inno-cently on the train, but if you're a non-*Mail* reader, by the time you get to page five you're already fuming at their fuming. It's a joyous meeting of righteous anger all round. They're cross. You're cross at their crossness. They're probably cross that you're cross at their crossness. That article condemning your muesli-eating lesbian vegetarianism can only be a matter of time.

Dallas

Who will J.R. screw next, either literally or figuratively? Will Sue Ellen stay on the wagon? Who will get the bejesus kicked out of him at the Cattleman's Ball? Such were the questions that ate at fans of this grandpappy of all glitzy American soap operas, which ran from 1978 to 1991. A monster hit, it shouldered aside Hilda Ogden's rollers in favour of outlandish plot twists and endless backstabbing without demanding a three-days-a-week commitment. Three hundred million worldwide viewers tuned in, shaking up British viewing habits as thoroughly as a longhorn steer at a Southfork lawn party. See also *Dynasty*.

'Dancing Queen' See ABBA.

Darkness, The

Clever, Very clever. Are they in on the joke or not? Are they legit or are they a tribute band? Do we care? Probably. From that growling testosterone-filled guitar riff from *I Believe in a Thing called Love* onwards, Justin Hawkins and his Ipswich-based colleagues have kept the world guessing. The music is stadium rock *par excellence*, but with that all-pervading scent of student union themed-tribute night about it. The worry that maybe you are being sold old lamps as new brings the guilt pouring out of the Marshall amps.

Dawson's Creek

There is a simple rule for people over a certain age when it comes to celebrity: if you don't know who someone is and they're British, they're probably from *Hollyoaks*. If they're American, they're from *Dawson's Creek*. There's nothing guilty about watching *Dawson's Creek* if you're under the age of, say, twelve, but for the rest of the cradle-snatching viewers, there's really no excuse. It's a children's show and a sloppy, puerile one at that. Yes, the actors and actresses are good-looking, but be honest, they're not really in your age-bracket are they? Wash your hands and go down the pub like everyone else.

Day, Doris

The former Doris Kappelhoff was never billed as one of cinema's finest actors, which is okay by us. If we want to gunk up the cinematic experience with sophisticated plots and well-developed characters, we'll get *Citizen Kane* out on DVD. When we're in the mood for a happy sing-along (*Lullaby of Broadway*), a formulaic romance (*Pillow Talk*), or a cute film about a small-town girl who brings out the good in people (*It's a Great Feeling*, *My Dream Is Yours*, *Young at Heart*), then it's off to the Technicolor Classics aisle we go, twirling our dirndl skirt all the way. Fans might be surprised to know, however, that the star of *The Pajama Game* wasn't all peaches and cream. In her early days she melted microphones as one of the most sultry swing band singers on the circuit, prompting someone to famously note, 'I knew Doris Day before she was a virgin.'

Daytime Talk Shows See Richard and Judy; Springer, Jerry; *Today with Des and Mel*; *Trisha*.

Deal or No Deal

Anything with Noel Edmonds in is a guilty pleasure by definition. And just as Chris Evans split from Billie and returned to our TV screens, so Noel returned from his self-imposed exile with Mr Blobby for the delights of a daytime game show, one in which a selection of contestants win money for doing nothing more than opening boxes. Really, that's it, apart from Noel and the 'banker' attempting to persuade the contestant to take the money and run. Think of it as a one-hour daily tax for the self-employed.

Death Race 2000

This 1975 American classic is one of cut-rate film producer Roger Corman's greatest triumphs – if you can call a film about a cross-country race in which the participants get points for running over pedestrians (40 for teens; 70 for children under 12; and 100 for oldsters over 75) a triumph. Still, there are reasons why it remains a video shop staple. There are plenty of car wrecks, plenty of breasts, plenty of camp humour, and, perhaps best of all, a very young Sylvester Stallone chewing up the scenery (and running down bystanders) as car driver Machine Gun Joe Viterbo. It was followed by a sequel called *Deathsport*, which was rubbish, and a computer game called *Death Race*, which ruled. See also **Corman, Roger**; **Stallone, Sylvester**.

Death Songs

The first time you hear 'Billy, Don't Be a Hero', you are justified in listening to the bitter end to find out if that fool *does* go out and try to be a hero, losing his life in the process. (Spoiler: he does.) The same morbid curiosity can lead you, once, through 'Leader of the Pack' (protagonist killed in motorcycle accident); 'Teen Angel' (train-car accident); 'Ebony Eyes' (plane crash); 'Tell Laura I Love Her' (racing mishap); and 'Seasons in the Sun' (dying singer). But when you listen *repeatedly* to such tunes, knowing how things turn out, it might be time for counselling. See also '**Escape (The Piña Colada Song)**'.

Death Wish

When three thugs (one played by a very young, very miscast Jeff Goldblum) assault the wife and daughter of a businessman (Charles Bronson), you pretty much know, based on watching a thousand other vigilante films, what will happen next. Except that when this film was released in 1974, the idea of taking the law into one's own hands was still taboo. Hard as it is to believe, many viewers were shocked and unnerved when Bronson switched into Payback mode, whipped out a gun, and started capping people. These days *Death Wish* is still shocking, but in a guilty way. The feeling of discomfort comes from realizing that absolutely *nothing* about Bronson's behaviour seems strange any more and that you are putting money into Michael Winner's pocket. See also **Rambo Films**; **Schwarzenegger, Arnold**.

Deidre's Photo Casebook

If you genuinely wanted relationship advice you might ask a trusted family member, a respected friend, or maybe splash a few quid on a professional counsellor. If you just wanted to look at some pleasingly trim young models wearing the legal minimum of clothing then look no further than Deidre's Photo Casebook. Every week an entirely predictable dilemma plays out in the style of a teenage girl's photo-love comic, but with added Ann Summers appeal. We know you're *far* too posh and brainy to buy the *Sun* for yourself, but we challenge you not to read the problem page every time you find a discarded Currant Bun on the train. See also **Advice Columnists**.

Demonic Children (Films about)

Kids can be devils. The little terrors ruin restaurant outings, annoy us at the cinema, and turn a trip to Alton Towers into the Bataan death march. Yet not since W. C. Fields was in his prime could we publicly admit that we'd like to see the diminutive miscreants get theirs – big time. Which is where this guilty pleasure comes in. As long as we know, for example, that young Damien in *The Omen* is truly the son of Satan (who else would knock Lee Remick off that balcony ladder), then it's okay to cheer for those who want to clean his clock. It's also okay to scream for blood in *It's Alive* and *The Bad Seed*. But you might want to curb your enthusiasm during *Home Alone*. See also **Blair, Linda**.

Denver, John

It is possible for someone to be *too* nice? Perhaps, if that person is singer/songwriter John Denver. His first early Seventies hit, 'Take Me Home, Country Roads', set the template for every tune to follow. It was a simplistic, naïve song that was nevertheless as relaxing as Valium with a white wine chaser. Denver was a looking-on-the-bright-side kind of guy and apparently lots of people saw things the same way. *John Denver's Greatest Hits* has sold more than 10 million copies and can be found (no doubt carefully hidden) in the collections of many a highbrow Music Nazi. See also **Carpenters, The**; *Muppet Show, The*.

Designer Labels

The ultimate conundrum of the fashion world: why pay less when you can pay more? Ever since man and woman emerged from caves they have needed something to keep them warm and cover their important little places, but fig leaves and woolly-mammoth fur doesn't really cut the mustard in Penge High Street. You *could* pop along to Marks and Spencer's or BHS and pick up something very serviceable for a tenner, but hold on a sec: D&G do a rather nice, almost-identical 'garment' for a much more reassuring £75; and when it comes to jeans, put all thoughts of a £30 purchase from Gap far from your mind, since those nice people at Gucci will sort you out with something in denim for a sensible £210. As Naomi Klein points out in *No Logo* there is of course a danger that the world will end up producing 'walking, talking, life-sized Tommy [Hilfiger] dolls, mummified in fully branded Tommy worlds' but we are happy to risk it because we wouldn't be seen dead in something machine washable.

Desperate Housewives

American Beauty meets *Dynasty* (well, sort of). This darkly comedic look at suburbia, where the secret lives of housewives aren't always what they seem, is a must-see that feels like an utter waste of an hour very soon afterwards. Every man (half the viewers are men) who watches will claim it's just to keep a female partner company. This is a lie. Every man indulges in a little fantasy: would he run off with ditsy, attractive but irritatingly naïve Susan (once the Internet's most popular pin-up and formerly Lois Lane); perfectly coiffed, red-haired Stepford wife Bree; Latina überbabe gardener-shagging Gabrielle Solis; Caprice-lookalike Evie; or long-suffering yummy mummy Lynette? Female viewers, on the other hand, who compulsively watch each episode, weigh up the relative merits of six-packed teenage gardener John; strait-laced but hooker-visiting Rex; poker-faced plumber Mike, who to no one's surprise rarely does any real plumbing; macho, possessive Carlos; and creepy, did-he-kill-his-wife? Paul. The formula for success? Secrets, glamour, the eternal sunshine of Wisteria Lane, cliffhangers. Also the fact that next week's episode is screened the same week on satellite, so you have to pretend you aren't a step ahead at the office the next morning.

Diamond White

In the days before Bacardi Breezers, women of a certain ilk had a different option when it came to going out and getting rat-arsed. Diamond White contained no diamonds and wasn't actually white, but it did have enough sugary alcohol in it to get a sixth-former seriously trolleyed after a bottle and a half. The first time we tried it aged fifteen, being too 'cool' to order straight cider, we lost our inhibitions after bottle one,  our wallet after bottle two, and our way home after bottle three. There was an amusing *trompe-l'oeil* cinema ad in which a man walked into an oversized bottle, but really, that was about as sophisticated as Diamond White got.

Diamonique

The rarest and most beautiful of the earth's precious stones, Diamonique is a glittering jewel that can only be discovered in the remotest and most inhospitable climes: satellite shopping channels. The secret of the stone's true worth is simple: it looks like diamond, but it's only a fraction of the price. That diamond-studded collar for your pit bull terrier that you've always dreamed of? It's yours, complete with this attractive mahoganish display box and free postage and packing. But hurry, the stocks won't last for ever. All we can say is thank the Lord Gollum didn't have access to QVC. It could have got very messy. See also **Pit Bulls** and **Bid TV**.

Dianamania

Media analysts have called it morbid, exploitative, and an out-of-control, merchandise-driven myth machine. But the truth of the matter is that everybody remembers what they were doing when they heard about Princess Diana's fatal 1997 encounter with pillar 13 of the Pont de l'Alma underpass. Us? We were driving a white Fiat Uno very fast out of Paris. No, but seriously – a 2002 History Channel poll revealed that us Brits considered Di's death to be our nation's most historic twentieth-century moment, edging out the Second World War. Diana's face launched thousands of magazine covers and adorned many books with sappy requiems such as *Diana: The*

People's Princess and *Diana: The Lonely Princess* – as well as a few juicy tell-alls, such as Windsor insider Lady Colin Campbell's *The Real Diana* and the countless Andrew Morton updatings of his classic, secretly authorized *Diana: Her True Story*. We can't seem to get enough of this story, with its tragic heroine and an entire cast of bad guys: the paparazzi, the icy mother-in-law, and the cheating husband. Years from now, long after we've put away our 'Shy Di' commemorative plates and Dodi Fayed is but a line on a Trivial Pursuit game card, we'll probably still get a little misty during the piano interludes of *Candle in the Wind*. See also **Royal Family, The**; **Queen Elizabeth II, Her Majesty**.

Dickinson, David

We all accept that he was the original plank of well-varnished wood from which *Lovejoy* was carved, but David Dickinson has a great deal more to offer us than a few hours of amiable post-card TV. Despite the protestations of certain Hoxton crimpers, David Dickinson single-handedly revived the much maligned mullet hairdo, and indeed his Ronseal-referencing retro style has set many of the key fashion trends of the last few seasons. David's TV show, *Bargain Hunt*, is glued together with a multitude of infectious aphorisms which have re-entered common parlance, like 'Cheap as chips', and . . . er . . . well, just 'Cheap as chips' really. As yet, Big Dave's maverick views on eyewear and gentlemen's tailoring have yet to enter the mainstream, but there is already a small coterie of Soho hipsters rockin' the 'specs on a chain' look and it's only a matter of time before these innovations too permeate worldwide street style. If only he wouldn't insist on dropping a teabag in his bath every night.

Dido

She provides such good value: simply put *No Angel* on repeat on a Friday night and it will provide you with the musical soundtrack for the whole weekend – perfect for a drink with the girls on a Friday night, staying up late sorting out holiday photos, having a lazy Saturday breakfast with the papers, a haircut, a manicure and a full Brazilian at the salon, a Saturday afternoon shopping trip with your girlfriends, a romantic night in with your boyfriend, a bottle of Chardonnay, a Marks and Spencer ready-meal, a furious argument about 'that girl' at work followed by really quite good sex and then perfect for a Sunday morning lie-in while your boyfriend washes the car before picking up some cushions from Habitat on the way down to Virginia Water for tea with your parents before returning home alone to spend an evening alone with *Bridget Jones* on DVD and an hour with your rabbit. Wave the *White Flag* someone – we surrender.

Diets (Not Sticking to Them)

Yes, we know that ninety-eight per cent of people who lose weight on a diet put it back on again and we know that yo-yo dieting is potentially harmful, but there is something fun about road-testing this month's fashionable diet – whether it is Atkins (no carbs), South Beach (no carbs), Cabbage Soup (no friends), Hip and Thigh (high-lycra content) or G-Plan (where you get so hungry you eat the furniture). Day 1 is great and you stick to the new regime letter by letter, Day 2 is a little bit more of a challenge and on Day 3 you have a lunch with a new client and slightly break the rules but decide to make-up for it by not eating in the evening. By Day 4, you have a hard day at work, decide to let your hair down and get some girlfriends round for a pizza and a DVD and then one of them tells you about a diet which sounds much more 'you' and which really worked for them. The next morning you pop into the bookshop and start again.

Dinner Parties (Snacks)

The few precious minutes before a dinner party are some of the best you can hope for: children and/or pets safely filed away in beds/gardens accordingly; your significant other wearing a clean(ish) shirt for once, and your domicile looking markedly tidier than it has been in weeks. Factor in a refreshing aperitif and the only thing to mar the perfection of the moment is the task of rearranging those nice Japanese rice crackers so that the bowl doesn't look quite so empty. It isn't your fault. Cooking is very demanding work and you can't be expected to do it on an empty stomach.

Dinner Parties (Tricking Your Guests)

This dinner party guilty pleasure comes in all shapes and sizes. It can range from pouring cheap own-brand mineral water into those expensive cobalt blue Tynant bottles, to pretending that all the ingredients are organic or the ultimate sin of buying an Indian takeaway, hiding all the packaging and pretending you have spent all day marinating choice cuts of meat in expensive herbs and spices. Do you want the recipe?

Dire Straits

In the mid-1980s, *Brothers In Arms* was the subject of a compulsory purchase order, with every household legally obliged to buy at least one copy of the album. But for all of Sting wanting his MTV and what can only be described as the mature cheddar of 'Walk of Life', the true reputation of the Straits relies on one earlier opus: 'Sultans of Swing'. The Elgin Marbles of air guitar, scientists have proved it is physically impossible for grown men to listen to this song without grabbing the nearest tennis racket. We know it's the truth, but it's best to keep your thoughts about Mark Knopfler's stunning musicianship to yourself. Dire Straits have never been cool. That's why Mark Knopfler wears a headband.

Dirty Dancing

Seventeen-year-old Baby (Jennifer Grey, pre-rhinoplasty) is on holiday with her family when she finds her way into the staff quarters, and gains a whole new appreciation for the resort's amenities – especially its hunky dance instructor, Johnny (Patrick Swayze). He teaches her some new dance moves (including the horizontal mambo), but misunderstandings ensue when Baby's father (pre-*Law & Order* Jerry Orbach) accuses Johnny of knocking up his dance partner. Of course Baby and her beau inevitably merengue their way out of trouble. You certainly shouldn't own up to having this on DVD. See also **Chick Flicks (Cinderella Fantasies)**; **Lambda, The**.

Disabled Loos (Able-Bodied Use of)

All public places now have a legal requirement to have a separate loo with a wide door and easy access. This is a good thing both for the disabled people out there who need to be able to get wheelchairs in easily and also, obviously, useful for anyone who can't be arsed to queue in the Gents' or the Ladies' and fancies making full use of such commodious, under-used and spotlessly clean facilities. Ideal for changing outfits, putting finishing touches to make-up and hair and even, so we've been told, for having acrobatic and experimental sex either alone or with a new special friend. One tip though: don't mistake the red emergency alarm cord for the light switch – you may get more company than you bargained for.

Disasters (Films about) See Allen, Irwin.

Disco (Dancing)

Before the Macarena, before hip-hop, before video killed the radio star, there was disco and its delicate tango of foot swivels, cross-steps, and Tony Manero bravado. Not that *Saturday Night Fever* started it all. Far from it. Before that 1977 blockbuster came along, the Bee Gees were harmonizing 'More Than a Woman', Shirley & Company was scolding 'Shame, Shame, Shame', and Diana Ross was suffering from a 'Love Hangover'. *SNF* didn't start a trend. It just told the folks in Devon that one was going on. The craze began to fade around 1981. Yet decades later, clubbers still pull out a few of the signature moves when they're feeling retro – proof that the dance craze that bankrolled ABBA *and* the gold lamé industry has survived. And why wouldn't it? Did you think it would crumble? Did you think it would lay down and die? See also **ABBA**; **Disco (Fashions)**; *Saturday Night Fever*.

Disco (Fashions)

Back in the day – when a man's worth was measured by the width of his collar – the dance floor dress code tipped quite clearly towards ostentation. Six-inch heels, glittery blouses and plunging necklines were de rigueur – and then there were the *women's* fashions. On any bare-shouldered diva who ever stood breathlessly next to Terry Wogan at the end of *Come Dancing*, a strappy Gucci pump with inlaid rhinestones was no mere shoe but an extension of her body. Is it any wonder that a new generation of Gloria Gaynors has adopted the sequined halter as the standard issue for dancing till dawn (followed by the mortifying Sunday morning 'walk of shame')? Or that every New Year's Eve party is marked by at least one brave chap who has decided to unilaterally repeal the laws of good taste? No denying it: a white polyester suit over a patterned 'burn baby burn' rayon shirt is a surefire conversation starter. Does it matter if the conversation is behind your back? See also **ABBA**; **Disco (Dancing)**; **Halloween**; *Saturday Night Fever*.

Disease as a Plot Device See **Chick Flicks (In Which Someone Dies)**; *Love Story*.

Dodge Ball

The most Darwinian, and politically incorrect, of all P.E. activities was only considered a guilty pleasure by those with strong throwing arms. Virtually forgotten in the UK until revived by the classic Ben Stiller movie in which underdogs 'Average Joe's Gym' face closure unless they can beat Stiller's 'Globo Gym' mega team, participants divide into teams and hurl balls (sometimes footballs and occasionally even softballs) at their opponents. Get hit and you drop out. The action continues until one side is entirely knocked out – or until some unlucky player is so entirely knocked out that he has to be carried to the nurse's office.

Dog (Pretending to Throw a Ball for)

This needs careful attention to the comedy 'rule of three' to work effectively. Deviate and your beloved dog will not . . . erm . . . play ball. Position dog some twenty feet away from you, but facing towards you. Pick up ball very obviously, maybe bounce it a few times to get his attention. Pull back arm and throw said ball beyond dog (another thirty feet is ideal). Dog will leap up madly, do a 180° turn and chase ball down, catch and return it to your feet. Praise dog madly and then send it back to its base camp position. Repeat. Praise dog madly again and return it to base camp once more. Ostentatiously bounce ball and then pass it behind back and shift it secretly to trouser pocket. Pull back arm and enthusiastically throw 'ball' over head of dog. Dog will react in predictable fashion: leaping, 180° spin, chasing madly for ball and then it will stop, run twenty feet in other direction, do a 360°, run backwards, look up in air again and then finally wander back to you looking as if he has failed you miserably. This never fails.

Dog Pooh (Fake)
Artificial dog pooh is available in almost as many varieties as the real thing, including a Mr Whippy twist, a comma-shaped log, and a moist, splatty mess. But just because you get someone to fall for this trick doesn't mean that you're the next Woody Allen. Or that he or she isn't going to get you back, when you least expect it, with some fake vomit. See also **Vomit (Fake)**.

Dog Shows
What could be more pointless and absurd than a beauty contest? How about a beauty contest for dogs? That, essentially, is the nature of dog shows. Staged since the mid-nineteenth century, they celebrate not the intelligence, fortitude and loyalty of canines, but rather how closely they adhere to a long list of technical parameters dreamed up for each particular breed. It's as if Miss World contestants were all herded onstage, weighed, measured, felt up, made to run in circles, and then judged. At least the dogs in these competitions (unlike the majority of the Miss World contestants) haven't the vaguest idea what's going on. As far as they're concerned, they're just being led around in circles by humourless women with thick ankles.

'Don't Stop Movin''
In the golden age of popular music, school playgrounds resounded with the question: 'What are you, Beatles or Stones?'. Pity the slow-witted child with a plaster over one lens of his spectacles that responded 'the Monkees'. If pop still divided along such Manichean lines today, the question would probably be: 'What are you? Keane or Coldplay?' It's a tragic notion, and we would probably applaud the freethinker who piped up

'S Club'. Unfortunately, life is no longer that simple and consequently the popular music aficionado who confesses to a fondness for the works of Bradley, Rachel and er . . . the other ones, risks almost certain mockery. To confess to liking their junior branch, S Club 8, will lead to an invitation to sign some sort of register at your local police station. As a result of this ignominy, S Club went their separate ways and are now involved in various exciting fast food retail opportunities. It's a shame, because 'Don't Stop Movin'' is undoubtedly one of the most perfectly crafted pop songs of recent years. Just don't tell anyone we think so.

Doom

The point of this most popular of all 'first-person shooter' computer games isn't to negotiate mazes or run races or gather tokens. It's to kill things. Lots of things. And not just with a gun, but with rocket launchers, laser cannons, even a chainsaw. When is it over? When everything else is dead and you aren't. See also **Computer Games**.

Doughnuts See Dunkin' Donuts.

Dumb & Dumber

Jokes about bowel movements are funny. Jokes at the expense of blind children and their dead pets are funny. And jokes about being stupid are the funniest of all. That's the mind-set behind this 1994 Jim Carrey vehicle, often hailed (though rarely in public) as the greatest film ever made about idiots on a cross-country journey. It's also, arguably, the pinnacle of Carrey's career – not the Jim Carrey who wants to be a serious actor, but the Jim Carrey who wants to swing from street lamps and use his backside as a ventriloquist's dummy. See also **Carrey, Jim**; **Jokes (Dirty)**; **Jokes (Sick)**.

Dungeons and Dragons

Developed in 1973, this mother of all role-playing games is basically a complex computer simulation that doesn't use a computer. Players become fantasy characters such as wizards and dwarves, equipped with varying degrees of intellect, strength and skill based on values assigned them by rolling dice. The players then go on 'adventures' that exist only in the mind's eye, guided by a 'dungeon master' – an all-powerful, all-knowing player who serves as the game's controller. For a while during the Eighties, D&D was so popular that parents, fearing the game was an occult plot, formed groups to combat it. The *Daily Mail* (of course!) ran articles warning of its dangers. Those concerned parents needn't have been so worried, because D&D was a threat to nothing but one's social standing. See also *Lord of the Rings, The*; **Computer Games**.

Dunkin' Donuts

Remember that childhood sensation of a sugar and hundreds and thousands sandwich that ended up half in your mouth and half-smeared all over your face? Well hurry along to DUNKIN' DONUTS and you can recapture that very feeling right now – a fresh batch of hot doughnuts are just out of the oven. From that fateful day in 1950, when Bill Rosenberg opened the first Dunkin' Donuts shop (in Quincy, Massachusetts) Dunkin' Donuts has built a worldwide business with an annual turnover of $3.4 billion. That's a lot of doughnuts, muffins, bagels and coffee. How much? If you lined up every doughnut they sell each year they would circle the Earth 5.8 times and they serve 2.7 million customers each day with everything from Caramel Apple Krunch Donut to Croissant Spanish Cheese Omwich. They sure as hell can't spell, but they know how to craft dif-ficult-to-walk-past shopfronts. A sharing-box of assorted Dunkin' Donuts, a couple of Dunkachinnos on the side and a huge double espresso to follow. Perfect to correct that post-gym tiredness.

Duty Free

'Say Hello to Good Buys' read the advert – as if we needed any encouragement. On the basis that the money you spend in foreign currency or, indeed, in any airport, doesn't really count, this is an opportunity to load up with industrial-sized quantities of things you don't really need in enough-to-last-your-entire-life quantities. Enormous bottles of Cointreau ('well it's always good to have some in for Christmas'), three-for-two bottles of Chanel perfume ('they'll make nice presents'), coffin-sized cardboard boxes of cigarettes ('for the people back at the office'), leather-clad magnums of Veuve Clicquot and £125 Dolce and Gabbana sunglasses – all find their way into the basket and before you know it, you have spent the best part of 300 quid. And that's not even taking into account the giant Toblerone which, by law, everyone entering a duty free shop has to purchase. See also **Cigarettes**.

DVD Box Sets

Television companies are such meanies, rationing out our favourite programmes at the rate of one episode a week. But now, thanks to the advent of the DVD box set, we can watch the whole series as we want to, when we want to. There are drawbacks of course: watching a whole series of *24* in one twenty-four-hour sitting is likely to leave you requiring heart surgery; watching a whole series of *Friends* is confirmation that you haven't actually got any friends. But who cares? Sofa, duvet, remote, Pringles; let's 'ave it.

DVD Extras (Wasting Time Watching)

If this book was a DVD then at the end of the text there would be a commentary from each of the authors explaining their motivation for writing the god-damn thing in the first place, a shot of the menu from the 'original lunch' at which the idea was conceived, some talking-head stuff with our agent discussing the negotiations behind the contract, and all the words and 'guilty pleasures' that were edited out just before it went to press. There would also be, hidden in the text, some 'Easter eggs' – i.e. hidden bits that depended on your reading the book in a certain order and unlocking a secret page or two printed in invisible ink. All sounds rather ridiculous, doesn't it, but in the DVD world we embrace it and confess to having two copies of *Star Wars* in our collection because the later one has a new commentary by George Lucas, and to feeling short-changed if there aren't at least half a dozen unused (because they are terrible and virtually unwatchable) scenes tagged on the end.

Dynasty

For nine years back in the 1980s, television viewers from as far afield as Serbia followed Aaron Spelling's decadent nighttime soap opera about a dysfunctional Colorado oil family that put the 'filthy' in 'filthy rich'. Bribery, extortion, seduction, cat fights and diamond-studded functions were regular occurrences in the Carrington household. In too deep to turn back, we followed the storyline through every ridiculous plot twist until the writing team's literary cop-outs (UFO abduction! Miracle recovery! Plastic surgery! *More* plastic surgery!) collapsed under their own weight. See also **Collins, Joan**; **Heston, Charlton**; **Soap Operas (Glamorous)**.

E

Eavesdropping

Who can honestly say they haven't done at least one of the following: moved closer to a couple having an argument on a train, turning the volume on your iPod down but continuing to tap your feet to the now-silent beat; or on the same train, tried to imagine what is happening at the other end of the phone call you are being subjected to? There is something comforting about discovering that other couples argue about who changes the loo roll, why their sex hasn't been what it used to be since 'your mother came to live with us', and something deeply amusing about watching the man with lipstick on his collar and a doe-eyed willowy blonde on his arm explain to his wife on the other end of the line that the 'whole team is being put up overnight in a hotel to brainstorm new product ideas'.

eBay

This online auction service calls itself a 'grand experiment in Internet commerce'. Others (particularly those who spend hours placing bids for things like Smurf Pez dispensers and *Thundercats* lunch boxes) think of it as a grand experiment in testing the limits of obsession. Founded in 1995 by former software developer (and current billionaire) Pierre Omidyar, the California-based company has reeled in more than 50 million such cyber scavengers, all clicking away at an array of items broken down into thousands of categories. To understand eBay's iron grip on e-commerce, consider that more than 100 Barbie dolls are sold on the site *every hour*. It's no exaggeration to say that you can buy anything on eBay. Some of us have tried. See also **Lunch Boxes**; **Pez**.

Edmonds, Noel See *Deal or No Deal*.

Electra, Carmen See *Baywatch*.

Electric Light Orchestra, The
Who hasn't at some point bought one of the numerous ELO greatest hits collections for an unloved brother-in-law and then ended up hanging onto it 'for the car'? Never fashionable, the ELO went for the same 'Bootleg Beatles' idea as that other revered tribute band Oasis, but had a few more violin exams between them. Nobody likes a swot, but everybody liked their tunes. 'Out of the Blue' alone featured four undisputed pop classics. Lots of bands get by with one classic per career. Then again lots of band members have better haircuts than Jeff Lynne, who looked like Noel Edmonds after three years on a desert island. 'Why do people need a Beatles reunion,' Paul McCartney once wondered aloud, 'when they've already got ELO?' It's a fair point, but still, nobody *hides* their Beatles records.

Elvis See **Presley, Elvis**.

Elvis Impersonators
They aren't Elvis. They aren't even close. But judging from their popularity there's still a large audience pining for an evening with a man (and, occasionally, woman) who would be King. The truly creepy, kitschy part is that lots of impersonators don't just want to make money. They want to bring people closer to the spirit of Elvis by (they keenly hope) channelling some of his Burning Love. How many impersonators are there? Let's just say that on the 16 August anniversary of Elvis's death, Graceland is always surrounded by jumpsuited, sequined, sideburned acolytes. See also **Presley, Elvis**.

Email (Offers of Free Money from Dodgy Nigerian Business Ventures)

The last time we checked, something like forty per cent of all email traffic in the world was spam. In the hierarchy of unwanted mail, the hands-down winner is the '419', or 'Nigerian Bank' scam. Of course no one on earth would be dim enough to actually fall for this well-known credit trick, but nonetheless every morning your inbox has at least one missive from the widow of former Palestinian leader Yasser 'Dries Up With His Hat' Arafat, or some other bereaved relative of a financially flexible politician. Why? Because people *do* reply to these implausible requests, people like us in fact, if only for the entertainment of receiving the Nigerians' incredulous reply. (*They* didn't expect it to work either!) With a little practice you can get at least five emails from the same increasingly-excited PC World (Lagos) employee before they realize that you're just jerking their chain and shut up shop.

Email (Pretending to be Someone Else When Sending)

We would have to kill you if you ever tried to do this yourselves as it is a violation of some federal laws somewhere, but we have a friend who once tried it and told us all about it. Basically, you can send an email from your own account to, say, your colleague at the office, which LOOKS LIKE IT IS FROM SOMEONE ELSE. Therefore, when it says 'Dear John – Your expenses contain many questionable items last month so please can you email me immediately with an explanation for all items. Sincerely, Head of Finance', it is actually from you. The joy of it is that when your victim clicks reply it will go NOT to Head of Finance but into your inbox. Imagine the tricks our hem-hem 'friend' could get up to: sending fat Julie in accounts an email 'from' painfully shy Fred in sales declaring his undying love; emailing the MD 'from' the Chairman saying there will be a 40 per cent paycut for all board members; or even emailing the whole company late on a Thursday 'from' the Head of Human Resources to say that from now on employees will have to wear black on Fridays. Our friend said he has had much fun, but has now learnt his lesson and wouldn't recommend ANYONE doing this themselves.

EMAIL

Emmanuelle (Films Featuring the Character of)

Many a teenager was introduced to the world of softcore porn courtesy of the Emmanuelle movies – a long-running series of French films usually shown in the early morning, after *Prisoner Cell Block H*, concerning a liberated woman who roams the world spouting fuzzy free love philosophy while freely loving pretty much everyone she encounters. The scripts are peculiar, the sex scenes brief, and the sequels so numerous, and with so many different actresses, that it's a wonder they haven't done an *Abbott and Costello Meet Emmanuelle* (which, by the way, we would gladly pay to see). See also **Abbott and Costello**; **Teenage Boys Losing Their Virginity (Films About)**; **Films (Pornographic)**.

End-of-the-World Films

If everyone in the world was annihilated except for you and a handful of other people, there would be a fair amount of tears, ennui by the bucketful, and a stink to end all stinks. But in Hollywood, where the last people on Earth might be played by Harry Belafonte (*The World, the Flesh and the Devil*), Charlton Heston (*The Omega Man*), or Ray Milland (*Panic in the Year Zero*), being around for the endgame can be a thrilling adventure. A sub-genre of science fiction, end-of-the-world films tap our desire to be left alone and take it to its ultimate extreme. Plus, such movies save money by eliminating walk-ons and extras. See also **Heston, Charlton**.

English (Insistence on Speaking Abroad)

The acres of pink shading on dusty schoolroom maps designating the British Empire may be long gone, but the Englishman abroad still believes in not only their inherent supremacy but in their linguistic prowess. They don't believe in the language barrier or in allowing taxi drivers, waiters or hotel receptionists to get in their way. Oh no. The English have actually gone to great lengths to ensure total comprehension, a system which shows unusual linguistic initiative: they speak fluently a new universal language overseas which they believe everyone understands, a form of Esperanto called ENGLISH SPOKEN VERY SLOWLY BUT QUITE LOUDLY

WITH ACCOMPANYING LIONEL BLAIR-STYLE GIVE-US-A-CLUE GESTURES. This is usually delivered in a way that suggests annoyance that Johnny Foreigner insists on speaking in their native tongue. Sadly, it usually works.

Enya

Connoisseurs of New Age music will point out the sonic incorrectness of listening to just *one* Enya song (namely her 1989 hit 'Orinoco Flow', played *ad nauseam* in shopping centres) instead of pulling up a comfy chair and enjoying a nice, leisurely repast of the Gaelic warbler's entire album from start to finish. Maybe we'll try that some time, even if it does sound a bit like crunching through the whole doughnut when all you want is the jam in the middle. For now, we just really like that 'sail away, sail away, sail away' part, which goes to show that there's a lot we don't know about Eithne Ni Bhraonain – including what she's saying in most of her songs. Muzak to our ears.

'Escape (The Piña Colada Song)'

Annoying but very, very catchy, 'Escape' is one of those tunes where everyone knows the chorus but not the verses. And no matter how much you like piña coladas, you still have to wonder: is anyone really 'into' champagne? (Incidentally, Rupert Holmes also co-wrote the fabled death song 'Timothy', which was aimed squarely at people who were 'into' cannibalism.) See also **Death Songs**.

Escape to Victory

Sylvester Stallone in goal. Pele up front. Michael Caine in defence. Ossie Ardiles in midfield. We don't know who came up with the idea for *Escape to Victory* (shame on you who just thought 'the writers of *The Great Escape*') but they should be applauded: it's so bloody awful, it's brilliant. It's difficult to decide which was worse – Sly's goalkeeping or Ossie's acting – and even the title is misleading (the match between this odd-ball collection of prisoners and Nazis ends in a draw) but as the accompanying pitch invasion lets them escape it's a harsh man who hasn't got a smile on his face. See also **Stallone, Sylvester**.

Eurotrash

In its original Jean-Paul Gaultier and Antoine De Caunes incarnation *Eurotrash* burst onto the TV scene over a decade ago, titillating and shocking in equal measure. Staged in a weirdly *Carry On*-meets-Austin Powers format, we laughed out loud at Antoine's Inspector Clouseau faux Frenchifying, as he cavorted in front of a gaudy set welcoming us as his 'leeetle Breetesh Bum-Chooms', the hilariously inappropriate British regional accents overdubbed on foreign documentary footage and, of course, at poor, tragic Lola 'When did she last see her feet?' Ferrari. Even now, every time you tune in you are guaranteed to see either that clip of the German man who likes to have his soiled nappies changed by a 'nanny' or a clip of an Austrian porn star whose parents are her biggest fans and like to visit the set.

Eurovision (Terry Wogan's Commentary on)

The pyrrhic victory of World War Two left Britain with few military advantages over our European cousins – a price we as a people were willing to pay in order to preserve our notion of civilization for the rest of the world. We managed to retain, however, one secret weapon that lesser nations will never be able to duplicate: we're better at pop music than everybody else. After a ten-year campaign of diplomacy and espionage, we managed to trick several European countries into thinking that it was their idea to have a Song Contest. What sweeter satisfaction than to create an arena where we could mock the inept musical efforts of hapless continentals year after year? How much sweeter the pleasure, then, that the cutting edge of our mockery was provided by a son of Erin, when the Irish Republic so memorably failed to throw in their lot in our titanic struggle against the dastardly Germans and their quislings. Rarely has the Blarney Weapon been deployed to such devastating effect. Most delicious of all is the fact that more and more countries have been drawn, moth-like, to the Eurovision flame. All we have to do is keep fielding colonial no-hopers like Gina G and the laughs will never stop.

Everett, Kenny

Genuinely an innovative talent on the radio, Our Ken was revelling in crap culture long before irony became the default state of British comedy. His *World's Worst Record Show* LP (subtitled, somewhat transgressively, 'Pain can be fun!') stitched together some jaw-droppingly awful singles in a crude style that still seems fresh today, and his array of comedy characters, every one of them bearded, did little other than run on and bang out a catchphrase in a manner which *Fast Show* or Catherine Tate viewers will recognize instantly. There's something irredeemably naff about his seaside postcard approach to human sexuality, you might say he's the missing link between Benny Hill and Chris Morris. See also **Hot Gossip**.

Expenses (Putting It on)

It's like stealing but with receipts. With a bit of imagination anything can be artfully added to your monthly expense account: the new *Sex In The City* Box Set becomes 'US market research publication', a dirty weekend in Paris becomes 'Fact-finding mission for expanding European business' a new Mountain Bike becomes 'Travel' and a night out at Spearmint Rhino for eight friends from college becomes 'Urban focus group hospitality'. And if you were to be writing a book on, say, guilty pleasures then there would be no end of things one could charge back to your publisher. Apparently.

Extreme Makeover Shows

We all have something about us that we would happily change, whether it be a slightly crooked nose, stubborn hard-to-shift love handles or a saggy bum – but most of us used to just lump it and get on with life. Until, that is, those evil Americans invented the whole 'extreme makeover' franchise and made us all think that anything is possible. Once you stumble upon Maureen from Basingstoke or Charlie from Tulsa who look like they have been made from the bits Dr Frankenstein left on the floor, you can't walk away until you have seen the end product of the *Pygmalion*-meets-Ugly Duckling experience.

Gasp as the dentist fixes their Dracula-like fangs; swoon as the plastic surgeon cuts away buckets of unwanted fat and reshapes their face and laugh as the hairdresser asks them what product they currently use on their hair. Finally, we reach the million-dollar moment, which is worth all the agonies you the viewer have gone through in the preceding hour. As they walk down the staircase, the camera angles milk it for all its worth and the tears and applause of friends and family are writ large. We are left with two thoughts: firstly, inescapably, 'it could be me'; and secondly, that the newly madeover beautiful people are so obviously going to dump their other halves and shag their way round the singles bars of their home towns. So romantic.

Facial Hair (Inappropriate, Humorous) See **Sideburns**.

Factory Seconds
Go to any second-rate tourist trap and you'll find a nearby 'factory outlet' allegedly selling discontinued merchandise and factory seconds direct to the consumer at huge discounts. However, the fact that there are so many such places begs a couple of questions. First, how can retail companies such as Tommy Hilfiger and Ted Baker have enough excess inventory to stock so many locations? Haven't they heard of just-in-time manufacturing? And secondly, how inept must their manufacturing staff be to produce so many seconds? See also **Booker Cash and Carry**.

Faggots
No character from *Silent Witness*, no expert from *CSI*, would be capable of dissecting a faggot and determining what kind of animal it came from. Constructed of a more loosely-packed assemblage of mystery meat than, say, Pepperami, it shares that snack's veiled origins and intoxicating flavour. Where the faggot triumphs over lesser snacks, though, is in its indefatigable Britishness. Born out of the same make-do-and-mend Blitz spirit as the rissole, it has transcended the austerity years and become a staple of . . . Well, no one knows who actually eats these things. Not after all that BSE business anyway. Still, someone's

still buying them. And we'd probably give them a go if you had some. They used to be lovely. Be careful if you order them in the US – you might be misunderstood.

Fairs

Sometimes, as with the deep-fried Mars bar, one guilty pleasure can lurk inside another guilty pleasure. For instance, you might find attending a summer fair – with its fried food, medieval re-enactments and, bizarrely, the world's largest pig – to be pretty embarrassing all by itself, but visiting the fair's 'amusements' takes shame to a different level. The rides will make you cough up whatever money the charity tins didn't get – plus those hot dogs you had for lunch. Enthusiasts don't come here for cutting-edge attractions (although some of the rides do have sharp edges). Instead, they board the likes of the Tilt-a-Whirl or Scrambler knowing full well that it was assembled in a matter of hours by people you wouldn't allow to change the oil in your car. See also **Funfairs**; **Meat on a Stick**; **Out-dated Fair Rides**.

Fake Tan

Gone are the days when you actually had to go on holiday to look sun-kissed and health personified. Now all you have to do is go into a little booth, take all your clothes off and a nice technician comes in with a huge spray-gun and effectively paints you whatever shade you desire. Of course you could turn out looking like Gloria Hunniford or Donatella Versace and be signed up immediately as a walking advert for Orange mobile phones, but at least the future would be bright . . .

Fame

'Remember my name' was both the tagline and an oft-repeated lyric from this 1980 film. And although few actually remember the names of stars Lee Curreri, Irene Cara, Maureen Teefy, Paul McCrane, and Gene Anthony Ray (okay, maybe you recall Irene Cara and recognize McCrane's face from *ER*), few from that era can forget the TV series, or the film's hit soundtrack. Set at New York's High School for the Performing Arts – and expecting audiences to believe that students do traffic-stopping dances in the streets and impromptu instrumental numbers in the lunchroom – *Fame* followed the intertwined lives of a group of students trying to make it in a pre-*Pop Idol* world. Was it just us who thought Doris was cute?

Family Fortunes

Public humiliation is part of the raison d'être of just about every television gameshow ever made. But *Family Fortunes* took the concept a step further by allowing entire families to humiliate themselves. Launched in the USA as *Family Feud* in 1976, it crossed the Atlantic two years later and has been hosted here by a veritable Who's Who of British light entertainment: Bob Monkhouse, Max Bygraves, Les Dennis . . . er . . . Andy Collins . . . Much of the hilarity comes from the answers that contestants give to apparently simple questions. Some were surreal: 'Name something you hide in your socks when you go swimming.' ('Your legs.'); some were incredibly lateral: 'Name a place you would keep a pen.' ('A zoo.'); some were joyously xenophobic: 'Name a dangerous race.' ('The Arabs.'). If those answers were up there on Mister Babbage, Les would give you the money himself.

Fancy-Dress Cinema Going

Have you ever been to a film musical and had the uncontrollable urge to dress up and burst into song? No? Don't knock it till you've tried it – it's like being back in year three and being chosen to star in the school play. In addition to the slightly more late-night fishnets, rice and toast experience that is *The Rocky Horror Picture Show* the inventive fellows at 'Singalonga' have widened this 'let's put the show on right here right now' subtitled experience to include *The Wizard Of Oz*, *Joseph and His Amazing Technicolour Dreamcoat*, *The Sound Of Music* and ABBA and Elvis in concert. So as long as you have an abundance of straw, some deckchair canvas, some lonely looking chintz curtains, some silver foil and a white dressing gown then the world is your oyster.

Fantasy Football

One of those viral schoolboy crazes that inexplicably infects the adult world, fantasy football *should* have flourished for a season and died. Instead, like some kind of nerd ebola, it goes from strength to strength, spreading via newspapers and the Internet and offering astounding cash prizes for, effectively, day-dreaming. Where do we sign up?

Fantasy Island
Real-life resorts brag about being all-inclusive. Yet no resort this side of Yul Brynner's Westworld was ever as inclusive as the one presided over by Ricardo Montalban in this 1978–84 ABC series. Guests arrived on the island ready to act out a fantasy – whether it was Bert Convy as an escape artist seeking to make the ultimate prison break, or a waitress (Adrienne Barbeau) who wanted to be treated like a queen. Sure it was cheesy, but viewers made it a hit in large part because they couldn't help wondering what *they* would ask for. See also **Barbeau, Adrienne**; **Bond Films Featuring Roger Moore**; **Midgets**; **Spelling, Aaron**.

Farrah Fawcett Poster, The
In 1977 the bedrooms of pretty much every male teenager in America were equipped with this le-gendary pin-up, some 8 million copies of which were printed by its creator, Pro Arts. But why did this image become one of the most widely used (and abused) masturbatory aids of all time? Just one (or, technically, two) reasons: nipples. OK, so, Farrah was leggy, tanned, and crowned with a mane of sun-kissed tresses. But you could also see her hi-how-do-you-dos poking against the swimsuit fabric. Schwing! See also *Charlie's Angels*; **Masturbation**.

Farting
From the squeaker at the church service to the silent-but-deadly shot in the lift to the bean-fuelled eyeburner in the car during a long, winter drive, breaking wind has always been a source of both discomfort and laughs. It wasn't until 1974, though, that we collectively acknowledged its importance as an object of humour. That's when *Blazing Saddles* hit movie screens. Thanks to Mel Brooks's groundbreaking (and pants-tearing)

bean-eating-around-the-campfire scene – and Brooks's refusal to cut it when studio execs put on the pressure – we as a people could finally acknowledge the beauty of expressively expelled human gas. There's no scientific proof, but perhaps that film and its endless imitators (it seems that no Disney movie these days is complete without some sort of fart joke) have made us all feel a little less guilty about letting one rip. See also **Whoopee Cushions**.

Fast Food See **Bacon Sandwich**; **Chicken Nuggets**; **Chip Butty**; **Fries, French**; **Grated Cheese (Pre-Packed)**; **Hot Dogs**; **Kebabs**; **KFC**; **McRib**; **Micro Chips**; **Pot Noodles**; **Scraps (Chip-Shop)**; **Wimpy Bars**.

Fast Show, The
'Hi, this is Ed Winchester.' This 1994–2002 BBC comedy sketch programme (featuring Paul Whitehouse, Charlie Higson, Simon Day, Mark Williams, John Thomson, Arabella Weir and Caroline Aherne) was loosely structured and relied heavily on wonderful characters, long-running gags, and endless catchphrases many of which still live on today and are enshrined in the *Oxford Dictionary of Quotations*. Which is nice. It is all but impossible to read the following list without smiling out loud: 'Ooh suits you, Sir','This week, I have mostly been eating . . .'; 'Does my bum look big in this?'; 'Scorchio!' We love the repetition, we love the silliness and we love the anticipation. As Louis Balfour from Jazz Club would say, 'Mmm, nice.'

Feature-Length Episodes of TV Series
All successful entertainments are carefully honed to fit the form that delivers them. This is why you can't make a good film out of a computer game, or vice versa. Comics adapted to films generally attempt to circumvent this rule by taking (sometimes constructive) liberties with characters and storylines and then dressing everyone up in leather. Most carefully crafted, though, is the extended adaptation of a half-hour TV comedy. Remove the exoskeleton of structure that both confines and supports a

quality show like, for example, *Porridge* and it will flop amorph-
ously around on a film script like some kind of unpleasant
jellyfish thing on a beach that you can't help hitting with a
stick. Nevertheless, we've all sat through enough feature-length
specials of *Knight Rider* and movie versions of *Please, Sir!* to
know that there's an ineffable kind of brand loyalty that keeps
us watching even though the whole affair is about as natural
as a budgie on a bicycle.

Female Impersonators (Professional)

As anyone who saw *Shakespeare in Love* knows, the stage didn't
always allow for actresses. In the Bard's time, men played every
role, regardless of gender. These days you can still see the same
thing, except that the men *want* to play girls – if the girls are
Judy Garland, Marilyn Monroe, Barbra Streisand, Cher and
other gay icons. A kitschy step removed from mere celebrity
impersonators, drag acts only ever flirted with the mainstream.
With Danny LaRue more of less retired, only entertainers like
Dame Edna's alter ego Barry Humphries, and Lily Savage, are
pursuing that odd kind of excellence. Unless you count Pete
Burns. In their heyday though, drag acts took audiences into
a gender-bending world where fabulousness was everything and
where we are reminded that, under the skin, we are all . . .
well, kind of creepy. See also **Celebrities (Impersonators)**; **Cher
(Without Sonny)**; **Garland, Judy**; **Streisand, Barbra**.

Ferrell, Will

Imagine an orang-utan shaved, given a mousy merkin for a wig,
and subjected to an interminable cavalcade of indignities. That's
our Will. From 'More Cowbell' to *The Producers* Will Ferrell
has specialized in portraying rangy goons with an extraordinary
lack of self-awareness and a face like a monkey. Many actors
could do that, but he does it with more charm, and with less
prosthetic make-up, than any other rangy monkeyfaced goon
in Hollywood. So much so, in fact, that the average British cin-
emagoer is willing to overlook his rare clunkers, like *Elf*, con-
siderately pretending it wasn't even showing and going to see
something else instead. As long as Will is prepared to keep
making films about simian naïfs with friends that look a little

like either Vince Vaughn or Owen Wilson (or both) we'll be there at the box office.

Ferrets

Cats and dogs are incontestably Britain's favourite four-legged pets. But look a bit further down the companion animal hit parade (past fish and birds and rabbits) and you'll find a surprising non-mover at No. 6: ferrets. Not as elegantly beautiful as felines, as obedient as canines, nor, arguably, as bright as either (a healthy percentage of ferrets never learn to use a litter tray), these domesticated relatives of polecats, skunks and weasels nevertheless enjoy enormous popularity, especially in Ambridge. The domestic ferret's Latin name is *Mustela putorius furo*, which means 'foul-smelling weasel'. There's a name dreamt up by a scientist, rather than a marketing executive. Certainly, ferrets do give off a rather pungent smell, not to mention a certain lowbrow aura that makes them a poor topic for discussion at, say, a gallery opening or symphony recital. Still, they have their place. Granted, they're not that cute, not that cuddly, and not all that bright, but you could say the same for a lot of men, and most of *them* manage to find homes.

Film Reviews (Use of Star Rating System in)

When it comes to films, we want to believe we can make our own choices, without guidance from the unelected guardians of pop culture. That's why we're more interested in a critic's reasoned opinion than in a glib, wordless assessment of a film's worth – unless we're in a hurry and our lift to the cinema is sitting in the driveway, beeping his horn. Then all we want to know is how many stars it got. Though few will admit it, the first part of a film review we study is the number of stars doled out. It's a guide, but also a weapon. Countless filmgoers have escaped being browbeaten into watching undesirable flicks by saying, 'I heard it's rubbish. It only got one star'. See also **Flops (Big-budget Films That Turn Out to Be)**.

Film Sequels

What so many studio execs seem to forget is that while making a hit is tough, going back to the well a second time, with the same characters and premise, is like asking to be struck down by the Film Gods. For every sterling effort such as *Bride of Frankenstein*, *Aliens*, and *The Godfather, Part II*, there are ten or more stinkers like *Staying Alive* (the sequel to *Saturday Night Fever*); *Grease 2*; *Speed 2: Cruise Control*; and *I Still Know What You Did Last Summer*. Of course, watching an awful sequel can sometimes be awfully entertaining – though not always in the way its creators intended. Another reason to like sequels: they can bypass such first-film technicalities as 'character introduction', 'plot development', and 'suspense', and get quickly down to business. Honestly, do you really want to have DNA explained to you again in a *Jurassic Park* sequel? See also **Rocky Films**; **Saturday Night Fever**; **Stallone, Sylvester**.

Film Soundtracks

There are two distinct kinds of film soundtrack. One is, essentially, background music – even if it's big and symphonic. Owning such recordings in any numbers pegs you as either a film snob (does anyone really sit around the house listening to Bernard Herrmann CDs?) or a film dweeb (do you really want to admit that, just last weekend, you were jamming to your *Star Wars Episode I: The Phantom Menace* CD?). The second type of soundtrack is a collection of songs, original or otherwise, that the producers of the film managed to acquire rights to. Depending on the quality of the flick, these can be either good albums in their own right (*Saturday Night Fever*), interestingly evocative (*American Graffiti*), or lame, lame, lame (did you really need the disc of the Mel Gibson/Robert Downey Jr film *Air America* – featuring Aerosmith and the Four Tops – in your collection?). Compilations like this are gathering dust in discount bins through the country, in part because buying one is about as uncomfortable as buying condoms at your local chemist. See also **TV Theme Tunes (Instrumental)**; **TV Theme Tunes (Vocal)**.

Films (Pornographic)

Back in the 1970s, when watching a dirty film meant putting on a trench coat and joining the rest of the perverts down at the local adult cinema, producers made valiant efforts to create productions that mimicked 'real' films. This golden age of porn spawned such near-mainstream hits as *Deep Throat*, *The Devil in Miss Jones* and *Debbie Does Dallas*. But the industry changed when video technology allowed consumers to ditch their raincoats and leer in the privacy of their homes. It also gave any bloke with a sleazy girlfriend and a camcorder the right to call himself a pornographic filmmaker. These days, hyperdescriptive titles like *Double Anal Entry* and *Dildo Crazy* occupy as much shelf space as the films that at least try to maintain some semblance of plot amidst the humping and bumping. But thank goodness the industry hasn't lost its sense of humour. A trip into the back room of your local video shop will still reveal that same whimsical zeal that led to such porn classics as *Foreskin Gump*, *Saturday Night Beaver*, and *Blazing Boners*. *The Ozporns*, anyone?

Films that Parody Other Films

Throughout the history of cinema there have always been tiny films that made fun of major projects. But the genre really blossomed in 1974 with the première of Mel Brooks's Western parody *Blazing Saddles*, followed that same year by the even funnier horror film parody *Young Frankenstein*. While Brooks (with ever-diminishing success) continues to mine this genre, in 1980 the torch of genius was passed to Jerry and David Zucker and Jim Abrahams, who co-directed the disaster movie parody *Airplane!* Among other things, it launched the comedy career of formerly dead-serious thespian Leslie Nielsen. These days the films-parodying-films line-up grows each year, with flicks such as *Scream* (a scary parody of slasher films), *Scary Movie* (a funny parody of slasher flicks that also parodied the parody *Scream*), *Repossessed* (mocks devil films), and *Spy Hard* (does likewise to spy films) marching into cinemas. Granted, some aren't all that funny, but at least they provide work for Nielsen. See also **Nielsen, Leslie**.

Final Demands

Playing the Final Demands game is a feat of brinkmanship that should be attempted only by those with the steeliest of nerves, the most indefatigable resolve. While other poor saps allow the utilities companies to rack up huge interest on early payments, so the less submissive among us lie in wait for the bailiff, ready to draw his teeth with a well-timed cheque, contumaciously ignoring the escalating redness of bills until the ultimate payoff showdown ends hostilities. For about three months.

Fireworks (Backyard)

There's a certain segment of the population for which no Guy Fawkes, New Year's Eve, or Diwali celebration is complete without risking life and, if not limb, at least a finger or two. We're talking about the backyard fireworks display, an ill-advised practice in which dads (it's always dads) set off a series of bottle rockets, Roman candles, and Patriot missiles. What these amateur pyrotechnomaniacs may not realize is that they're part of a growing trend: firework injuries rose by over forty per cent between 2000 and 2001. It's nice to be part of a trend, isn't it?

First Class (Getting an Upgrade to)

Most of us only ever glimpse the joys of turning left when you enter a plane: through the curtains you feel certain you caught a glimpse of the hanging gardens of Babylon, the Niagara falls and an unlimited smorgasbord of fine wines and fancy foods. As you sit in coach class sandwiched between a large sweaty man eating his own weight in lard out of a bucket and a family from Solihull arguing with their teenage daughter about binge-drinking the untold luxury of first class seems an impossibility, but when you are chosen from the many to be part of the few the feeling is a mixture of euphoria, smugness and beautiful guilt. For one flight only, you can pretend you are the only child of an Internet billionaire, an artist who has just had his entire collection bought by Charles Saatchi or a fashion designer on their way to have their first collection shown in New York. The sky's the limit. Enjoy it while it lasts.

Fish Fingers

Eating these requires a wanton disregard for the nature of the fish itself – kind of like eating meat on a stick without knowing if it's cow, lamb, or dog, for that matter. A fixture on infant-school lunch menus and in lower-to-middle-class freezers, fish fingers – or 'fish sticks' as they're called in the States – actually enjoyed brief notoriety in 1988, when they were used as a plot device in the film *Rain Man*. See also **Meat on a Stick**; **Mentally Impaired (Films Whose Stars Pretend To Be)**.

Flambé See **Flaming Food and Drink**.

Flaming Food and Drink
No matter how much you're in the mood for Christmas pudding, baked Alaska, or just a shot of Sambuca, it's difficult not to be embarrassed when pyrotechnics are involved in the serving of your meal.

Flash Gordon
In the wake of the incredible success of *Star Wars* dozens, nay hundreds, of sci-fi and fantasy films were greenlighted by eager Hollywood executives. Most of these were, frankly, forgettable, but one of the pack stood head and shoulders above the others. The ancient black and white serial *Flash Gordon* was no one's idea of a hot property when it was optioned by Dino de Laurentis, and former *Playgirl* centrefold Sam J. Jones was no one's idea of a movie star. In fairness, he still isn't. Once surrounded by quality thesps such as Timothy Dalton and Brian 'The Shouter' Blessed, however, his shortcomings were somewhat masked. It's difficult to concentrate on nuances of characterisation and script when a tubby guy with a beard is yelling 'Diiiive, my hawkmen!' with all the power at his disposal. Factor in the deliciously squealy soundtrack from Queen and you have a stone classic Sunday afternoon film to enjoy with the blinds closed.

Flatley, Michael See Riverdance.

Flat-Pack Furniture (Assembly of)
Guided only by a vague recollection of what your life-enhancing new product should look like, you tip open the box and are faced with a hermetically sealed bag of washers, nuts, wooden

pegs and the ubiquitous allen key. Add this to the badly drilled, dusty pile of wood-effect chipboard and a leaflet printed in *Star-Trek* English (that's English, Jim, but not as we know it) and you are only three hours away from turning your house into a skip. There are two rules of thumb about the experience ahead: (a) you won't have the additional tools needed to complete the project; (b) part 'a' will only fit into part 'b' if you hit it with part 'c'; (c) something will be left over afterwards which looks important but has no obvious role . . . until it collapses a week later. See also **Ikea**; *Star Trek*.

Flavoured Coffees

If you think taking a shot of vanilla or cinnamon in your coffee is sophisticated, think again. It's pretty much the same thing as putting tomato ketchup on steak. The practice began in the mid-Seventies, when skyrocketing coffee prices forced low-quality beans onto the market – beans so unpalatable they had to be augmented with chocolate hazelnut and Irish creme. Nowadays, most purists believe that if you need flavourings in your cup, you're either drinking crap coffee, or you're a ponce. See also **Coffee-mate**.

Flintstones, The

A satire of contemporary consumer culture? You could make that argument. An endless series of stone-, rock-, and slate-puns? Absolutely. Not particularly funny? God, yes. And yet generations of TV addicts can quote *The Flintstones* (original title: *The Flagstones*) chapter and verse, citing the birth of Pebbles, the appearance of the Great Gazoo, and the disappearance of Barney's sabre-toothed tiger as if those events changed the face of television. One thing is certain, however: Fred and Barney definitely did well for themselves. For blokes, choosing between Betty and Wilma is as popular a pub game as deciding between Girls Aloud and the Pussycat Dolls. See also *Scooby-Doo* (**Daphne**).

Flops (Big-budget Films that Turn Out to be)

Watching films such as *Hudson Hawk*, *Cutthroat Island* and *Ishtar* (or, more likely, fast-forwarding through DVDs of them) offers several different kinds of fun. In the case of straight-up abominations such *Hawk*, it comes from wondering if anyone involved in the project understood the magnitude of the travesty being perpetrated. With such earnest efforts as *Ishtar*, one can ruminate about what might have been achieved had there been just one grown-up on the set. Or (as in the dreadful *Heaven's Gate*, for which an entire nineteenth-century town was constructed from scratch in a remote corner of Montana) seeing the frankly daft ways money can be wasted. Occasionally, such morbid interest in a potential Flop can work to its advantage. For instance, intense audience fascination with the soggy Kevin Costner vehicle *Waterworld* actually helped it to break even. See also **Prince (Films of)**; *Xanadu*.

Fluff (Collecting from the Tumble-Dryer Filter)

Usually set into the front door of the dryer is a release catch which gives you access to a circular dinner-plate sized plastic framed mesh. On the surface of the mesh is all the fluff spun loose from your rotating clothes. Running your hand over this mesh to gather the fluff into a rollable ball of warm fluff is pure heaven. Like a lot of guilty pleasures you look stupid if anyone spots you doing it, but believe us it is pure pleasure.

Fonda, Jane

The Vietcong's favourite pin-up girl has sparked guilty pleasure with almost every one of her career changes. Early on she starred in *Barbarella*, a film packed with powerful images that can still make viewers blush even though it was made in 1968. Later, during her 'Hanoi Jane' period, when many thought her anti-war activism crossed into the traitor zone, liking a Fonda film made audiences risk feeling unpatriotic. In the Eighties she became a fitness guru, spreading guilty inferiority among the doughy millions who bought her tapes, used them twice, and then set them out at the next car-boot sale. In recent years, Fonda has denounced her Vietnam-era antics.

Fondue

Originally pioneered by the Swiss as a way to get rid of old, dried-up cheese (namely, melt it and dip stuff in it), fondue came into its own in the 1950s, when the method was applied to cooking meats in hot oil (and, shortly thereafter, dipping fruit and cake in melted chocolate). The technique goes in and out of style, but if you're in the right frame of mind, cooking your dinner one bite at a time can be quite entertaining. But the guilt – nay, the horror – comes at the end of the meal, when you look at the fondue pot and realize the oil level has dropped by several inches.

Fonzie See *Happy Days*.

'Food Centres' (American-Style, Double-Fronted, Refrigerated)

The kind of fridge in your kitchen says a lot about you – if it contains any (or all) of the following items: lager, mouldy cheese and a traffic cone, then you are a student; if it is a fridge freezer with pre-washed salad, four kinds of cheese and a bottle of champagne then you are newly-married; and if it stands as tall as you and as wide as your car, is resplendent in grey chrome and dispenses ice (of both crushed and cubed varieties), and contains more culinary wonders than are to be found in the combined vaults of the Harrods Food Store and Waitrose then you are our kind of person – but you know your marriage is in trouble when you spend more time choosing which fridge to buy than you do naming your first-born. Ice anyone?

Food Courts

These days, no shopping centre worth its Accessorize can be without a food court – basically a load of tables and chairs surrounded by food stands selling everything from pizza slices to kung pao chicken. Food courts are a glutton's dream, because they generally serve big portions and don't cost much. They're also a godsend to parents when little Paris pleads for pizza while Brooklyn begs for a Big Mac. Getting the most out of the experience requires only two things: a high tolerance for background noise (particularly the sound of screaming children) and the ability to use a spork. Advanced food court aficionados can create impromptu multicultural banquets by purchasing individual meal components from every franchise on the court; put it all together and you've got a veritable United Nations on your plate – followed shortly thereafter by World War Three in your stomach.

Foosball

There is little argument that football (we need not refer to it as soccer here) originated as a brutal competition between English villages, and indeed so it remains. Table football, or 'foosball' as we are obliged to call it in a post-*Friends* environment, has a more mysterious provenance. Some say the game was developed in Germany – a logical conclusion, since 'foosball' is a corruption of the German for 'football'. Others, infuriatingly, credit the French. Whatever the case, Belgian foosball leagues were formed in the 1950s and the European Table Soccer Union was founded in 1976. Today the game is a staple in hundreds of pubs and bars, as well as in trying-to-be-cool offices. By the way, official foosball rules (not that anyone uses them) call for no spinning of the rods.

Football (Non-League)

Football at the top level is all about tactics and skill: a sublime moment of genius that changes the course of the game, a clever substitution that turns things around. Non-League football is all about having a big 'fella' up front, hoofing the ball to him and hoping for the best. Put it this way, it is not a form of football that involves passing the ball along the floor. But by the same token, the players are not paid an obscene £100,000 a week, and it doesn't cost £50 to get in. You can roll up at five to three, have plenty of time to get yourself a tea and something to eat, and find a nice place to stand (yes, that's stand) on the terraces. With everyone as bad as each other, anyone can win, which means none of the stale predictability of the Premiership. An interesting game of football? Now there's a novel experience.

Footballers (Swearing)

Cricketers use the full variety of the English language to 'sledge' during a match. Footballers, by contrast, use a maximum of four or five words. We don't know much about lip-reading, but even we can work out what footballers are saying when the camera focuses in on their face. 'Offering his opinion there,' the commentator blandly opines as the neck-bulging centre-forward shouts 'Fuck Off, You Fucking Fuck!' at the referee's back.

Footballers Wives

A show so fundamentally based on an endless cavalcade of excess in sex, drugs, alcohol and gambling would normally have been taken off the air after the first episode, but even TV censorship watchdogs can't get enough of that weird thing Zoë Lucker does with her eyes, where they flick from side to side in a hypnotic fashion that snakes seeking to mesmerize small mammals would do well to emulate.

Footballers' Indiscretions (Tabloid Coverage of)

What do young lads do when they have a bit of cash? They go out and get drunk. What do young lads do when they have thirty, forty, fifty grand a week to blow? The answer is: pretty much whatever they want. Cristal champagne is normally in the mix, as is Chinawhite's nightclub. A breathless 'sexclusive' in the *News of the World* the following Sunday is merely the icing on the football cake. All of which tends to be far more interesting than the football they actually play. After all, what would you rather read about: Another boring hat-trick or fun with geriatrics?

Ford, Anna

As newsreaders go, Anna Ford is first class. Age hasn't dented her severe good looks – will Katie Derham shape up so well in twenty years' time? Add in a dash of discipline, a soupçon of posh and a hint of a racy past (we may be making that last one up) and the announcement of a change in tax brackets can only point upwards. It may just be our warped imagination, but Anna, we think, would be up for a laugh, and outrageously indiscreet off-camera. Maybe it's time we had a cold shower.

4x4s

 Think of your classic four-wheel drive advert on the telly – a rugged farmer saves a flock of sheep from frostbite by fighting his way through Snowdonia to deliver extra feed; a district nurse drives through flooded fields to deliver a baby just in time. All this despite the fact that the majority of us live in an urban environment where the nearest we come to off-roading is when we have to park with our wheels on the pavement. So why is there this obsession for huge need-a-ladder-to-get-in-them four-wheel drive vehicles in towns? Why does a yummy mummy need a gas-guzzling monster truck to drop little Jack to school or to pick up Helen from her ballet class? Because 4x4s look the business, grant you instant don't-mess-with-me status and give the subliminal impression that you have an estate in Hampshire and are just visiting – even if the only mud that ever comes near the vehicle is from a spray-on can. No kidding – you can buy the stuff on eBay.

Franklin Mint, The

Launched in 1964 by Joseph Segel (also the founder of the QVC shopping network), the Franklin Mint has been mocked ruthlessly for offering junk 'collectibles' to the lowbrow masses. Yet almost everyone has been enticed, at one time or another, by an advert offering an Irish Princess Ring or the near-legendary *Star Trek* chess set. These days, however, the company's line-up has swollen to include a long list of over-the-top items that look like they were developed during the Cross Promotional Meeting from Hell. How else to explain such you-have-to-see-them-to-believe-them items as Kristy: The Ultimate Harley-Davidson Bride Doll; the *Gone With the Wind* Miniature Egg Collection Display; or the John Wayne 'Little Duke' Porcelain Collector Doll? See also **Museum Gift Shops**; **QVC**; *Star Trek*; **Wayne, John**.

Free Gift with Purchase

There is some shopping you can do where technically you end up cash positive. Well – when we say 'cash positive' what we mean is that you will have an astounding array of free gifts bestowed on you that it will feel like you are cash positive but actually what you have experienced is the equivalent to legalized shoplifting. Cosmetic companies are the best at this – pop into Debenhams or Selfridges and single-mindedly take your one lone purchase to the nice lady at the till. There will be a pause when she looks at you and dangles a rather beautifully packaged ribbon-wrapped box under your nose. She will then very politely explain that were you to buy JUST ONE MORE item then she would GIVE YOU THIS PRESENT FOR FREE. You just can't say no and you zip off to ferret out the cheapest additional item you can find. You rush home, not daring to open this valuable gift in public and then the moment is finally upon you. Inside is a tiny sponge bag packed full of tissue paper, about five diddy samples of moisturiser, eye gel, lipgloss, lotions and potions. Ah. These are then hidden away at the back of the bathroom cabinet because you wouldn't want your friends to think you had been an unwitting victim of a cynical marketing ploy.

Freemans Catalogue (Lingerie Section)

Cast your mind back to a simpler age. The time before the Internet, when Spam was what you had with a salad and only Germans had heard of felching. In that primitive age, up until about 1997 or so, the only way most young men could gain access to actual pornography involved a somewhat embarrassing transaction in his local newsagent's involving the purchase of a broadsheet newspaper that he would never read and another, smaller publication pulled furtively from an inaccessible shelf with little or no opportunity for prior appraisal. No great surprise, then, that very few bold souls actually put themselves through that trial, and settled instead for a mixture of ill-informed imagination and an occasional browse through the ladies' underwear pages of their mum's catalogue. The images therein were not particularly racy by today's standards – you can see more skin in any nightclub – but for the priapic postwar male they were a veritable *Kama Sutra* of longline bras and slightly medical-looking girdles. Even today, you can still find happily married men idly flicking through mail-order catalogues, slowing perceptibly as they reach the 'bra pages'.

Friday, Nancy

Nine out of ten women surveyed only read Nancy Friday books for their insightful critique of sexual mores in a post-feminist cultural landscape. A similar proportion of men only consult these influential texts in an attempt to understand the changing desires of modern women. The fact that these tracts are dead, dead fruity is merely a bonus. Well, that's our story, and we're sticking to it.

Fries, French

What pleasure could be guiltier than choosing a less substantial Continental alternative to the beloved British chip? Linguists argue over which came first, the French or the frenching. Specifically, some say that even though they originated in Paris (as *pommes frites*), French fries get their name not from the country, but from the fact that they are cut in long strips, or 'frenched'. Others contend that the term 'frenching' arose in response to French fries. Whatever the case, apart from on school trips to Calais, they arrived in the UK consciousness at around the same time as a sinister clown set up his first shop here in the 1970s. Today they're eaten by the handful by fast-food customers who couldn't imagine a hamburger without them.

Frostrup, Mariella

Recently voted the sexiest female voice in the UK with her unbeatable honey over gravel combination, Mariella is an über-brainy posh-totty polymath who is as likely to be seen hanging out with Salman Rushdie at some literary event or escaping from the paparazzi with George Clooney. Men love her and fantasize about flirting with her in some dark corner of a private members club, whereas women want to be her.

Fruit (Juggling with)

Is fruit in a bowl there to be eaten? Don't be daft. Is it there to look decorative? Not really. There's only one reason for fruit to be sitting out in a bowl and that's because it's there to be juggled with. Badly. How long can YOU keep three oranges in the air as your partner shouts at you to 'put them down before you bruise them!' The golden rule of juggling is that you carry on until you drop one. If not more. How come we can only land one on the back of our neck when no one is watching?

Fruit Machines in Pubs
After a few drinks it is impossible not to wonder at the potential riches that might be waiting inside this fridge-sized box of flashing lights and come-back-ring-tones-all-is-forgiven sound effects in your local pub. Whether it's the traditional one-armed bandit sport of waiting for three gold bars to drop into place, or a slightly rubbish general knowledge quiz machine, the fun is as endless as the loose change in your pocket. And obviously there is a possibility that the *Fast Show*'s pub bore Billy Bleach might wander over and tell you what you are doing wrong. See also **Casinos**; **Las Vegas**.

Fruit-Juice Cartons, Mini
Yes, parents realize that excess packaging creates more landfill clutter. But that doesn't keep them from praising (and using) mini drink cartons. Thanks to this remarkable rectangular creation, annoying Thermos bottles that require regular cleaning have largely vanished from school lunch boxes. In their place are highly disposable, straw-already-attached containers of fruit juice (or, more likely, fruit 'drink'). Savvy mums and dads freeze them prior to hot days, and savvy commuters know that cartons are safer to drink while driving than other, tilt-your-head-back beverages.

Funfairs
Many of the same people that express genuine trepidation before boarding an aircraft will happily risk their lives on a whirling *something* that has been hastily assembled that very morning by a rootless pikey with more tattoos than qualifications. Any sane person would quail at the sight of those rusted bolts and ill-adjusted stanchions, and indeed there are so many irresistible

attractions at ground level that the more suicidal attractions can be left to teenagers with delusions of immortality. The dodgems and the doughnuts will do for us. The doughnuts available at fairgrounds are like no other doughnuts commercially available: hotter than lava, they roll off that funny conveyor belt thing and into a (literally) heart-stoppingly large pile of sugar which adheres to them by force of lard alone. The first two you eat will be too hot to appreciate and just serve to remove a few layers of skin from your mouth. This oral exfoliation is essential though, in order to expose virgin tastebuds to the vertiginous sugar rush that comes from the following three doughnuts. The moment when the sugar reaches its intoxicating peak in your bloodstream is the moment to climb into your dodgem: slamming your car sideways into a vehicle ineptly operated by two adolescents is a thrill that can otherwise only be experienced on an inner-city sink estate. Guess which one does least harm to your no-claims bonus.

Furnish, David

His CV says he's a filmmaker. One of his films is a documentary about his boyfriend. It's a bit like you videoing one of your pals falling over outside the pub and sending it to the Motion Picture Academy for consideration, instead of to *You've Been Framed*. Still though, those suits: hilarious. Can't knock the fella.

Fuzzy Slippers

Footwear fashionistas might consider UGG's Australian shearling boots, Manolo Blahnik's Orientala slippers, or Agent Provocateur mules to be the height of home footwear style. But rare is the woman who can deny her deep-seated love of fuzzy slippers – even though they're trailer-park tacky and impractical (unless worn as mobile dust mops), and no amount of machine washing can weaken their lint-collecting, dust-mite-harbouring propensities. And yet, there's not a microfibre moccasin on the market that elicits so many warm childhood memories – especially the pastel (particularly pink or baby blue) models.

G

G, Kenny

Why feel guilty about liking the best-selling instrumental artist in history? Because, at least to critics and music purists, this performer's smooth jazz stylings are so languid they don't even qualify as jazz. Maybe as Muzak, but certainly not jazz. And such questionable career moves as G's 'virtual' duet with the late Louis Armstrong border on sacrilege. Even those who don't hold the man in abject contempt understand that getting caught listening to his music won't win them any style points – unless you're a bloke trying to show a not-very-cool woman your sensitive side.

Gadget Shop, The (Buying Useless Stuff from)

The words 'gadget' and 'shop' to a bloke are like 'designer' and 'sale' to a woman – they induce a feeding frenzy within nanoseconds, so it is a public scandal that this fine chain of shops is going through a tough financial patch. It's a great concept, beautifully realized. Where else can you buy such essential products as 'Arse/Face reversable towels' for the confused in our lives, huge paperweights with lightning storms contained therein and an inflatable massage chair with questionably-shaped rubber spikes?

Game Shows

A TV contest can be either so difficult it makes you feel like a moron (*University Challenge*), or so simple it makes you feel like everyone associated with it is a fool (those multiple-choice questions on *This Morning*). But one thing they all have in common is their power to grab the attention of even the most intelligent viewer and, in short order, have him screaming, 'Brazil, stupid! BRAZIL!!' at the TV screen. Quiz shows have been a staple of television from its earliest beginnings, with now-forgotten shows like *Double Your Money* and *Take Your Pick*. But until the comparatively recent advent of *Who Wants To Be A Millionaire?* prizes were comparatively feeble on British TV quizzes, with only the occasional speedboat (inevitably awarded to a landlocked Midlander) on *Bullseye* or *Sale of the Century* for us to aspire to. Even today, in the cynical era of coughing majors, we still find ourselves yelling at Anne Robinson's prey with all the vigour of our deprived forebears. See also **Deal or No Deal; Family Fortunes**.

Games, Drinking

Most students don't need an excuse to get drunk, but they can sometimes use an excuse to get drunker quicker. That's where drinking games come in. The fact that the loser is usually the one who has to neck a tequila doesn't quite make sense, considering that getting boozed up is the raison d'être for such gatherings. But no matter. Drinking games not only kick the inebriation factor to a higher level, they also provide a convenient cure for party awkwardness. Immerse yourself in a game of, say, Fuzzy Duck, and you can stare at your opponents' open legs with impunity. See also **Games, Party**.

Games, Party

'Spin the Bottle', 'Truth or Dare'and other such party games dreamed up by hormone-crazed teenagers allow for lip-locked pairings without the bother of actually selecting and talking to a potential partner. You still think Speed Dating is clever? See also **Games, Drinking; Twister**.

Gangsta Rap (If You're White)

Hey, it's a great big world and we should all be allowed to listen to whatever music we like, right? Right. But that doesn't make white hoodies look any less ridiculous – or more utterly

Caucasian – as they sit at traffic lights with N.W.A. or Tupac blasting from the stereo of their parents' car. Still, without these bone thugs from the cul-de-sac, today's hip-hop stars wouldn't be living like pimps. Because the sad truth is that while rap is undeniably about the African American experience, industry statistics show that a large percentage of the music's buyers are white.

Gap Adverts

Often more entertaining than the programmes surrounding them – and with better production values – television ads for Gap are inevitably oddly watchable. Whether it was L.L. Cool J and Queen Latifah introducing us to the word 'aight', dispassionate slackers singing 'Mellow Yellow', or dancers freezing mid-motion, *Matrix*-style, in the groundbreaking 'Khakis Swing' ad, the minds at Gap always seem to know how to mock conformity while, at the same time, pushing it.

Garland, Judy

Gay men long ago deified the former Frances Ethel Gumm. Credit the woman's appeal to her dynamic voice, over-the-top personality, tortured life, and drag-show-friendly costumes. But when a straight man admits to loving Judy, that's when the eyebrows rise. Enjoying *The Wizard of Oz* and appreciating *A Star Is Born* is acceptable – barely. But owning soundtracks of *The Harvey Girls*, *Summer Stock*, or *Meet Me in St Louis* is as hard for a hetero to rationalize as watching gladiator films with your mates. Not that there's anything wrong with that. See also **Female Impersonators**; **Streisand, Barbra (as Actress)**; **Streisand, Barbra (as Singer)**; **Gladiators (Films Featuring)**.

George and Lynne

A mainstay of the *Sun* newspaper for as long as we can remember, this sweetly married couple fill a single row of cartoon strip every day. There are only two elements to this successful formula. Firstly, there's a punch-line that isn't very funny. And secondly, Lynne isn't wearing many clothes. She should have died of hypothermia by now, but instead the old girl remains as perky as ever.

George Foreman Grill, The

In 1993, the former heavyweight boxing champion of the world made our kitchens safe for preparing a range of meaty snacks when he attached his name to a table-top grill. Slanted to drain off excess grease, the product (full name: George Foreman Lean Mean Fat-Reducing Grilling Machine) sold millions. It's difficult to say whether more guilt comes from having an as-seen-on-TV item so prominently displayed in your kitchen or from using it as an excuse to consume even more toasted sandwiches and burgers than you did before.

Gerbils (Dancing, Singing) See Big Mouth Billy Bass.

Gere, Richard See Urban Myths.

Getting the Last Seat on a Bus or Train

Parking your posterior on public transport is something of an acquired art form. Ostensibly musical chairs for grown-ups, the winner of this particular game must show no mercy; those stickers about 'priority seats' for the pregnant and the elderly must always be taken as nothing more than a serving suggestion. Then there is the guardian of the seat to be overcome: the curmudgeonly traveller who has taken the aisle side of the double seat, and deposited a collection of coats and bags by the window. So much do they hate the question 'Is this seat taken?' that rather than saying no, a variety of answers are offered: 'Isn't there somewhere else you could sit?' is one classic; 'Yes' is the response of a particularly outrageous liar; but our particular favourite is the pleading 'Where am I going to put my bag?' Yeah, why don't I stand while your bag puts its feet up? Sitting down is all the more satisfying for the harrumphing at your side.

Giant Creepy-Crawlies (Films About)

There's something about films featuring enormous, rampaging insects that touches us – and not in a good way. Maybe, when we see the world terrorized by huge ants (*Them!*), giant mosquitoes (*Skeeter*), or an aircraft carrier-sized spider (*Tarantula*), it makes us think of the payback we deserve for all those times we've poured a kettle of boiling water on the ants on the back patio. See also **Rampaging Animals (Films About)**.

Gimmicks, Film

Producers considering ways to pump up interest in the 1974 Charlton Heston disaster movie *Earthquake* at first considered hiding large Styrofoam blocks in the ceilings of cinemas that would fall during on-screen tremors. That didn't work out, but *Earthquake* (and *Midway*, and *Rollercoaster* after it) *did* get tarted up with Sensurround, a low-frequency sound system that caused objects in the cinema to vibrate. It was just one in a pantheon of gimmicks that have been used to attract attention to otherwise dubious films. The master of the form was producer William Castle, who sent a skeleton on a wire out over audiences' heads for 1958's *House on Haunted Hill*; rigged special shock seats to spice up 1959's *The Tingler*; and stopped 1961's *Mr Sardonicus* in mid-reel so the audience could vote in a 'punishment poll'. None of these effects caught on, but the most popular gimmick, 3-D, still occasionally rears its right-in-front-of-you head (witness 2003's *Spy Kids 3-D: Game Over*). Then again, we now take for granted two of the biggest – at the time – movie gimmicks: sound and colour. See also **Heston, Charlton**.

Girl Drinks

From the Babycham and Pink Lady of yesteryear to the Fuzzy Navel and Flirtini of today, girl drinks have long been an embarrassing pleasure for both women and men. Lady drinkers know that they are being treated like second-class citizens of the alcohol world, with assumptions made that their libation needs to be tarted up with fruit, umbrellas, gimmicky names and other accessories. Meanwhile, barstool-perching guys are forced by their gender roles to order a whiskey and water or a Rusty Nail, even as they secretly covet their lady friends' strawberry Margaritas or crave a nice white Zinfandel.

Girlfriends (Telling the Truth when Asked Questions About Their Appearance)

Relationship should be built on trust, mutual honesty and a sense of loyalty but, let's face it, where is the real fun in telling the truth all the time? Nowhere – it's far better to save up your truth serum for those pivotal life questions such as 'Do you like what I am wearing?', 'Does my bum look big in this?', 'You don't like my haircut do you?' and 'Do I look older than your last girlfriend?' How you tackle these questions is a good barometer of the relationship but if, God help you, you tell the truth ('You looked better in the first outfit you tried on'/'A bit'/'Not really – it makes you look like your mother'/'Erm . . . a lot') then you are either mad or a masochist.

Girls Aloud

Firstly, they're reality TV fodder and therefore not real. Secondly, they're aimed at thirteen-year-old girls. Thirdly, Cheryl Tweedy was found guilty of assaulting a nightclub worker in Guildford. But despite all this, Girls Aloud are the twenty-first-century Bananarama, except better looking and with better songs. Occasionally there are reviews in posh newspapers which give the girls five stars and blether on about how pop music has never been better, but though in our opinion they may be right, use this argument in public at your peril. Best to play the records in private, particularly if you don't have a thirteen-year-old daughter. We say: four stars out of five (one docked for the ginger one).

Gladiators

Was this ultra-low-budget programme truly a gameshow? Maybe, but instead of answering lame-brain questions from an emcee, contestants tried to overpower a pack of muscle-bound, spandex-clad 'gladiators' with bad stripper names like Wolf, Colon and Jade, fronted by Ulrika (who famously had an affair with Hunter). Hapless participants, most of them half the size of their opponents, would do everything from running obstacle courses to jousting with big padded stick-things on rock-climbing walls whilst attached to large bungee ropes. The show ran from 1992 to 2000 and ushered in a whole new type of 'game show': the trial by ordeal, as perfected by the likes of *Survivor* and the *I'm A Celebrity* . . . 'Bushtucker challenge'. See also **Game Shows**; **Reality TV**.

Gladiators (Films Featuring)

On the one hand, there's all the fighting, gore, and bloody-minded thinking any Mitchell brother could want. On the other, all the men wear dresses and seem excessively well oiled, and there aren't many women around. See also *Gladiators*.

Gobstopper Machines

As kids, we saw the gobstopper machines chained strategically outside the supermarket as our just reward for not being total pains in the backside while mum shopped. As adults we can visit them as many times as we want – if we're willing to block the stream of trolleys exiting the shop while we stoop down, drop in some change, turn the crank, cup our hands, open the metal slot cover, and receive a pretty tawdry sweet. Of course the experience itself has been dressed up in recent years. Modern machines offer plastic jewellery, toy cars, and for all we know blocks of Semtex imprisoned in those little plastic globes.

Godzilla

The first instalment in this series, 1954's *Godzilla, King of the Monsters*, can rightly be called a classic. In that film the huge, radioactive dinosaur served as a chilling and very effective parable for nuclear war. But its creator, Toho Co., Ltd., couldn't leave well enough alone, converting its atomic lizard into a cash cow. Yet through it all, the creature never lost its hold on the imaginations of the world's youth. Witnessing the destruction of tiny cardboard cities and legions of radio-controlled tanks was, somehow, mesmerizing. Not bad for a dinosaur that was named after a hulking stagehand on the Tojo set. His nickname, Gojira (the monster's original Japanese moniker) means, roughly, 'gorilla whale'. See also **Rampaging Animals (Films About)**; **Professional Wrestling**.

Going Commando

Picture the scene: you have an important business meeting or are attending a Buckingham Palace garden party, where formality and decorum are everything – and you decide not to wear any pants. No one else knows (unless of course you are Vivienne Westwood) but you do, and that's the important thing.

Goody Bags
Our love of posh parties with lush goody bags must be a throwback to when we used to come back from a kids' party with a bag stuffed full of balloons, a whistle, a slice of cake, one of those circular games with a little plastic maze and silver balls, some stickers and an orange. These days if you trip down the red carpet past the paparazzi, you can expect to bag yourself a whole better class of booty. At the jackpot level, whoever presents the Oscars can expect a goody bag worth $50,000 of holidays, treatments, clothes, sunglasses, gadgets, mobile technology and flights, but even at a more commonplace corporate event like a health and beauty product launch your loot could include a message-from-the-sponsor brochure, a pen, a notebook, loads of free product, a logoed Swatch watch, some vouchers, a T-shirt and a CD or DVD or three.

Google (Wasting Time Searching for Dirty Images on)
Oh grow up. The Internet is a purely educational facility and its use should take that into account at all times. What kind of sicko are you?

Graceland See Presley, Elvis.

Grated Cheese (Pre-Packed)
We're busy people. We like cheese. This leaves us as you can imagine, in a difficult situation. Just where are we going to find the time in our hectic schedule to spend a few seconds grating that nice lump of cheddar on top of our pasta? Well that's where pre-packed grated cheese comes in. It's like cheese, but get this: someone's already grated it for you. Could life get any better? Probably not, though the cheese possibly could.

Gravy
Bad architects plant vines. Bad cooks ladle on the gravy. This golden broth of forgiveness (in most cases made from a foolproof tub of granules) can cover a bevy of mistakes, from a dry

Christmas turkey to a steak that lingered too long under the grill.

Greatest Hits Albums

These compilations, in which artists repackage previously recorded songs, are the musical equivalent of those American sitcom episodes where everyone gets trapped in a meat locker/closet/empty missile silo and spends half an hour recalling the funniest and/or most touching moments from the last few seasons. What fan would say that *1* is her favourite Beatles album? Or that Sinatra's high point was *Greatest Hits Volume 2*? Still, none of this stops these career-spanning retrospectives from flying off shelves. For instance, *Eagles: Their Greatest Hits, 1971–1975* is now the biggest-selling album of all time, surpassing even Michael Jackson's *Thriller*. See also **Jackson, Michael**; *Thriller*.

Greetings Cards (Dirty)

You know that sweaty/excited feeling you get when visiting the curtained-off room at the back of the video shop? One gets pretty much the same feeling cruising the dirty card aisle in card shops. Here you find naked fat women, horny nuns and naked gay couples dispensing such subtle witticisms as 'Two's company, three's a BLAST!' and 'You can't have your cake and Edith, too'. Your reaction? A guilty snigger, a quick look to see if you know anyone else in the store, and then a reach to see what the next card says. See also **Greeting Cards (Sentimental)**.

Greetings Cards (Sentimental)

Stock photos of adorable puppies. Poems that begin, 'What is a friend?' And of course, sunsets, sunsets, sunsets. It's easy to be cynical about the greetings card industry, which preys on our guilt over, in the most literal sense, not being there for friends and family. To assuage our conscience they imply we can make everything better by purchasing a folded piece of paper for two quid. But then, while trolling the aisle of the card shop, past the, well, troll keyrings, you find that one, perfect card – the one that says, in words and picture, exactly what you'd like to say if you could write from the heart, take better pictures, and had a cuter puppy. See also **Greetings Cards (Dirty)**.

Grier, Pam

Though she was the queen of seventies blaxploitation flicks, Grier never seemed all that blaxploited. She was too busy kicking ass – back in the days when such distaff death machines as Angelina Jolie weren't even born. For women, watching Grier in action was empowering. For men, watching Grier in action was arousing – even the parts (*especially* the parts?) where she got riled and called someone, say, a jive ass m——r. Director/groupie Quentin Tarantino paid homage to her in his 1997 opus *Jackie Brown*, named after Grier's character. See also **Blaxploitation Films**.

Ground Force

Alan Titchmarsh has some claim to being a proper gardener. He must know that a proper garden takes a good while – seasons, if not years – to mature. But hey, what kind of dull telly would that make? Let's give him, Charlie and her Dimmocks forty-eight hours to knock up a cheap bit of decking and a sprinkling of token flowers, the last plant being put in place as the owner's car pulls up the drive. Oh Alan it's . . . say it someone, please! Say, 'Well it's a bit cobbled together Alan, isn't it? It's a shame you didn't have a bit more money and a bit more time to spend on it.' And what the hell did Nelson Mandela ever do to deserve having his garden 'transformed'? Did he really suffer twenty-five years in prison for that?

Guest Lists (Being on)

Live gigs are a particularly inconvenient means of listening to music: by comparison to listening to a CD in your front room – live gigs lack sofas, volume control and a mud-free listening environment. One of the few compensations available to the intrepid live music lover is, of course the guest list. Admission to this golden circle is generally obtained via a nodding acquaintance with one of the band or one of the record company. The most obvious advantage to being on the guest list is the price. The second and third advantages, however, are in conflict: on the one hand, the guest list queue will generally be shorter than the one for general admission. On the other, the short wait will only serve to attenuate the amount of time you can bask in the admiring gaze of lowly ticket-buyers who will be engaged in *sotto voce* debates as to the exact nature of your celebrity. You're probably that one off *Big Brother*, they're saying, or *Crimewatch*. And they're probably right.

Guinness World Records

How appropriate that the book that has settled countless drunken pub bets was invented by a beer company. It all began in 1951 when the managing director of the Guinness Brewery got into an argument over which was the fastest game bird in Europe. It occurred to him that people might enjoy a book that complied such useless drivel in one place, so a London fact-finding agency was commissioned to dig up the necessary data and the first *Guinness Book of World Records* was published in 1955. It has since sold some 94 million copies, branched out into TV, and gained regular headlines for the stunts people do in order to gain a mention in its pages. One of the most commonly broken records is for the DJ who can prattle on the longest – well over sixty hours at the last count. One of the most painful is for the most clothes-pegs clipped on the face: 153. See also **Stunts (Insane, Televised)**.

Gym (Going to the)

Does going to the gym get you fit? Possibly, but that's a side product to the basic point: you go to the gym to get smug. The warm glow of satisfaction you leave with isn't because you've exercised your body properly, it's because you're feeling virtuous. The more you go to the gym, the smugger – sorry, the fitter – you become: not only that but the cost of membership per visit starts coming down. Though when you start referring to yourself as a 'gym bunny' it's probably best to keep your smugness to yourself.

Gym (Not Going to the)

Does not going to the gym get you fat? Possibly, but that's a side product to the basic point: you don't go to the gym to feel naughty. The warm glow of satisfaction you get from that third pint isn't because you've satisfied your thirst properly, it's because you're behaving badly. The less you go to the gym, the more satisfyingly wicked you feel. So you may have been smooth-talked into taking out gold membership with a twelve-month minimum contract, but so what? By not turning up, you're really sticking it to them. Who's laughing now, gym owner? Exactly.

Hair-Straighteners
Even on the worst bad hair day ever you too can plug in your sleek GHD straighteners (a snip at £100) and with two minutes deft handling you can look like Christina Aguilera. Try to ignore the fact that what you're effectively doing is ironing your hair with two flesh-meltingly hot ceramic sheets and that if you do it twice a day for ever you will probably look like Gary Glitter.

Hairstyle Magazines
Anyone who has ever pondered a major change of coiffure already knows the calming qualities of a dog-eared copy of *101 Celebrity Hairstyles*. Page after page of covetable manes can move a redhead to chunky blonde highlights and make a woman with flowing tresses think 'pixie cut'. But it's all just a tease. We see the sideways glances every time we fold down a corner of *Soap Star Hairstyle Magazine* while waiting for our turn in the stylist's chair, and we realize that no step-by-step illustration will ever deliver us to perfectly tousled Meg Ryanhood. But that doesn't mean we won't try.

Hallowe'en
When most of us were young Hallowe'en was a pretty niche festival, celebrated exclusively by expat Americans and the kind of English people who talked loudly about 'vacationing' in 'the

States' last 'fall'. Nowadays, of course, every opportunity to sell specialized seasonal merchandise is seized upon by card shops that have sprung up on every British high street. You can't fault the card shops for trying to make an honest bob, and you shouldn't begrudge the kiddies risking molestation as they wander the dark winter streets in search of some free fun-size Mars bars. But adults dressing up as witches and wizards before congregating in tipsy companionship at Hallowe'en parties? It's a bit desperate isn't it? Well, if anyone but us does it, it is.

Halloween (The Film Series)
This massive 1978 hit kicked off, for better or (mostly) worse, a new cinema genre: Films in Which Teenagers Have Sex and Are Then All Killed by an Unstoppable Masked Psychopath, Except for the Town Virgin, Who Manages, Somehow, to Stop the Unstoppable Masked Psychopath. *Halloween*, directed by John Carpenter and now considered a classic of sorts, was followed by an avalanche of dreary clones that were hack work in every sense of the word. Remember *Friday the 13th*, *Prom Night*, *My Bloody Valentine*, and *Silent Night, Deadly Night*? Or, for that matter, the seven (so far) *Halloween* sequels? See also **Barbeau, Adrienne**; **Serial Killers (Films About)**; **Shatner, William**.

Hammer Films
Christopher Lee and Peter Cushing were the Lugosi and Karloff of Hammer films, a British company that one-upped the classic American creatures (Drac, the Frankenstein Monster, the Mummy, the Wolf Man) by adding the key elements of colour, sex, gore and torch-bearing crowds of yokels hungry for revenge. The results offended purists but offered a new generation the guilty pleasure of garish monster films. That plus endless sequels with exactly-what-it-says-on-the-tin titles such as *Frankenstein Must Be Destroyed* and *Taste the Blood of Dracula*.

Hanna-Barbera Cartoons
It's hard to believe that the animation team of William Hanna and Joseph Barbera shared seven Oscars, gleaned

between 1943 and 1953 for their animated Tom and Jerry cinematic shorts. When the market for big-screen cartoons dried up, the duo formed their own company in 1957 and flooded TV screens with low-quality 'limited animation' cartoons. Not that this stopped Hanna-Barbera from creating a string of massively successful programmes and characters, including *The Flintstones* (the first animated series on prime-time telly), Yogi Bear, Huckleberry Hound, Scooby-Doo, *Captain Caveman* and *The Jetsons*. See also **Cartoons (Adult Interest In)**; *Flintstones, The*; **Saturday Morning TV**; *Scooby-Doo*.

Happy Days

A five-foot-six-inch, twenty-eight-year-old graduate of Yale with next to no real acting experience, Henry Winkler was the surprising choice for the part of leather-clad, motorcycle-riding high-school tough guy Arthur Fonzarelli (a.k.a. Fonzie). By the time Richie Cunningham (Ron Howard), in theory the star of the show, bailed in 1980, the Fonz was clearly the main draw, managing to turn a simple thumbs-up salute and 'Aaayyh' into an embarrassing catchphrase/gesture that everyone seemed to try. *Happy Days* also provided the genesis for the phrase 'jumping the shark', which is used to indicate the exact moment when a show/band/career begins its downward arc towards oblivion. In this case, it refers to a *Happy Days* episode in which Fonzie water-ski jumped over, yes, a shark. See also **TV Catchphrases (Quoting of)**.

Hard Men Playing Soft

We guess it seemed a good idea at the time: action hero playing against type. That's got to be a box-office draw, hasn't it? Have you ever seen *Kindergarten Cop*? Or *Twins*? *Stop, Or My Mom Will Shoot*? Or, God help us, *Junior*, in which Arnold Schwarzeneggar is – we're not sure how, either – pregnant. We blame Tony Danza, the dumb guy on *Taxi*, who starred in the Eighties sitcom *Who's the Boss?*, which took the standard 'unlikely nanny' premise and milked it to death. We say, just give the guys their guns back. Please.

Hard Rock Café See Theme Restaurants.

Harris, Rolf

When this particular writer was young, he was told what can only be described as a bare-faced lie by his parents. The story was that Rolf Harris was so loathed in his native Australia that he was deported from Down Under and told never to return. That was why he was always on UK television screens: we let him in and gave him a job because we felt sorry for him. Years on, even when the truth was revealed, a sympathy vote for Rolf still exists. I can forgive him his cartoon club. I can tolerate his pet hospital. I can almost – almost – allow him his cover of 'Stairway to Heaven'. Can you tell what it is yet? No Rolf, but I will hang around to find out, sport.

Hasselhoff, David

Lesser men than Hasselhoff would have been content with a six-year stint as William 'Snapper' Foster Jr on American day-time soap *The Young and the Restless*. But fate had more in store for The Hoff. During his stint on the Eighties series *Knight Rider*, he became not only a star around the world, but a star in a programme with a talking car. But was that enough? Not a chance. Hasselhoff topped the pop charts across continental Europe with the song 'Looking for Freedom', before whipping his shirt off as head lifeguard on the TV jigglefest *Baywatch*. Although the programme flopped on its first run, the six-foot-four-inch hunk boldly helped line up the finance necessary to take the show into syndication, where it became an international phenomenon, launching the careers of Pamela Anderson and Carmen Electra. We say, Respect the Hoff. See also **Anderson, Pamela**; *Baywatch*.

Having Four Seats to Yourself on a Crowded Train

Once you have secured that precious InterCity 'double seat facing forward with integral table' pole position, the last thing you want is to have it spoiled by the arrival of a large bloke with smelly sandwiches and dandruff and a couple of ASBO kids. One simple but effective method to secure all four seats is to take off coat, jacket and tie and strew them liberally on the other three seats along with free newspapers and rubbish, and then either feign sleep right across the table or sit there innocently, saying 'I think they've popped along to the buffet car/loo/guard's van', if questioned. But be warned: one man's guilty pleasure is another's red rag to a bull. See also **Getting the Last Seat on a Bus or Train**.

Hawaiian Shirts

The official uniform of gone-to-seed slobs world-wide, the Hawaiian shirt can conceal a beer belly or a ketchup stain with equal aplomb – provided the pattern is busy enough. See also **Tracksuit Bottoms**.

Heat Magazine

After a brief period as a not-very-successful general entertainment title, *Heat* was retooled as a gently bitchy celebration of all things Celebrity targeted principally at glamour-deprived female twenty-somethings and their gay mates. Its irrepressibly happy tone exults in the tawdriness of reality shows, the implausibility of soap story-lines, and the almost complete pointlessness of photographing actors in the supermarket. It's almost a compendium of guilty pleasures: every page you turn is just as likely to reveal an inter-view with Dale Winton as a Hollywood tit-tape disaster and frankly, we love it. The fact that every issue also furnishes us with a guide to the week's essential television (which generally turns out to be *EastEnders*) makes it a completely indispensable read.

Heated Car Seats

We don't know who invented car seats, but they must have been pretty pleased with themselves. Standing up on a long journey? Not in our vehicle. But wait, what if we told the car seat inventor that we could better his design? That not only could someone drive *and* sit down at the same time, but have their arse warmed as well? We reckon we might have to get the car seat inventor a chair as he takes that one in. For particular pleasure, we re-commend switching the heat on when you have passengers in the heat-free back seat. Or when it's hot, just because you can.

Heavy Metal

Social critics see it as a metaphor-laden commentary on the bleakness of modern life. Others treat it like rock and roll's Special Needs cousin. Yet heavy metal, the musical genre of choice for rebellious adolescent white males, has endured from its Black Sabbath Seventies roots to today, overwhelming audiences with music anchored in death imagery, satanic showmanship and outrageous album covers. Liking it when you are no longer a 'misunderstood' teenager isn't exactly cool, but that doesn't stop some fans. And besides, what's wrong with being sexy?

Henman, Tim (Losing)

We know it's not very patriotic, but the best bit of Wimbledon every year is when 'Tiger' Tim fails to win yet again – that's your destiny, Henman, and we can transfer our allegiances to another player who is a) talented and b) interesting. It's partly to shut up all those middle-aged, middle-class women waving their Union Jacks and shouting 'Cam orn Tim!' Then there's all those numbskulls watching the match on Henman 'over the' Hill. And what's with those pathetic pumping punches Tim insists on to gee himself up? We only hope that when Tim finally faces reality and throws in the towel, he ends up trying those punches out on *Celebrity Boxing* – though no doubt even after being beaten into a pulp by, I don't know, Keith Chegwin or someone, Tiger will whisper through bruised lips that he still has it in him to be heavyweight champion.

Here and Now Tours

When you were a teenager, you lacked the freedom and the finance to see all the hip bands you cared about so much. Now you're an adult, you've got money that your teenage self could only dream about and you're allowed to stay out all night if you want to. The only thing is, you've got no idea what all these new hip acts are called and if truth be told you don't really 'get' grime or nu-metal at all. Enter the 'Here and Now' tour: seven assorted Eighties bands just playing the hits and getting off before the babysitter starts charging double. God knows you spent enough of your pocket money on these people's records, but they frittered it on rapidly depreciating sports cars instead of a nice safe ISA and now need to go out and play all the hits again so that the generation that once paid for their cocaine can now pay for their omega-3 oils. Lovely.

Heroes (Lying About Having Been Chatted Up By)

To you this is a defining moment: you are punching way above your weight, having blagged an invitation to an A list party from a friend who works in PR when you suddenly spot him standing on his own in the middle of the room. Having taken a quick emboldening swig of chardonnay, you wander over and launch into some corny lines like 'Ooh I'm such a big fan' and 'What are you doing next?' before they give you that bored 'I'm off-duty – leave me alone' face and wander off without looking back or making eye contact. Nursing your wounds, you head back to the bar and then home soon afterwards feeling a real sense of disillusionment. The next day at the water cooler you tell anyone who will listen how 'he wouldn't leave me alone', 'he came over and started chatting me up', and 'I've already had a text this morning.'

Heston, Charlton

You have to acknowledge Charlton Heston's cinematic range, even if you don't like his politics. After all, who else could keep a straight face while appearing in so many of the major unintentionally comic cinematic genres? Heston has done biblical epic (*The Ten Commandments, Ben-Hur, The Greatest Story Ever Told*), futuristic adventure (*Planet of the Apes, The Omega Man, Soylent Green*), disaster (*Earthquake*), films that sound like porn (*The Last Hard Men*), aeroplane-in-distress (*Skyjacked, Airport 1975*), horror (*The Awakening*), and films featuring Tim Matheson (*Solar Crisis*). All with the same chin out determination that we too will aspire to when the monkeys take over the world. See also **Pre-*Star Wars* '70s Sci-Fi Films**; ***Planet of the Apes* (Films)**; **Biblical Epics**.

Hill, Benny See *Benny Hill Show, The*.

Hilton, Paris

Far too many of the very wealthy pay at least some lip service to the notion of using their privileged position for the good of the less fortunate. Not Paris. The anti-Sting in almost every respect, she appears to spend more on fake tan every minute than the average person will spend on *The Big Issue* in a life-time. Her entirely sanguine attitude to becoming an accidental Internet sensation as a result of her infamous sex video merely serves to cement her position at the pinnacle of our celebrity pantheon. If we suddenly became teenage heiresses, we'd be like Paris too: solipsistic, well-groomed, and owners of the finest quality consumer electronics available to man.

History Channel, The

At school, history seemed like a wilfully dull parade of dates, punctuated by thrill-a-minute dissertations on rotten boroughs or the Corn Laws. The History Channel gets its frankly less than stellar ratings by dispensing with these minutiae in favour of a steady stream of programmes on the one historical topic no one can ever get quite enough of: Nazis. Those eternal vil-lains with their curious trousers and unconscionable beliefs pop up at least once an hour and viewers can spend all day hissing at their patently evil ways while marvelling at the elegance of their tailoring without once rising from the sofa. We have lost many a damp afternoon basking in the hypnotically black-and-white glow of the Nazi Channel and we suspect that you may have too.

Hitman and Her, The

If you were ever pissed and/or lonely at one o'clock on a Sunday morning between 1988 and 1992 the chances are you would have turned on the telly and been confronted with Pete Waterman and the impossibly bubbly children's TV presenter Michaela Strachan fronting *The Hitman and Her* – a vibrantly garish and 100 per cent downmarket yoof show from a Mecca dancehall somewhere in the north of England. Regular fea-tures included 'Pass the Mic' (a sort of rip-off karaoke game with drunk Northerners) and the unmissable 'Kiss, Touch and Feel' intellectual gropefest, all set against a backdrop of lots of swirly magenta lighting and close-ups of gurning yobs leering at lairy slappers. With the 'Hitman' fronting the show like an embarrassing Dad trying to get down with the kids and 'Her' whipping the clubbers into a frenzy aided and abetted by a bloke with a platinum wig called (unsurprisingly) 'Wiggy' it was a joy to behold. As the Hitman once said 'People switch on the telly and think, "It's that bad – I'll watch this."' It was and we did and we want it back – although this time we may record it and watch it when we get up.

Holiday Inns
Kemmons Wilson is the man who, in 1952, lifted the name from a popular Bing Crosby film and opened the first Holiday Inn. From a single Memphis location, his children-eat-free empire has expanded to tens of thousands of rooms around the world, all equipped with tiny bars of soap. Did he steal those from the Oompa-Loompas?

Holidays From Hell
This should be renamed *Smug TV*, since it enables you to sit back and marvel at the enjoyable predictability of the whole proceedings, safe in the knowledge that the terrible events about to unfold would never happen to you . . . A family from Middle England book a 'bargain holiday of a lifetime' which then turns out to be a bit rubbish. They don't complain at the time, but do have the piece of mind to video the whole thing and then run screaming to the media on their return. The footage and inter-cut talking heads are usually along the lines of 'The hotel wasn't finished and the swimming pool was a building site'; 'Raw sewage filled our bath when my husband boiled the kettle'; and 'The flight was two days late and we had to share a bath-room with a colony of lepers.' Hell is truly, as Jean-Paul Sartre once said, other people.

Hollywood Walk of Fame
It's easy to spot the tourists on Hollywood Boulevard. They're the only ones looking down. The Hollywood Walk of Fame is

an unintended object lesson in the shallowness of worldly acclaim, since most of the names honour people you've never heard of (Licia Albanese? Edward Sedgwick? Henry B. Walthall?). The result resembles both a giant trivia quiz and a serious pedestrian hazard. Woe to the walker stuck behind fans seeking a particular star, be it Sharon Stone or Lassie. See also **Olsen Twins, The**; **Lassie**.

Holy Moly!

If Popbitch is the mother of all gossip sites, then Holy Moly is very much the daddy. Firstly, with its invite-only message board, it boasts an air of exclusivity that any budding 3am Girl is desperate to break into. Secondly, with its harsh but fair features (Cunts Corner, for example), it pushes the whole celebrity-as-scum ethos to its very limit. And then goes over the other side. Thirdly, its weekly mailout is funnier, ruder, and more revealing than anything you'll find in the tabloids. When the story broke about BBC chief Mark Thompson biting a chunk out of a news colleague's arm, who a) got their hands on the email exchange between Jeremy Paxman and the story's source and b) mailed the entire exchange to its collective readership? Got it in one. Subscribe now.

Home Wireless Networks

This is Britain. No one's house is *that* big; we went to Windsor Castle once and it wouldn't have taken us all that long to pop along to the back bedroom and Google the date of one of the paintings if we'd wanted to. Assuming we'd known where the back bedroom was. And also assuming for a minute that we'd have been allowed. Nobody *needs* a wireless network at home. It just seems so modern, and the magazines we read keep telling us how everyone else has got one. Still, you haven't lived until you've checked something on imdb.com while you were sitting on the loo.

Homebase (Spending More Time than You Planned in)

The fateful words 'I'm just popping to Homebase to get some light bulbs' usually heralds a shopping-browsing-buying trip of unexpectedly gargantuan proportions through the aisles of DIY heaven. Who can fail to admire the paint-mixing machine and integral colour-scanning device, the in-store product demonstration videos and the 'hose accessories' section. On the return journey, the car will usually contain most of the following items: a) a power tool of dubious usefulness but of stunning ergonomic design – and on special offer (this will be used once, badly, and then rediscovered when you next move house); b) an assortment of drill bits and Rawlplugs that duplicate equipment you have at home 'but can't quite find at the moment'; c) a number of Cillit Bang cleaning products; d) a curtain rail (not measured but 'it looks about right' for the spare bedroom); e) two fencing panels and f) four tins of Hob Rejuvenator which were on special. Damn – you've forgotten the light bulbs. Might have to pop back later . . .

Horoscopes

Google the word 'horoscope' and you'll get more than 6 million hits. Pretty good for a system of nonsense with no track record of accuracy, no basis in science, and no reason for existing except to convince the gullible that their lives are somehow influenced by the positions of the stars in the night sky. And to make Mystic Meg a few quid.

Hot Dogs (From Street Vendors)

The old saying 'Any port in a storm' is never so sorely tested as when a hungry traveller contemplates eating a hot dog from one of those metal trolleys in the street. But once you get past the unknowable (how long has it been waiting on that grimy grill?) and slather it with the requisite mustard and ketchup from the Day-Glo bottles, such hot dogs provide a secret thrill when you discover that your reconstituted gristle sandwich is not just edible, but enjoyable. (Of course, other times you are just thankful when it stays down.)

Hot Gossip

Essentially the same act as Pan's People, but with a slightly less subtle sexuality, Hot Gossip burst out of Kenny Everett's *TV Show* to spearhead the horde of legwarmer Lolitas that invaded dance classes across the country in the 1980s. Thanks to the indefatigable efforts of Mary Whitehouse they came to the attention of spoonfaced genius Sir Andrew Lloyd Webber, who hired their choreographer, Arlene Phillips, and married the singer they hired to front their solitary hit single – the brilliant and incomprehensible 'I Lost My Heart to a Starship Trooper'. Arlene is now best known for her Cowellesque appearances on *Strictly Come Dancing*. The rest of the troupe are firmly ensconced in the 'Where Are They Now?' file.

Hotel Rooms (Stealing Things from)

When one has spent approximately a week's mortgage on one night in a Corby-trouser-pressed hotel room, one forgets that the normal laws of the land apply and one might even find oneself justifying taking some of the experience home with you. For the entry-level light-fingered guest, items such as ashtrays, sewing kits, shower caps, soap and shower gels find their way into the Samsonite; but for the seasoned 'borrower' out there the likes of towels, pillow-cases and even bathrobes have left the premises under cover of the night. Of course the real professional at this was the late, great Who drummer Keith Moon, who tried to smuggle a television set out by . . . er . . . throwing it through the window to land in the swimming pool. Not the most perfect of crimes.

Hot-or-Not Web Sites

'Judge not, that ye not be judged' is an often-quoted line from the Gospel According to Matthew. It's not, however, an often-followed tenet. The desire to judge seems hardwired into our system. Witness the new-millennium Web craze for hot-or-not web sites in which photos of real people are presented for the rating pleasure of you, the person sitting at your PC. On most such sites, your score is averaged with those of everyone else who voted, so you can see if your score matched the masses (or, at least, the part of the masses that sits at their computers wasting time on silly web sites). Amihotornot.com started as a lark and went on to attract 3 million page views a day after only six weeks. Of course, that could be three really lonely men judging a million women each, but that's probably not the case.

More likely, this amazingly addictive site (now called simply hotornot.com) and its copycats have tapped into the guilty kick of anonymously assessing someone's visual allure without putting our own on the line.

Howard from the Halifax (Adverts Featuring)

One day, banker Howard Brown is sitting in the Sheldon branch of the Halifax Building Society, stamping cheques and engaging in polyester-suited banter. On a whim he enters the company 'Search For A Star' competion and before you can say 'Your home may be at risk if you don't keep up your repayments' he is climbing on the back of a swan and swooping through clouds, performing terrible Karaoke-on-a-wet-Friday-in-Wigan-style versions of 'Sex Bomb' and 'Something Stupid', and dressing up as P. Diddy and having a hit record with a cover of a cover of Barry White's 'You're the First, the Last, My Everything'. As an ad strategy it sounds like suicide – a toe-curlingly corny, terrible 'performance' with a ghastly 'feelgood' collection of irresistibly toe-tapping music covered by a man you would happily push down a darkened stairwell if no one was looking. But when you find yourself singing along and, worst of all, taking more notice of your local Halifax branch the next day, then you know it has worked.

HP Sauce

How dirty is HP sauce? Let's be honest, it's filthy. Tomato ketchup is somehow so middle class by comparison, proudly boasting its five-a-day fruit and vegability, or at least its transparently direct association with something you can actually pick and eat. HP sauce, by contrast, is common as muck, and looks like it too. 'The highest quality ingredients', boasts the label. Malt vinegar and spirit vinegar? Sugar and glucose-fructose syrup? Dates and molasses? What are molasses, anyway? The only bit of the label you need to bother with is the following serving instruction: everything goes well with HP sauce. Couldn't agree more.

Hughes, John (The Films of)

When we're talking about John Hughes's films we are of course ignoring 90 per cent of his long and successful Hollywood career and concentrating instead on the extraordinary run of movies he wrote, and in most cases directed, between 1984 and 1986. These films – *Sixteen Candles*, *The Breakfast Club*, *Weird Science*, *Pretty in Pink* and finally, triumphantly, *Ferris Bueller's Day Off* evoke a sunkissed teenage wonderland few of us (all right, none of us) have known and yet for which most of us (all right, all of us) feel a baseless nostalgia. Hughes's movies are steeped in a nostalgia of unknown veracity for his own high school years in Illinois, and most of them are set there. The English equivalent would probably be a series of films set in a Newcastle comprehensive, and we've all seen enough episodes of *Byker Grove* to guess how much fun *that* would be. After he completed *Ferris Bueller's Day Off*, Hughes went on to create the wildly successful, although virtually intolerable, *Home Alone* and *Beethoven* franchises. Don't be fooled by the label; if Molly Ringwald isn't in it, or at least near it, it isn't a proper John Hughes movie. Here's a trivia fact to remember for a day or two: Molly was born on John's eighteenth birthday. There. Don't let people tell you that books like this aren't educational. See also *The Breakfast Club*.

Humperdinck, Engelbert

You gotta love a guy who decides to bin his bland-but-record-label-friendly name (Gerry Dorsey) and adopt the sprawling moniker of a nineteenth-century German composer. Career suicide? Not for Engelbert Humperdinck. Fame found him in 1967 when the newly-renamed Engelbert was a last-minute substitute for Dickie Valentine (remember him? Thought not) on the televised London Palladium show, plugging his new single, 'Release Me'. It would remain Humperdinck's signature tune throughout his career, which included everything from the Grammy-nominated album *After the Lovin'* to the song 'Lesbian Seagull', recorded for *Beavis and Butt-head Do America*. Never a critics' darling, Humperdinck, like his contemporary Tom Jones, built his reputation on give-the-audience-all-you've-got live shows. Which is why, while your neighbours may not admit to being fans, Humperdinck has nevertheless played to sold-out crowds for three decades. See also **Beavis and Butt-head**; **Jones, Tom**; **Sideburns**.

'100 Best' TV Countdown Programmes (Interminable)

It's cheap telly. It's wall to wall Jimmy Carr. It's full of C-list celebrities (plus Stuart Maconie) pretending to remember some oh-so-hilarious episode from *Blue Peter* where Simon Groom makes a crass joke about knockers, a 'memory' that the researcher has obviously just prompted them towards. But despite the increasingly barrel-scraping nature of the genre – first the list is chosen by a panel of experts, then it's based on actual sales, then it's selected by a bucket of frogs – the gut-wrenching truth is that once started, it's all but impossible to switch the sodding thing off. Once you've grumbled through the choices from numbers 100–76, there's no way you're not going to stay up to 1 a.m. to find out that *OK Computer* is the number one album yet again.

Hunt, Mike See **Crank Phone Calls**.

Hurdy Gurdy See **Outdated Fair Rides**.

I Dream of Jeannie

This 1965 to 1970 series tapped into the same adolescent fantasy as *Weird Science* and countless porn films: What if a beautiful woman suddenly appeared out of nowhere and agreed to do your bidding? In this case, the woman was a genie who, the lyricless opening sequence showed us, was released from her bottle by astronaut Tony Nelson (pre-*Dallas* Larry Hagman). The fact that Jeannie displayed a bare midriff, lived with her bachelor friend and called him 'master' added a frisson of guilt to the otherwise innocent proceedings. See also *Dallas*; *Weird Science*.

I Know What You Did Last Summer

Imagine getting together all the best looking actors and actresses in Hollywood – Sarah Michelle Gellar, Ryan Phillippe, Jennifer Love Hewitt, Freddie Prinze Jr. Now add in some dodgy plot about accidentally killing someone in a car accident, except he isn't dead (or is he?) and get some fisherman with a hook for a hand to scare the willies and wobblies out of them. *I Know* . . . is shit but reckons that if it knows that it's shit, then that's OK. It's not really, but you do get lots of gorgeous young folk running about screaming as compensation. The glorious rubbish was reprised in *I Still Know What You Did Last Summer*, which considering it was set a year on from the first film, is factually wrong. It should have been called *I Still Know What You Did Not Last Summer, But The Summer Before That.*

Ice Magic

Your mouth will water during this paragraph. Guaranteed. This handy ice-cream accompaniment is served in a neat plastic bottle with a cute little snow-covered mountain top effect around the top. Simply squeeze the gloop (available in Mint, Choc or Vanilla) over the top of your ice-cream servings and then spend the most frustrating two to three minutes of your life whilst it sets. Maybe you could listen to a song from the collected works of Kylie Minogue or count backwards from 400, but the important thing is that you WAIT because 'ice magic' is indeed taking place. When fully set, you can crack open the top of your ice cream with a spoon and then pick off little bits of pure chocolate. If you are a connoisseur then apparently you can pick off the entire chocolate hat and use it to scoop up ice cream with. Either way it won't be too long before you are experimenting and writing your name and that of your loved one in chocolate, drawing pictures of Bart Simpson or whatever takes your fancy. Irresistible.

Ice Pops

It's like a summer version of SodaStream. Ice – with flavour! We don't know who invented Mr Freeze (we're guessing it's not his real name) but we say hats off to the man who came up with the idea of selling kids frozen water with a violent squirt of colouring, all wrapped up in a thin strip of plastic. Of course, the colouring created problems, what with fruits, particularly of the berry kind, all being the same kind of reddish tint. The loser in this particular fight was the raspberry, who after long discussion was offered the not-remotely artificial shade of Day-Glo blue. Have you ever eaten frozen raspberries? Us neither, but put it this way, if they went bright blue, they'd be straight in the bin.

Ice Skating Shows

Combining the glitz of a Vegas revue and the athleticism of a figure skating exhibition, such bygone shows as the Ice Capades and its contemporary 'on ice' counterparts (*Disney on Ice:*

Princess Classics, *Wizard of Oz on Ice*, et al.) satisfy our desire to see grace, elegance, men in bolero jackets and/or women in short skirts.

Iceland

No one actually admits to buying anything from Iceland. There's some evidence to suggest that it isn't even a shop at all, just a conceptual art installation commenting on the loss of connection between the food we eat and any naturally occurring substance. The Turner-winning aspect of the exhibit is, of course, the rolling TV ad campaign. First of all you are offered a box of frozen pizzas, which look edible enough in the photo, for some derisory sum like 99p or so. Then you're told, to your mounting amazement, that you'll also get an artery-hardening Sara Lee gateau, a tooth-weakening tub of ice cream, and your own jet airliner, all for under a pound! Of course, you know it's some sort of situationist gag, but there's always a point, around forty-five seconds in, where the pile of savoury pancakes and GM-free cola that they're offering to give you becomes so huge as to weaken the stoutest resolve. It would be so easy to give in, to wander still dazed into the shop only for Tracey Emin to burst out of a dummy freezer and guffaw at you until she almost drops her fag. They used to offer a home delivery service too, until Damien Hirst's van packed in.

Ideal Home Exhibition, The

An opportunity to wander around a perfect world – a world where scatter cushions look tidy, wooden flooring gleams, everything is colour-coordinated and water features play lovingly on bronze and decking terraces . . . before returning to a world where the front door sticks, the carpet still shows signs of that accident the cat had at Christmas, the sofa has a nasty stain that can only be disguised by a cunning use of the *Guardian*'s 'Media' section and the garden has what looks like *Scrapheap Challenge* in progress.

Ikea

No matter how strong your resolve and no matter how many times you repeat the pre-arrival mantra of 'I am not hungry, I am going to go straight to the downstairs store section and I am not going to buy any more candles', something weird will happen once you have grabbed your yellow shopping bag, your free paper tape-measure and stubby wooden pencil. Two hours later you will have consumed a healthy meal of Swedish meat-balls, visited every room-display, had a life-threatening dispute with your Significant Other about the relative merits of the Hurdy-Gurdy sofa as compared to the Ulrika sofa-bed, filled your flatbed trolley with piles of self-assembly Swedish renewable forest, found that your car is miraculously full of tea-lights – and that you've spent in excess of £200. Two hours later still you will be sitting at home wondering what madness came over you; and then you will wake up on Sunday morning and trip over the boxes of self-assembly furniture. See also **Flat-Pack Furniture (Assembly of)**.

Imitation KFC Outlets
Here's a problem: people love the taste of Kentucky Fried Chicken, but not even Colonel Sanders can have a branch on every street corner. What is this chicken-loving nation to do? Worry no more, dear reader, for step forward the Imitation KFC Outlet owner. This is a person who might not quite pos-sess Colonel Sanders's secret recipe, but he does have an atlas that contains the names of all the American states. Voilà, Tennessee Fried Chicken! Hello Alabama Fried Chicken! Oh look, if that isn't Mississippi Fried Chicken! (Or is that KKKFC?) It's interesting that KFC have suffered such blatant copying, while other fast-food chains have got off scot-free. Why is there no Burger Prince, McDougalls, Pizza Shed or Gimpy? It's inter-esting, too, that no one has ever knowingly entered one of these establishments sober. And to think you were worried about how much chicken there was in a KFC . . . See also **KFC**.

Impostor Perfumes
Who would pay £30 for a 100 ml bottle of White Diamonds perfume by Elizabeth Taylor, when you could get the same amount of its impostor, Ice Gems, for £1.50? Certainly not any fake-fragrance aficionados we know. Never mind that the

imitators never smell exactly like their uppity originals. You can always blame it on body chemistry. See also **Cheap Perfume (From the Chemist's)**.

Impulse Buying

It's so wrong, we know. We know we should be scouring copies of *Which?* magazine in order to make an informed purchase. We know we should be walking the entire length of Oxford Street to make sure that we have checked all the possible alternative shoes for sale before we plump for some. But doesn't it just feel fantastic to pick the first pair you see, think: I'll have these, slap it on the plastic, and take the rest of the afternoon off? It's not laziness. It's instinct, darling. Now, do you take American Express?

Inadequate Parent TV Programmes

Imagine (for a moment or two) that while you're reading this book there's a rather stern lady's voice in your ear commanding you to smile to yourself, nod, chuckle appreciatively, turn the page and then repeat. Every now and then it tells you that you're doing really well. Soothing, yes, but it rather removes some of the free will from the equation. Makes us feel like we needn't have tried so hard, frankly. Welcome to the world of Doctor Tanya Brier. There's been a mini-boom in the 'Just how bad are these kids?' sector of the reality TV market, and we can't decide which of the Tanya-come-latelys we like the most. The point isn't of course the mock S&M trappings of *Supernanny* or the baffling American-ness of *Nanny 911*, it's the fact that every single one of these kids is *worse than yours*.

Incredible Hulk, The

This not-so-jolly green giant first appeared in a Marvel comic in 1962. (He was originally grey, but a printing error turned him his famous green.) Since then the Hulk has appeared in innumerable comics, a big-budget feature film, and, most famously, a television series which always ended with the saddest music in the world. Featuring Bill Bixby as scientist David Banner and

Lou Ferrigno as his snarling, car-crushing, tiny-denim-shorts-wearing alter ego, the programme earned muscular ratings by taking the revenge fantasy to new heights. Banner, who was exposed to an overdose of gamma radiation, turned into the Hulk whenever he got stressed. Which meant that if anybody messed with Bixby (and people *always* messed with him), Ferrigno (wearing a fright wig, Billy Bob teeth and a couple of tins of leprechaun-hued body paint) would suddenly appear and give them flying lessons. And the best part, from the vicariously thrilled audience's perspective, was that all that ass whooping *wasn't Banner's fault.* He was just a regular guy who had a *condition.* See also **Rambo Films**; **Superheroes**.

In-flight Safety Demonstrations (Not Watching)

You've settled in, adjusted your seat belt and worked out how you can stash your illegal duty free; you recline the seat to get maximum legroom, and suddenly the chief steward comes on the tannoy and tells us how important it is to watch the safety demonstration. Of course, there are far better things to do with the next three minutes – playing with the sick bag, laughing at the incredibly parochial nature of the in-flight magazine and reading the shopping catalogue – than watching how to fasten the toggle to button B and understanding the importance of tying both straps around your waist and of not inflating the life-jacket before leaving the plane. You can sense that the stewardesses know the futility of this routine and would much rather instruct us in how to scream and how to remove red-hot engine casing from our loved-ones before jumping to a certain death but, for some reason, she doesn't.

Innovations Catalogues

Who among us has not leafed through the Innovations catalogue that fell from their Sunday supplement and pondered, however briefly, how nice it might be to have a row of solar-powered gnomes in the garden. Let he who is without sin cast the first stone – or, in this case, solar-powered, self-throwing stone. Innovations were very much the innovators in this area, but now dozens of imitators are hawking vast remote-controlled airships and special toenail-cutting scissors to us from catalogues secreted within the pages of the Sundays, all too aware that after a weekend of sybaritic indulgence our critical faculties tend to be somewhat impaired and, frankly, that we'll buy any old tat.

Inspirational Books

Inspirational books are quickly read, quickly abandoned, and just as quickly forgotten. Still, books like *Life's Little Instruction Book* and the endless incarnations of *Chicken Soup for the Soul* are addictive and, in some cases, capable of inspiring readers to, if not actually change their lives, at least *think* about changing them. Unlike self-help books, inspirational titles are all about simplifying philosophy and theology for the layperson (and by 'layperson' we mean anyone who considers Khalil Gibran to be a deep thinker and feels that angels on a cover imply a heavenly endorsement). See also **Buscaglia, Leo**; **Mills & Boon Romances**.

Instruction Booklets (Not Reading)

What sort of boring anorak takes delivery of a gleaming new gadget, sets it to one side and sits down for forty minutes reading the step-by-step instruction booklet before finding the 'On' switch? Are you kidding – this is moment when man and machine step forward into an arena for a moment of mortal combat. It is time for the male of the species to crack the whip, break in his new wild stallion, wrestle it into a headlock and then ride it bareback off into the glowing sunset with only a cigar and a horse blanket for company. It is not time to spend weeks at Pony Club being taught how to groom your little pony before finally being allowed to 'trot on' behind fat girls whilst wearing a hard hat. Get a grip – please. Instruction books are for wimps.

InStyle Magazine

Originally launched in the US in the mid 1990s, this glossy mag devoted entirely to celebrities and fashion practises the four Ws of journalism: Who Wore What Where. *InStyle* gives its readers a monthly dose of high-quality fluff, including a retrospective of Jennifer Aniston's hairstyles, a tour of Jennifer

Lopez's wardrobe, a peek inside Reese Witherspoon's make-up bag, and a shopping guide full of dropped names. No hand-carved antique wood coffee table (like the one in Macy Gray's Los Angeles living room) would be complete without it.

Interactive Telephone Menus See Call Centres (Listening to Soul-Destroying Music while on Hold with) as your enquiry is important to us.

Internet Message Boards (Spreading False Information on)

Coldplay splitting up? Robbie Williams having a sex change operation? Pete Doherty behaving himself? Dear reader, do you ever find yourself on a gossip web site, but sadly bereft of any grade-A gossip to contribute to the discussion? We say, no matter, not when you can make up some heap of celebrity horseshit instead. Revel in the glow of people suddenly thinking you're cool. Delight in the fact that some people actually believe what you've written. Snort with uncontrolled mirth as the rumour appears in the next day's tabloids.

Internet, The (Downloading American TV Shows From)

So Sky have taken *24* off air? So Channel 4 are sticking *The West Wing* on Digital only? So *The L Word* is only available on Living TV, whatever that is? Well worry not, for thanks to the joy of the Interweb and the brainchild of the person who invented BitTorrent, that time delay of six months/a year/never for the next series of your favourite programme is over. OK, so it's not entirely legal, but it's not like anyone's losing any money over it – if you download a film, sure, you might not pay to see it at the cinema; if you download a TV series . . . exactly.

Internet, The (Downloading Music From)

Few criminal activities are so easy to learn, or can be executed in such a convenient location. After all, comparatively few magazines run 'how-to' features on housebreaking and with the possible exception of sodomy, most crimes inconveniently require one to leave the house. Downloading music also gives the impression of being a victimless crime – after all, all you're doing is subtracting a pound or so from David Furnish's weekly suit budget, and based on some pictures we've seen in *Heat* lately, that's a major service to mankind. Of course you shouldn't do it, but the joy of collecting yet another Van Der Graaf Generator bootleg that you'll never listen to is sharpened by the feeling that you've just done something uncharacteristically clever. As each successive iteration of the iPod line has even more intimidatingly vast capacity than its predecessor, it becomes less and less likely that the average individual will own enough CDs to feed their MP3 habit legally. Consequently many iPod owners turn to crime: first the entry-level stuff like Limewire, but that gateway drug will inexorably lead to harder kicks like BitTorrent and eventually hacking into the US Military's computers, like Matthew Broderick.

iPod

Of course, we got ours at the beginning. Oh yes. We carry round our original heavy, cumbersome model as a badge of honour, looking down on all those newbies with their feather-light Shuffles and Minis and Nanos. The sad fact is that the 'Pod is now so ubiquitous that possession of one now is all but sheep-like. And ok, so maybe we have swapped our white headphones for a black pair so no one on the train actually knows we are listening to one. And yes, hands up, we may have to plead guilty to the occasional bout of I-Willy Waving. But even given all that: as a concept, as a piece of design, as a thing that we own, it is still bed-wettingly fantastic.

Iron Chef

A peculiar combination of cooking show and sporting event, this demented Japanese programme enjoys a cult following, even though most viewers would never consider eating the exotic dishes prepared here. The 'iron chefs' are four Oriental culinary masters, each specializing in a different cuisine: Japanese, Chinese, French

and Italian. Each week one of the four, overseen by a bizarre emcee in matador costume (really an actor named Kaga Takeshi), is challenged to a food fight by an outside chef. The two then spend one hour creating dishes based on a surprise ingredient (anything from cucumber to sea urchin). Makes *Ready Steady Cook* look a little kindergarten, by comparison. See also **Cooking Programmes**.

It'll Be Alright On The Night
The sight of cadaver-like Denis Norden seemingly rising from the dead to stagger on stage clutching a BBC standard-issue clipboard, delivering bewilderingly terrible links in the style of a stroke victim on Mogadon and introducing a bunch of tired fluffs and blunders from television programmes from around the world is enough to get you reaching for the remote control. But then, just for a moment, you start watching and before you know it you are revelling once again in the sight of the *Blue Peter* elephant's bowel movements, laughing at Chris Tarrant fluffing his lines on *Tiswas* and calling your loved ones in from the kitchen to see some American newscaster battling with a stripper and a misbehaving python.

It's a Wonderful Life
Frank Capra's 1946 classic (unsuccessful on its initial release) makes even the most hard-hearted man want to run down the street shouting 'Merry Christmas' to strangers. See also **Tearjerker Films (For Men)**.

iTrip
Technically illegal in the UK, iTrips (and their imitators) are little gadgets about the size of a packet of Polos which dock onto your iPod and enable you to play the audio through a radio. Normally, we have found, a car radio – hence the 'Trip' part. The iTrip precludes the requirement for one of those surgical-looking cassette-on-a-string things and generally makes you feel quite modern while creating your own private radio stations entirely devoid of advertisements, inane prattle and Crazy Frog ringtones. The fact that it needs re-tuning every couple of minutes in no way detracts from that terribly

futuristic feeling that you will get from having a radio station in your pocket. If you actually had such a pirate radio station in your home, someone from the Department of Trade and Industry would pop round and kick your door in, confiscate your equipment and enquire politely if there was any chance of a cuppa. In a moving motor vehicle you are afforded an additional degree of security, analogous to the pioneering broadcasters of the early 1960s. Unlike them however, you're unlikely to end your days pushing old ladies around in wheel-chairs while wearing a tracksuit with an MBE pinned to it.

Izzard, Eddie (Films Featuring)

We have nothing but admiration for the genius that is Eddie Izzard. As a comedian, he is uniquely brilliant. As an actor, he's not bad. But as a person choosing which films he wants to be in, he is absolutely rotten. We don't know if it's just plain bad luck, but if Izzard's name is down on the cast list, you know it's going to be an absolute stinker. There was *The Avengers*: shit. Then there was *The Cat's Meow* and *Ocean's Twelve*: also shit. We don't remember Eddie's role in *Ishtar*, but given how bad it was, he must have been there somewhere.

J

Jackass

The stars of the 2000 to 2001 MTV series *Jackass* and the bafflingly successful *Jackass: The Movie* demonstrated both a propensity for tackling dangerous-looking, poorly-thought-out stunts and a remarkably high pain tolerance when those stunts went wrong. The crew 'urban kayak' in city fountains, test the protective power of the American equivalent of a cricket box by firing paintballs at each other's family jewels, swallow and then vomit up live fish, and spray each other in the face with fire extinguishers. Such can-you-top-this acts of idiocy, plus lots of scatological stunts and a steadfast refusal to explain what the point was, made *Jackass* a chance to release the 'dare you' clown in us all. See also **Kicked in the Nuts (Watching Someone Get)**; **Morons (Entertaining, Untimely Deaths of)**; **Stunts (Insane, Televised)**.

Jackson Family, The

What does it take to found a musical dynasty? If you believe the 1992 American mini-series *The Jacksons: An American Dream*, it takes practice, talent, persistence, and a good beating from your perfectionist, borderline-abusive father. Over the decades, in addition to some fine dance tunes, the Jackson clan has provided connoisseurs of guilty pleasures with enough scandals to fill an entire series of *Dynasty*. See also *Dynasty*; **Jackson, Michael**.

Jackson, Michael

Remember, in the video for the title song from his album *Thriller*, how Michael Jackson said, 'I'm not like other guys'? Well, truer words were never spoken. Back when he served as the diminutive front man for the Jackson 5, and during his early twenties as the force behind the albums *Off the Wall* and *Thriller* (which has sold over 50 million copies to date), Jackson may well have been the undisputed King of Pop. But during the Nineties his high-pitched squealing and dance-friendly melodies were muscled off the charts by grunge and rap. Still dressed in what looked like cast-offs from the *Beat It* video, he became a David Dickinson-like anachronism. That is, if David Dickinson had outfitted his home as an amusement park, complete with rides and a petting zoo; married one of his viewers and then fathered two children via artificial insemination; dangled his son off a hotel balcony in front of dozens of photographers; and underwent so much plastic surgery that his face looked like a waxwork model left under a sun lamp. All of which makes it harder and harder for fans to say, 'I like Michael Jackson', without drawing quizzical stares. See also **Jackson Family, The**; *Thriller*.

Jade (Not to be Confused with the *Big Brother* Non-Celebrity)

Jade is a different kind of horror movie by William Friedkin, director of *The Exorcist*. A script by Joe 'Showgirls' Eszterhas? Yes, it was never going to rival Friedkin's *The French Connection*, was it? This sub-*Fatal Attraction* romp may appear to exist only to strip Linda Fiorentino of any credibility she may have garnered from *The Last Seduction*. In fact, it appears to exist only to strip Linda Fiorentino.

Jade (Not to be Confused with the Risible William Friedkin Film)

Jade Goody is one of the few success stories to emerge from the reality TV genre, which pretty much tells you everything you need to know about reality TV. Taking the girl out of Essex, the Big Brother experience was very much unable to take Essex out of the girl. Surely, when the rest of the housemates made her take all her clothes off, someone should have intervened. We've never enjoyed a 'kebab' in quite the same way since. Now appearing in an *OK!* magazine near you, Jade is forever letting us into her life, her house, the secrets behind her amazing new look . . . We know it's bad to look. We can feel ourselves sneering even before we turn the page. But we just can't help ourselves.

Jameson, Jenna

Since she first came to public attention (and her public first came to attention) after her appearance in *Up and Cummers 11*, Jenna James (born Jenna Marie Massoli, fact fans!) has been the world's favourite pretend lesbian. She has fought drug addiction and a chronic lack of clothes to become the acceptable face of hardcore pornography, appearing on US TV whenever CNN or NBC need something rude explained by a full-breasted woman in a tight dress. There is an almost limitless supply of young women that are prepared to do something unmentionable on camera – you need only examine your local shopping precinct's CCTV records to determine that for yourself – but Jenna is one of the very few that has managed to parlay her early sauciness into a multi-million dollar business empire.

Janus, Hugh See Crank Phone Calls.

Japanese Animation (Adult)

You live in a strange yet vaguely familiar post-apocalyptic, amoral world. Your girlfriend is an android, an alien or a demon. And your 'job' involves lumbering around inside a great feck-off robot, battling other great feck-off robots. Welcome to the world of adult Japanese animation, or 'anime'. While most American animation (even the stuff that attracts adult audiences) is inherently child-friendly, in Japan that's definitely not the case. Nothing, and we mean *nothing*, is off limits. Which is why parents cruising the video shop for cartoons for the kids should never, ever snap up an unfamiliar anime without first reading the box. And then, just to be safe, watching the whole thing before the babysitter arrives.

Jehovah's Witnesses (Getting Rid Of)

The cat has just eaten the Sunday roast, two of your children are fighting and your partner is nowhere to be seen when the doorbell rings – two very polite besuited men with attaché cases are standing there smiling, asking a simple question, 'Have you ever wondered why we are here?' Biting back the impulse to say, 'To waste my time perhaps?' you need to devise a swift but effective strategy to rid yourself of these turbulent priests. Saying anything sensible will result in a twenty-minute Bible-reading and saying anything rude just isn't cricket, so we recommend one of the following: a) I am a Liberal Democrat and would like to talk to you about proportional representation; b) I am able to offer your church substantial savings on double-glazing; or c) I'm so glad you called – Satan told me to pray for potential new converts.

Jelly

Believe it or not, this so-easy-it's-embarrassing dessert was once the height of haute cuisine. Gelatin, in case you didn't know (or had banished it from your mind), is usually derived from cow bones, hides, and connective tissue. In the nineteenth century only the gentry ate enough meat to accumulate the spare body parts needed to make this wobbly treat. But in 1845 American inventor Peter Cooper developed a way to preserve gelatin in a stable, powdered form. Two years later, fellow American inventor Pearle Wait developed a fruit-flavoured version of Cooper's gelatin. His wife, May, came up with the name 'Jell-O'. In 1899 Wait, unable to create a market for his invention, sold the formula and name to manufacturer and salesman Orator F. Woodward – for $450. Woodward made it a success by sending out salesman armed with cookbooks explaining how to create fancy-looking dishes just like the rich folks. Shortly thereafter (and forevermore), puddings made from rendered cow parts became staples of children's birthday parties, family reunions, and lowbrow wedding receptions.

Jeremy, Ron

The horny hobbit of porn exists, it seems, purely to give hope to men of a certain age who are insulated almost too well with a draught-proof combination of body hair and subcutaneous fat. 'If Ron can make the two-backed beast with a dozen or so curvy lovelies in a day,' the somewhat erroneous logic goes, 'then so can we.' Of course we can't. Ron probably can't either, but the magic of great cinema is that it shows us our very dreams.

Jetsons, The See Hanna-Barbera Cartoons.

Jiffy Pop Popcorn

Want to re-create that essential cinema experience at home? Not happy about charging your family £7 to enter the sitting room and inviting fat/tall/talkative people to sit between your sofa and your screen? Then a good alternative is to visit those nice people at iwantoneofthose.com (a haven of guilty pleasures in itself) and order a Popcorn Maker. Switch it on, chuck in a beaker full of 'popping corn' (available at all good retailers) stand there for about as long as it takes to do three movie impressions (we suggest 'You were only supposed to blow the bloody door off', 'Of all the gin joints in all the world you had to walk into mine' and 'Are you lookin'at me?') and hey presto before your very eyes real popcorn starts exploding out of the machine like a styrofoam puppet having an orgasm. Simply add salt or sugar to taste and proceed to your home cinema, surround sound, Dolby 5.1 experience.

Jimmy Five Bellies

We looked up the truth about Jimmy, but it was a bit dull, so we decided to print the legend: there are enough tales of Jimmy's pranks while travelling the world with Paul Gascoigne to fill a book. He seems mainly to have been the butt of Gazza's jokes, being set up with a transvestite hooker, having his nose incinerated, being ordered about by Gazza's robot, that kind of thing. Given that Gazza himself occupied the National Jester spot for a few years back in the Nineties, being the jester's jester is either the greatest accolade in comedy or just a little bit tragic. We think he's hilarious. He's the kind of pal every man, and quite a few women, would like – he can take a drink, and never gets upset if you feed him a cat poo pie or set fire to him.

Johnson, Boris

The love child of Billy Bunter and a mop, Alexander Boris de Pfeffel Johnson is currently the only member of the Conservative Party known to have a personality. Whether it's insulting the people of Liverpool, threatening journalists, or getting jiggy with colleagues at the *Spectator*, there's never a dull moment when Boris is around. It's almost worth voting Conservative to enjoy the spectacle of Boris breaking the land speed record for resigning from the cabinet.

Jokes (Blonde)

Once it became deeply un-PC to tell jokes about the Irish, the butt of the classic 'isn't that person stupid' joke became blondes or their interchangeable partners-in-crime, Essex girls. Not only did this prove an effective way of recycling old gags (How do you make a blonde's eyes light up? A: Shine a flashlight in their ear; or, even better: She was so blonde, she spent twenty minutes looking at the orange juice carton because it said 'concentrate'); it also gave the teller and the laugher the guilty sense that they were getting away with something in a post-*Female Eunuch* world.

Jokes (Dirty)

Dirty jokes are huge with teenage boys still figuring out what goes where, and with grown-ups who like to embarrass their kids, or tell them 'ironically' to their dinner guests. But there's a rich history here: Chaucer, Shakespeare and other 'respectable' writers owe much of their popularity, at least among their contemporaries, to the fact that they had fun with the down and dirty. How different, after all, is Shakespeare's one-liner 'Is it not strange that desire should so many years outlive performance?' from the classic joke in which the old man thinks, 'My God, if I knew she was a virgin, I would have been much more gentle with her!' while his young lover thinks, 'My God, if I knew he could actually get it up, I would have taken off my tights'?

Jokes (Emailed)

It might be a list of Tommy Cooper one-liners not actually written by Cooper. It might be an anonymous cartoon featuring a celebrity in a compromising position. Anyone with a hotmail account knows what it's like to feign annoyance while guiltily sneaking a look at jokes sent from friends . . . and then to forward them along to everyone in your address book.

Jokes (Michael Jackson)

Much intellectual effort has been expended on the nature of humour, how the function of laughter is to help us face and manage our deepest fears. All nonsense of course; humour exists because it's sort of funny. Most of the time. The sole exception is the Michael Jackson joke. The MJJ is the most recent variant of a kind of linguistic virus that propagates by making the teller feel as if he's some kind of topical stand-up, and the tellee feel like some kind of square if they don't at least do that special laugh that's reserved for pædophile and serial killer gags. Other oddballs may come and go, but Michael will always be the headline act, just by dint of being the number one weirdo on the planet. Long may he reign.

Jokes (Sick)

Quadriplegics. Helen Keller. Dead babies, 9-11, Diana and Dodi. All are the subject of sick jokes designed not so much to be gags as to elicit them. Mysteriously passed from generation to generation of teenagers, sick jokes show a remarkable ability to adapt to whatever is in the headlines (What was X's last hit? The dashboard.') and a remarkable ability to get us to repeat them even after we've said, 'That's gross.'

Jonathan Livingston Seagull

From the dedication ('To the real Jonathan Seagull, who lives within us all') to the final words ('His race to learn had begun'), Richard Bach's slim volume is an exercise in simplistic philosophy. This tale of a free-spirited gull whose narrow-minded fellow birds keep him from maximizing his potential was more than a hit – it was a critic-baffling best seller that made even the most simple-minded reader think semi-deep thoughts.

Jones, Tom

He's got the looks, the style, and the talent, all wrapped up in one very large, very obvious package. Born into a coal mining family in South Wales in 1940, Jones rode to fame on the wings of the worldwide smash hit (and, now, karaoke classic) 'It's Not Unusual'. Jones had other hits, but it wasn't his singing that made him an international sensation. It was the fact that he appeared to be hauling around a couple of pounds of saveloy in the front of his extremely tight trousers. Perhaps inevitably, Jones became a Vegas headliner, where his ability to mesmerize his (largely female) audiences was so legendary that Elvis is said to have incorporated some of his moves into his own show. See also **Chick Flicks (Cinderella Fantasies); Humperdinck, Engelbert; Las Vegas; Presley, Elvis.**

Jools Holland's New Year's Eve Hootenanny

Just as sitting at home watching TV on a Saturday night carries a measure of shame, so sitting at home watching TV on New Year's Eve – the ultimate Saturday night – carries with it the ultimate ignominy. The Hootenanny has pretensions to hipness but is ultimately just a millennial retooling of the vaguely tartan variety shows our parents made us watch before we were old enough to go out and throw up in other people's homes. The show itself has a tried and tested formula: two worthy 'world music' acts to every one you've heard of, and only one band you genuinely like, who will be on last to make sure you sit through all the other stuff. It doesn't matter if you polish off the last of the Christmas gin and fall asleep before the people you wanted to see actually appear, because Jools will play inappropriate boogie-woogie piano over both their songs anyway and it will sound dreadful.

Jordan

Is the joke on us? On one level she is easy to dismiss as a lairy, huge-breasted cartoon character who falls out of nightclubs wearing some bondage tape and a filthy smile, who has dubious taste in men (think Dane Bowers and Dwight Yorke for starters before we even get anywhere near father of her second child and husband Peter Andre) but on another she is a role model for hundreds of thousands of teenage girls, a shrewd, switched-on business woman whose autobiography *Being Jordan* was the best-selling book of 2005, a woman with lucrative multi-media deals sewn up and who is so adept at keeping the press on her side that she could teach Alistair Campbell a few tricks. You decide.

Jurassic Park See **Alan Partridge (Quoting)**.

Just A Minute
Four celebrities (usually from a mix of the likes of Paul Merton, Tony Hawks, Sue Perkins, Clement Freud and Graham Norton) compete to talk on a subject for one minute without deviation, hesitation or repetition in this BBC Radio 4 panel game hosted by the (one imagines) blazered and brass-buttoned Nicholas Parsons. It is utterly, utterly (sorry – a bit of repetition there) pointless, very English, will never transfer to television (they have tried and failed twice on that front) and is everything radio comedy should be. In its heyday it was a weekly showcase for the weird comedic talents of Peter Jones, Derek Nimmo and Kenneth Williams. Like all great comedy, everyone takes it terribly seriously.

Karaoke

What began in Japan as an after-work stress buster has evolved into a cheap way for pubs to avoid hiring entertainers. Instead of paying a singer, just get the karaoke machine going and the crowd will amuse itself by struggling through such classics as 'I Will Survive' and 'New York, New York'.

KC and the Sunshine Band

The music of Harry Wayne Casey (KC) and his big, loud, horn-intensive band wasn't what anyone would call 'complex'. No one debated the hidden meaning in lyrics such as 'That's the way; uh-huh, uh-huh, I like it, uh-huh, uh-huh'. Instead they joyously did what everyone else did during the group's Seventies heyday: put their brains on hold, headed for the dance floor, and tore the place up to tunes such as 'Get Down Tonight', '(Shake, Shake, Shake) Shake Your Booty', and 'I'm Your Boogie Man'. See also **Disco (Dancing)**; **Summer, Donna**.

Kebabs

Unkempt sandwiches of mysterious meat and wholly disposable 'salad', never knowingly eaten by a sober man and only even considered by the drunkest possible woman. Some statistics we've just made up: 68 per cent of every kebab sold ends up being dropped down the front of the purchaser's shirt. 0 per cent of those phallic pepper things are eaten on purpose. Guilt rating: 97 per cent. Pleasure rating: off the scale.

Kendal, Felicity

Some film and TV stars bear an uncanny resemblance to the entertainers of an earlier age. We're still yet to be convinced, for example, that George Clooney hasn't been cloned from one of Tyrone Power's eyebrows. No star though has ever reminded one of 1940s cinema sensation Jerry Mouse quite so much as does dear Felicity Kendal. One might think that resembling a cartoon mouse would represent some sort of disadvantage, but on the contrary she has been the chosen pin-up of middle-income men of a certain age since they were a certain other age. The way she filled a pair of dungarees in *The Good Life* won her an entire generation of admirers of one gender, while her murine features ensured that she did not entirely alienate viewers of another, more influential, sex. The persistence of her success long after those obvious charms have faded, and her ability to continue to enchant even in anodyne piffle like *Rosemary and Thyme* bespeaks her status as a British institution of infinite endurance.

Ketchup

The term actually derives from a Chinese term for a fermented fish sauce. Yum. So ubiquitous is modern tomato ketchup that it's estimated to be in 97 per cent of American homes. While one can assume that most of that red lead finds its way onto oven chips, fish fingers, beef burgers and the like, true guilty pleasure comes from globbing it onto a good steak. Shamed US president Richard Nixon reportedly put it on cottage cheese, an embarrassment that rivals his implosion during the 1974 Watergate scandal.

KFC

Let's clear up one thing right away. That urban myth about how Kentucky Fried Chicken had to change their name to KFC is complete and utter cobblers. You've got to hand it to Colonel

Sanders, he's turned around the fact that KFC is as greasy as hell into something of a USP: it's finger lickin' good! That's balls. Balls as in his determination, rather than what they're selling. Not only does KFC taste great, but it comes with a free warm glow of self-justification. Pigging out is fine because it's white meat, isn't it, not like a burger or anything, and therefore it's not actually that bad for you. That's what we say, anyway. Bargain buckets all round! See also **Imitation KFC Outlets**.

Kicked in the Nuts (Watching Someone Get)

A man who takes a swift blow to the scrotum will experience severe pain, difficulty breathing, feelings of extreme nausea, and perhaps a fainting spell. A man who *watches* another man take a swift blow to the scrotum will experience a severely puckered facial expression, difficulty hiding his amusement, feelings of extreme mirth, and perhaps a laughing fit. While it's a mystery why so many people find the sight of someone getting kicked in the man sack entertaining, the spectacle is so popular that it is screened repeatedly on everything from *You're Been Framed* to commercials to numberless martial arts movies. But these films are made by people who have obviously never been kicked in the nuts. Otherwise they wouldn't show antagonists taking one, two, three, or even four swipes at the family jewels before folding. The truth is, one shot to the sperm bank ends a brawl quicker than a bullet to the temple. This move isn't called The Closer for nothing. See also *You're Been Framed*; **Kung Fu Movies**.

Kim Bauer (The Perils of)

24 is one of the best TV shows of, like, ever. Kiefer Sutherland, as maverick CTU agent Jack 'You Don't Have A Choice!' Bauer is brilliant. His daughter, Kim, played by the not unattractive Elisa Cuthbert, is not. For some unfathomable reason, the writers decided that a *Perils of Penelope Pitstop* style sub-plot was exactly what the drama needed. Kidnapped in series one, Kim finds herself captured again in series two, escapes only to be caught in an animal trap and cornered by a cougar, survives that to be trapped in a underground bunker with a loon, breaks free only to walk into a garage that is just that moment being robbed . . . By series three, even Jack had had enough and got his daughter (previous career: nanny) a posting at CTU Headquarters (new job: computer expert). Surely she couldn't get kidnapped in the middle of a high security government building. What do you think?

King, Stephen

There are a lot of books in the world. There are even a few not written by Stephen King. Beginning with 1974's *Carrie*, the master of page-turning-horror-usually-involving-dysfunctional-families-that-are-scary-even-without-the-supernatural-stuff has dominated the market, even when exploiting premises that literally no other big-name novelist could get away with (a killer car in *Christine*, a rabid St Bernard in *Cujo*). Critics, academics, and die-hard fans like to pretend there's literary merit in his pages, but you know better. This bloke just has a brilliant ability to scare the piss out of the masses.

Kiss

Okay, they're not the Beatles – or even Aerosmith. Their songs, most of them stadium rock anthems, have all the melodic sophistication of an explosion in an oil refinery. But when you're thundering down the motorway in your Fiesta . . . , there's no one you'd rather have on the stereo than the self-described 'hottest rock band in the world'. Best? No. Most talented? Double no. Most made-up? Definitely. See also **Concert T-shirts**; **Greatest Hits Albums**.

Kitten Posters/Cards

Even the most cold, unfeeling, dogcentric person will glance up at the poster above his dentist's chair and grasp the tender 'Just hang in there' sentiment of a terrified kitten dangling by a paw from a branch. The point is, a single furry face carries a vast amount of emotional information. Plus, nothing warms the cockles like a tabby in a teacup ('May your cup runneth over'), a kitten in a hammock ('Cat Nap'), or a feline wearing sunglasses ('Kool Kat'). Their dewy pink noses, disproportionately cute ears and knowing cat eyes leave impulse card shoppers with only one question: 'How many of these can I take to the till without looking like a freak?'

Knievel, Evel

Watching this man make motorcycle jumps was interesting. Watching him *almost* make motorcycle jumps – which happened fairly often – was fascinating. Knievel, who invented the art of leaping over things with motorbikes, accomplished possibly the most undesirable feat in the *Guinness Book of World Records*. Having sustained thirty-five documented skeletal fractures, he's listed as the human with the most broken bones in history. See also **Morons (Entertaining, Untimely Deaths Of)**; **Stunts (Insane, Televised)**.

Knight Rider See **Hasselhoff, David**.

Kournikova, Anna

For irrefutable proof that life is unfair and that most people are superficial idiots, consider the career of tennis 'phenomenon' Anna Kournikova. She's never won a singles title in her life. After peaking at number eight in the women's world rankings, she's slid below seventy. Serena Williams, Venus Williams, and probably their *mum* could hit her off the court. And yet, she has legions of fans, has been called the most recognizable face in sport, and makes about £15 million a year in endorsements. That's because she possesses something far more important than skills: looks. Instead of labouring in the obscurity she so richly deserves, Kournikova has transformed her babehood into lucrative promotional contracts, modelling assignments, even her own calendar. Who cares about making the cover of *Sports Illustrated*? She's on the cover of *Maxim*. See also **Lads' Mags**.

K-Tel Records

Bringing a K-Tel album to a party during the Seventies or Eighties was tantamount to publicly acknowledging that your ability to discriminate good music from bad was about as finely developed as a blind man's appreciation for painting. For years the company led the world in compilation discs that boasted 'original hits/ original stars' – which in practice meant albums resembling a Band Aid get-together from hell. In one 100 per cent true example, K-Tel's *Believe in Music*, Donny Osmond, Rod Stewart, Cher, Eric Clapton and Bobby Vinton were all slapped on the same piece of vinyl. With K-Tel a bankruptcy casualty, the format has more recently been dominated by the *Now That's What I Call Music* series, which might be better titled *Now That's What I Call Teenage Music That Next Year You're Going to Be Embarrassed to Admit You Liked*. See also **Cher (Without Sonny)**.

Kung Fu Films

Kung Fu films are made in such numbers that it's possible to find everything from kung fu science fiction (*Zu: Warriors from the Magic Mountain*) to kung fu romance (*Crouching Tiger, Hidden Dragon*) to kung fu comedy (anything by Jackie Chan). It's somewhat tougher to locate fighting flicks that don't bear an unsettling structural resemblance to porn films. Most begin with a one-on-one encounter, followed by some sort of group thing, perhaps spiced up with toys. A little girl-on-girl action is thrown in. Finally, there's a big, loud, sweaty free-for-all. See also **Films (Pornographic)**.

L

Lacoste Polo Shirts

There are lots of misconceptions about these Eighties fashion icons. First and foremost, the reptile featured on the left breast of every polo shirt is a crocodile, not an alligator. It got its name from French tennis star René Lacoste, whose impressive conk earned him the nickname 'Le Crocodile'. In 1934 Lacoste, who must have been an unbelievably good sport, added a reptilian logo to his tennis whites. Thus a legend was born. See also **'Members Only' Jackets**.

Lads' Mags

Salacious, leering and highly successful, *FHM*, *Maxim*, *Nuts* and the rest have climbed to the top of the men's magazine business by admitting that gentlemen really do buy girly magazines just for the pictures. The genius of these publications is in realizing that the girlies in question don't have to be totally naked, à la *Playboy*. This strategy has netted it a better class of celebrity T and A. Women who wouldn't dream of sitting for a nude shoot (at least, not yet) don't think twice about doing three *Maxim* spreads wearing nothing but thong underwear and a feather boa. Thus the magazine can snag the likes of Paris Hilton, Shania Twain, Lucy Liu, Jessica Simpson and even Helena Bonham Carter, while *Playboy* whines and begs to get a couple of scrubs from *Big Brother*. See also **Playboy**, **Thongs**.

Lager (Cheap European)

The British first developed their taste for mystery-brand Continental beers as a result of the package tour boom of the 1970s and 1980s. As that boom evolved into the twenty-first century E-tourism to Ibiza and Faliraki, that affection has only intensified. The classic Cheap European Lager is a watery concoction that appears to evaporate on contact with a dry throat, leaving the drinker with an unquenchable thirst for more. Generally purchased in boxes containing an unconscionable number of improbably small bottles, CEL is now a standard feature of the post-booze cruise barbecue, and as the climate of our small, damp island becomes increasingly arid, the trend for us to abandon our traditional fine quality beers in favour of this inferior brew is likely to sharpen. Guilty? A little. Pleasurable? Most definitely.

Lakeland Catalogue, The

You know you are hooked on the delights of the Lakeland Catalogue when you discard the rest of the newspaper it falls out of and read it first. The Lakeland story goes back forty years to when Dorothy and Alan Rayner, who made a living selling agricultural feed, started supplying local farmers with polythene bags for packing poultry. Well it's all got a bit fancy since then and if we had to choose just one product for our desert island kitchen it would be the best-selling Banana Guard, which enables you to 'transport your mid-morning snack to work or school without it looking as if it's gone five rounds in a boxing ring! Designed to accommodate virtually every shape and size of banana, it's especially useful for slipping in a rucksack when hiking on the fells – after all, a bit of extra energy will always be welcome.' Marvellous.

Lambada, The

Dance crazes are like one-night stands. After a brief, intensely passionate encounter comes a sudden 'what were we thinking?' moment followed by intense denial. Such was the case with the Lambada, a salsa offshoot featuring intensely sexy moves when done right and intensely embarrassing injuries when done wrong. The dance hit the mainstream when a musician and filmmaker visited Bahia, Brazil, in 1988, heard a unique sound, returned to France, and cut a record with a band called Kaoma. A craze was quickly born in late 1989 and quickly died less that a year later – leaving behind at least two quickie cinematic cash-in attempts, which opened at the same time: *The Forbidden Dance* and *Lambada: Set the Night on Fire*. Either one makes *Breakin' 2: Electric Boogaloo* look like *Citizen Kane*. See also **One-Night Stands**.

Lambrusco

Was 1987 a good year for the Syrah harvest in the Rhône valley? If, like us, you couldn't give a toss, then you're probably a Lambrusco drinker. This Italian table wine, low in alcohol content and typically possessing the shelf life of mayonnaise, comes in red, white, and rosé. Teenage girls across the country thought they were drinking champagne – an illusion their cash-strapped boyfriends did nothing to discourage. See also **Wine in a Box**.

Land of the Giants See **Allen, Irwin**.

Landon, Michael

It wasn't until the première of *Little House on the Prairie* in 1974 that we came to know Landon (born Eugene Maurice Orowitz) in all his suntanned, big-haired, U-rated glory. Playing the Ingalls clan's ever-patient 'Pa', he became a surrogate dad to an entire generation of latchkey kids. Which is why, even today, sophisticated adults can be stopped in their tracks by a repeat of *Little House*. Even his attempts to bare his 'troubled' side seemed inordinately wholesome. Landon wrote, produced, directed and appeared in a pretty-much-autobiographical 1976 film for TV called *The Loneliest Runner*, about a young boy suffering from a debilitating social problem. No, not a crack habit or alcoholism or even bulimia. The kid was a bed wetter.

Las Vegas

Even if you hate gauche excess, despise gambling and loathe Celine Dion, Vegas, a.k.a. Sin City, is still a blast. It's fun precisely *because* it's so lame. Originally a parched, end-of-the-line desert hell-hole, it got its big break when Nevada legalized gambling in 1931. These days the place has mutated from the semi-sleazy gambling den the Rat Pack made famous into some sort of bizarre entertainment Mecca – what Disneyland might be if they let you drink. And smoke. And gamble. And marry someone you met three hours ago. What's not to like? See also **Casinos**; **Elvis Impersonators**; **Jones, Tom**; **Presley, Elvis**.

Lassie

If the dog is man's best friend, then Lassie is man's *bestest* best friend. Debuting opposite a pre-teen Elizabeth Taylor and Roddy McDowall in the 1943 cinematic release *Lassie Come Home* (the collie was actually a male named Pal who was given to animal trainer Rudd Weatherwax to settle a $10 debt), he/she went on to star in a radio show, then a series of TV programmes running, without interruption, from 1954 to 1971. The pleasure came from watching a very talented dog (all subsequent 'Lassies' are male descendants of the original Pal) repeatedly save its accident-prone owners from disaster. The guilt (sometimes realized years later) came from thinking how much your own flea-bitten mutt suffered by comparison. See also **TV Programmes Featuring Animal Protagonists**; *Riverdance*.

Late-Night Phone-Ins

Apparently there was one on Election Day where this taxi driver called in and complained that Michael Howard was soft on asylum seekers and then last night this woman from Harlesden revealed that she'd always had this thing about Donny Osmond which came on just before the 'Pillow Talk' feature where post-coital couples shared their fantasies and then do you remember that time when they got through to the White House switchboard and asked if . . . Hang on a sec – I mean – honestly! Who listens to this rubbish?

Lava Lamps

The lava lamp (officially called the Lava Lite) works by heating a blob of specially formulated wax that's suspended in a jug

 of coloured fluid. As the wax heats and expands, its density becomes less than the liquid around it and it rises to the top of the lamp, forming all sorts of cool shapes as it does. Then it cools and drifts slowly to the bottom. Then it gets hot and rises again. On and on and on. Think of it as satellite telly for stoners. See also **Marijuana**.

Lawless, Lucy See *Xena: Warrior Princess*.

Lesbians (Film Scenes Featuring)
How did Salma Hayek and Jeanne Tripplehorn save the otherwise unbearable *Timecode*? How did Sarah Michelle Gellar and Selma Blair save the otherwise risible *Cruel Intentions*? How have scores of unknown actresses saved otherwise unwatchable straight-to-video films? By participating in lesbian scenes, of course. Whether it's a wet one on the lips or a full frontal attack, hot girl-on-girl action can make all the difference – at least for men whose wives are asleep upstairs. See also **Prison Films Featuring Women**.

Leslie, John
What is there to say about *Blue Peter* BFG turned gangling love rat turned lofty hermit John Leslie? Rarely are celebrities more entertaining than when they have fallen, and few have fallen from such a height as John Leslie.

Lewis, Jerry
Given his difficult reputation, his heart-on-his-sleeve charity work, and all the dud flicks mixed in with his hits, being a fan of Jerry Lewis isn't for wimps. But true believers know that it's not just the French who love him. From his first Atlantic City performances with Dean Martin (during which he pretty much redefined the term 'manic'), through such classic films as *The Nutty Professor* and *The Bell Boy*, to his 'rediscovery' at the hands of Martin Scorsese in the film *The King of Comedy*, Lewis has proven himself to be a one-of-a-kind entertainer.

LAVA LAMPS

Liberace

An oversized grand piano, a gaudy candelabra and a penchant for smiles not seen this side of the Chesire Cat led Wisconsin's strangest son to nightclub shows, TV gigs movie roles, and, in 1953, record Madison Square Garden crowds. Part of the guilty pleasure came from the 'Is he or isn't he?' question, which was fuelled in large part by Liberace's unmarried status and his devotion to his mother. Okay, and maybe his outrageous costumes (in one show he appeared in pink llama fur trimmed with rhinestones). But there was more to his appeal than mere gossip. Liberace could actually play the piano well. And even if he wasn't to your taste (one critic called him the 'biggest sentimental vomit of all time') you had to admire a man who could offer up 'Ave Maria', 'Yesterday', and then a little Chopin, all in one evening. See also **Cher (Without Sonny)**; **Las Vegas**.

Lidl

It's very hard to classify exactly what kind of shop Lidl is. Stacks of Mystery Brand cola jostle for shelf space alongside lawnmowers, disposable nappies, jeans that you would never ever wear, and more barbecue paraphernalia than the inhabitants of a small, damp island could ever need. All this, of course, and enough groceries for your weekly shop. Best of all, these groceries are generally exotic brands stocked by no other UK outlet, giving you the feeling of a continental self-catering holiday in your very own high street. In the technological paradise of the twenty-first century, where you can order all your grocery requirements with a simple click of a mouse, there's no need for you ever to buy anything in Lidl. It's just endlessly fascinating to wander the aisles playing a form of consumer roulette, trying to guess what will come up next.

Lifeguards

Lifeguards, male and female, have always enjoyed a high standing in the hierarchy of fantasy sex objects. Not only do they go around rescuing people and watching out for others (a sure turn-on for women), but their job requires them to be buff and pretty much naked (a sure turn-on for men). Not that this was always the case. Early lifesaving services used to row out during rough seas and try to rescue shipwreck victims. Not until the twentieth century, with the rise of beach culture, did the lifeguard become a tanned, toned, nose-smeared-with-sunblock model in a high chair. See also *Baywatch*.

Limousines

These days the truly wealthy travel in well-appointed but reasonably nondescript luxury sedans – the better to avoid kidnapping. Which means the 'high rollers' behind the smoked glass of most stretch limos are probably businesspeople sharing a ride to the airport, or a hen party. But still, even though the car is hired and, often, not all that clean inside, there's nothing like rolling around in a thirty-foot land yacht to pump up the ego – even if you're only catching a flight to Newcastle.

Line Dancing

Offering virtually the only chance for people with two left feet to hit the dance floor without making utter fools of themselves, the concept of the line dance goes back thousands of years. Early American settlers enjoyed a version called the contra dance (two lines, men in one, ladies in the other). Today's versions have everyone standing side by side, executing carefully choreographed steps at more or less the same time. Line dancing is popular among country and western fans – it's what Billy Ray Cyrus was invented for – but Michael Flatley has offered his own Irish version, and the craze is even responsible for the musical career of Steps – '1,2,3,4' being their debut hit single. See also **Lambada, The**; **Macarena, The**; **Riverdance**.

Lineker, Gary

Impeccable anchor of *Match of the Day*, former England captain, squeaky-clean, no-bookings on-pitch record. Lineker truly can do nothing wrong – damn him. Not even those annoying adverts for Walkers Crisps can make us dislike him – much as we try. We've seen him dressed up as a nun, a punk rocker, a headmistress, a menacing devil, reducing Gazza to tears and of course appearing as Mr Universe plotting mischief against boy-wonder Michael 'Cheese and' Owen – but he still emerges as good old lovable Mr Perfect Gary Lineker.

'For God's sake, please do something filthy and out-of-character,' we think, but frankly he could have a punch-up, a 112 mph speeding ticket, be caught spit-roasting Jordan with Colonel Gadaffi whilst dressed as Adolf Hitler and snorting coke off Des Lynam's moustache and the tabloids would only write about his boyish good looks, those gleaming teeth and the unflappable mateyness.

Little Chef
In the old days, stuffing your face on the motorway left you with the tricky dilemma of whether to stop at a Happy Eater (great slides) or a Little Chef (free lollipop). The Lollipops won out, and the Happy Eater franchise became consumed within Little Chef's greasy empire. And though the familiar high street chains are swiftly taking over most of the road network (Costa, Burger King, MacDonald's), we still prefer the simpler, more British charms of a full English with a mug of tea. If that isn't enough to fill you up after four hours crawling through the contraflow system round Newport Pagnell, there's always their gargantuan Olympic Breakfast. We're not sure which particular Olympic athletes eat that, mind. Maybe the shot putters?

Little House on the Prairie See **Landon, Michael**.

Local Radio DJs
There's never a dull moment on Local Radio. As a DJ fronting a 'pot-pourri' of local weather, Wine-Bar promotions ('See you down there on Thursday with the whole team for a crazy night out') school fête reports and drivetime cheese-tastic requests ('For Gavin – the light of my life' or 'For Donna – from all the lads at the Rugby Club') your broadcasting career is either almost over or only just begun. As a listener one can almost smell the Partridgesque desperation emanating from the Simon Bates soundalikes or the Johnny Vaughan wannabees and it is pure joy.

Loose Women
Hosted by Kaye 'a riot in beige' Adams, ITV's daytime talk show *Loose Women* is seemingly on every day of the week and

is worth watching through your fingers because it takes banality to an altogether more enjoyable level. It is simple low-rent telly: bung four women behind a desk and get them to moan on and on about lightweight 'ishoos'. Groundbreaking topics include 'Mid-life crisis – good or bad?', 'Do blondes have more fun?' and 'Hot flushes – does the menopause save money on your heating bills?' Panellists all belong to the 'I know the face but . . .' group of celebrities and include the likes of Coleen 'ex-pop star and ex-wife of Shane Ritchie' Nolan, Carol 'broadcaster and ex-wife of Chris Evans' McGiffin and Kerry 'ex-pop star and ex-wife of Bryan from Westlife' McFadden. And all hopefully soon also 'ex-panellists on ex-TV show *Loose Women*'.

Loosener

In cricketing terms, a loosener is a warm-up ball, pitching lazily outside the off-stump, as the fast bowler builds up his rhythm and speed. In drinking terms, a 'loosener' is that post-work pint, the taking away of the day's stress, the warm-up pint before an evening's entertainment, before the serious drinker builds up his rhythm and speed. As we say, it's not about appreciating the taste, it's about warming up. So get that down you, and landlord? Same again if you please, and whatever you're drinking.

Lord of the Dance See *Riverdance*.

Lord of the Rings, The
Millions of fans have read J. R. R. Tolkien's *Rings* trilogy since its initial publication in 1954 and 1955. Countless more watched the highly successful films based on the books. And literary critics have praised *LOTR* not just as great fantasy, but great literature. This means that absolutely anyone should be able to read or watch the story of Middle-earth without a twinge of guilt. There's just one catch. This most perfectly realized of all fantasy worlds is still larded up with the usual cheesy cast of nursery rhyme staples (trolls, elves, wizards, etc.) almost all of whom have silly-sounding names like Elrond, Legolas, Gandalf, and Éomer. And whether you like it or not, being a fan means you have something in common with the Dungeons

and Dragons crowd. Even if you were once *part* of that crowd and all that ten-sided-dice rolling is behind you, there's still that lingering feeling that you should be doing something more grown-up with your time. See also **Dungeons and Dragons**.

Losing Weight (Being Told You Look Like You Have When You Know You Haven't)

You go to a party, see a friend you haven't seen for a while and they utter the golden phrase, 'You're looking wonderful – have you been doing Atkins?' Inwardly you are thinking, 'Not unless Atkins involves loads of pasta, chocolate, Twiglets, white wine, a takeaway on a Saturday night and a pizza every now and again,' but outwardly you hear yourself saying, 'Yeah – it's great – you should try it.' Who needs diets, eh? See also **Diets (Fad)**.

Lost in Space See Allen, Irwin.

Lottery Scratchcards

Do you find waiting half a week for the National Lottery draw too much to bear? Thankfully, help is at hand. The instant-win scratchcard has become the impulse buy of choice for corner shop patrons picking up a four-pack of Carling and a packet of Marlboros after work. Okay, most of the people who play these games aren't total chavs, but you can sure *feel* like one when you belly up to the cash till and choose between the stunning variety of no-real-difference games. Still, in the time it takes to walk to the car, fish a pound out of your pocket, scratch off the numbers, and see that you've lost, you can have fun imagining what you'd do with the cash if you'd won. See also **Casinos**.

'Louie, Louie'

This 1963 song by the Kingsmen might have staggered quietly into obscurity if the state of Indiana hadn't banned the record (even though the lyrics, which are completely unintelligible in this version, are actually quite innocent). Sniffing a cult hit, its label reissued the tune in 1964. And in 1965. And in 1966. Eventually it landed at No. 2 on the *Billboard* charts. During the Seventies it enjoyed a resurgence thanks to its presence on the *Animal House* soundtrack. See also **Games, Drinking**; *Animal House*.

Love Story

If chick flicks were a pack of Brownies, *Love Story* would be its Brown Owl. In 1970 there was simply no escaping this three-hanky cry-fest, in which rich boy Oliver Barrett IV, played by Ryan O'Neal, falls for poor girl Jennifer (Ali MacGraw). They frolic around together, and then she dies. And that's pretty much it. See also **Chick Flicks (In Which Someone Dies)**.

Loyalty Cards

In the 1990s, you might have found it hard to imagine that coffee could be made more addictive than it already was. Far away, marketing men with intelligences far superior to our own looked at our wallets with envious eyes and laid their plans to empty them. Thus the loyalty card was born: a simple scrap of heavy paper designed to bring you back to the same coffee shop again and again in the quest for something for nothing. Scoffing at the notion that the price of the tenth one is concealed within the profit margin of the preceding nine, we jealously guard our dog-eared loyalty cards, bringing them out only behind cupped hands to count again the stamps thereon. Sensitive to the notion of a good idea, sandwich shops, barbers, and for all we know high-class madams have all created their own loyalty card schemes luring customers back again and again in pursuit of the elusive free sandwich/trim/happy finish.

Lucozade

Ian Rush, according to the advert, drank milk. Daley Thompson, clattering hurdles down to the sound of Iron Maiden, drank Lucozade. A sort of Tizer with additives, when we were growing up Lucozade only ever appeared in our houses when someone was sick. Did it really make people better, or did their mild hysteria at being allowed to glug gallons of sticky sweetness just take their mind off their chronic diarrhoea? We're not sure, but we miss the glass bottles with all the wrapping and all that congealed gunk that made it difficult to screw the cap back on.

Lunch Boxes

One sandwich with beef-paste in it. An apple. A mini carton of fruit juice. Those were the grim realities of a primary school child's packed lunch. But who cared, when the garishly-coloured plastic box it came in had KITT from *Knight Rider* or a My Little Pony on the cover? We loved our lunch boxes, and interestingly, scientific studies have shown that there is no quicker way to assess the favourite film, cartoon character or TV programme of a sample demographic of five-year-olds than to ask to see their lunch box. Wait, I'll rephrase that, Officer; I can explain; you see, I'm researching a book on guilty pleasures . . . Wait! . . . See also **Fruit-Juice Cartons, Mini**; **Hasselhof, David**; **My Little Pony**.

M

Macarena, The

Not since the hokey-cokey has there been an easier-to-follow dance craze. The song upon which it was based, originally a hit for Los Del Rio in Spain in 1993, was remixed by a group called the Bayside Boys and became an international musical, and dance, phenomenon. Too bad all those parents teaching it to their five-year-olds didn't pay attention to the lyrics (which, depending on the version, were either in Spanish or almost unintelligible English). Apparently, the song is about a girl named Macarena who, when snubbed by her soldier boyfriend, decides to hook up with two blokes she meets out on the razzle. Hey, Macarena! See also **Lambada, The**; **Line Dancing**.

MacGyver

If you're fighting crime, what could be more useful than an arsenal of weapons? How about a safety pin, or a credit card, or a light bulb? Such were the tools of the trade for MacGyver, the character played by Richard Dean Anderson on this popular adventure series. Loyalists kept the show going for seven seasons, during which MacGyver used a bicycle inner tube as a slingshot, nearly blinded an enemy with a packet of soy sauce, built a baby crib out of ice-hockey sticks. Hey, whatever works.

Madame Tussauds

Even if you live in London, home to many a celebrity, there's little chance you'll see an honest-to-goodness star on the street. But fear not – you can hit Madame Tussauds and ogle wax figures of famous people instead. This most notorious of all wax museums was begun by Marie Grosholtz (later Tussaud). Having learned her trade in Paris – including a stint moulding guillotine victims' heads – she inherited her mentor's collection, toured it around the British Isles, then settled in on London's Baker Street and opened up her permanent display in 1835. One can only imagine what the museum's namesake would think of the place now. Transplanted to larger digs and to other locations, it includes a talking Simon Cowell and a squeeze-the-bum Brad Pitt.

Madonna (Non-Music Projects)

The Material Girl has proved her lack of acting skills in romantic adventure (*Shanghai Surprise*), courtroom drama (*Body of Evidence*), movie cartoon (*Dick Tracy*), revenge drama/softcore porn (*A Certain Sacrifice*) and musical (*Evita*), although she would have excelled in the laugh-out-loud comedy *Swept Away* had it been a laugh-out-loud comedy; it wasn't, but it does have the distinction of being the first film to 'win' both the awards for Worst Picture and Worst Remake or Sequel at the Razzie Awards. Yet we continue to, if not buy tickets, at least gravitate to tabloid stories about her latest movie flops. She has also branched out into publishing with a line of children's books ('That story's nice, Daddy, but tell me about her hot girl-on-girl action with Britney Spears'). And of course, who can forget 1992's *Sex*? That portfolio of Madonna-intensive gynaecological pictures made an excellent coffee-table book – if the coffee table was in the *Playboy* mansion.

Magic Eye

The buzz of Magic Eye isn't just being able to see 3-D without daft glasses. It's also the fun of watching your friends straining to see what's right in front of their faces.

Magic Roundabout, The (Theories About)

The Magic Roundabout was, to our young eyes at least, bizarre enough without trying to extrapolate some high concept out of it as well. But that didn't stop the nation trying – and failing – to pin one on it. All *Magic Roundabout* theories suffer from what philosophers call 'The Dougal Problem', namely that beyond the character of Dougal, the theories never actually work. So the 'French political satire' theory starts off well (Dougal, De Gaulle, do you see what they haven't done there?), and peters out quickly. The 'each character is a different drug' theory (Dougal, hairy Woodbine)? Time for bed. See also *Captain Pugwash* (**Invented Stories About**); **Carrott, Jasper**.

Magic Tricks

As an adult in a world where special effects can do anything and where Google will break the secret code of the Magic Circle in the click of a mouse, you have split loyalties. Your mind tells you that magic tricks are all an illusion, but your heart wants to believe that live women can be sawed in half and still wiggle their sequined toes. Whether it be through the good offices of Paul Daniels, David Copperfield or even Siegfried and Roy, watching magic tricks can have a strange effect as we swiftly regress from ironic omniscient adult to being five years old again and marvelling at Uncle Joey conjuring a sixpence from behind his ear and guessing which card you had chosen. Ace of Hearts? Wow, how did you do that?!

Magicians

Merlin was a lovable old man who took young King Arthur under his wing. Just about every magician since then has been a tosser who considers making audiences feel stupid to be his life's work. Yet we guiltily watch, knowing that all the mumbo jumbo is just a distraction and that whatever we're looking at – usually the magician's barely dressed assistant – is exactly where he *wants* us to look while the big switcheroo takes place elsewhere.

Makeovers, Make-up Counter

Whether you're the type of woman who can go for years without so much as buying a new Chap Stick, or a CoverGirl savant who can recite all twelve of the brand's signature LipSlicks from warmest to coolest, the chances are that at some point in your make-up career you have enjoyed the redeeming powers of a free makeover. The secret, as you know, is to succumb. You can't help but feel beautiful and loved when you're getting so much undivided attention, especially once you get past the initial humiliation of perching on a tiny barstool in the middle of Boots while a woman with a China doll complexion studies you like a plumber looking at a blocked drain. See also **Avon**; **Clinique Pore Minimizer Make-up**; **Fake Tan**.

Male Singers Who Sound Like Women

It's been scientifically proven that high-pitched female voices cut through background noise more effectively than male voices. Perhaps that's why such falsetto superstars as the Bee Gees and Frankie Valli enjoyed huge success. What's harder to understand is how Valli and the brothers Gibb, all of whom have normal speaking voices, decided to take this particular tack. Of course singing like a girl sometimes isn't a conscious career move. Michael Jackson sounds like a woman on his albums because, well, *he just sounds like a woman*. See also **Jackson, Michael**; **Bee Gees, The**.

Manchester United (Losing)

Every country has their football hate team. In Germany, it's Bayern Munich, whose financial clout is epitomized by their nickname, FC Hollywood. In Britain, it's Manchester United. Why do we love it so when the ball squirms under Van der Saar's body, Gary Neville starts complaining to the referee and Sir Alex Ferguson breaks the world speed record for chewing gum? We think it's called karma. All those Manchester United merchandising stores on the high street. All those Red Devils fans in satellite towns of Manchester such as Guildford and Tunbridge Wells. So 'avid' fan Malcolm Glazer had never been to Old Trafford before he bought the club? Sounds like he's the perfect owner.

Manilow, Barry

The music of the nasally blessed Manilow seemed to blare out of every radio in the world during his reign as the king of ultrasoft pop from the early Seventies to the early Eighties. Can't Smile Without You? Actually, we can.

Maraschino Cherries

The original maraschino cherries were a true gourmet delicacy. The ones you get at Tesco's are not. Instead of bathing in a rare nectar, they linger for days in sugary water (not to mention food colouring), after which a touch of bitter almond is added to give them a flavour somewhat similar to the traditional maraschino. Hardcore fans eat them straight from the jar, while the rest of the world uses them as nothing but a quickly-brushed-away garnish on everything from iced buns to Happy Hour cocktails.

Marijuana

If you are just a regular law-abiding citizen who likes the illicit thrill when the decriminalized weed appears alongside the After Eights and Colombian (coffee), you have plenty to feel guilty about, including (but not confined to): a) The knowledge of how hypocritical you are for making anti-drug speeches to your own children; b) The realization that your sainted mother wouldn't approve (and wouldn't this break her heart?); c) The difficult-to-avoid fact that you are supporting oppressive foreign regimes with your hard-earned money; and d) The fact that you never can really get the hang of how to roll your own.

Marks and Spencer's Microwave Baked Potato with Cheese

The purpose of a convenience food is to transform something difficult into something easy. Yet one of the easiest dishes in the world to prepare – a Baked Potato with cheese (recipe – turn oven on, throw spud in, 90 minutes later take out, grate lump of mousetrap cheese, add knob of butter, eat) has now been packaged (after a huge amount of brainstorming and product testing one imagines) by those good people at Marks and Spencer into an even easier dish to prepare. Their cunning recipe has totally done away with the need to turn the oven on or, and here's the clever bit, grate the cheese or cut a knob of butter. All you do now is remove packaging, open microwave door, shut microwave door, select timing, press start, wait, open door and then eat your steaming Baked Potato with a beautiful cascade of stunningly grated cheese sitting in a glorious sump of pre-knobbed butter. Genius.

Marmite

Users of this word – be warned! It produces strong love-hate reactions (therefore useful as an instant ice-breaker). This gloopy stay-on-your-breath-all-day-no-matter-how-many-times-you-brush-your-teeth yeast extract is best eaten on cheap, thinly pre-sliced bread cut into soldiers and covered with cholesterol-inducing dollops of butter, to be accompanied by a big mug of builder's tea. They love it Down Under – just eat your way into an Aussie's heart. But don't make the mistake of ordering it at breakfast in a French hotel. They will look askance before bringing you a small, covered earthenware casserole.

Mars Bars (Fun-Size)

Since 1920, the Mars bar has been one of the world's biggest confectionery successes, even though our American cousins tend to get them mixed up with Milky Ways for reasons that defy explanation. The layers of chocolate, caramel and mysterious wall-cavity insulation combine to make one of the most delicious taste sensations available to the human tongue. For generations, our finest minds have striven to improve upon this tooth-loosening perfection to no avail; no amount of nut adulteration or deep-frying can improve upon the faultless original recipe. But what if you could eat three times as many in one sitting? By the simple expedient of making the bar one-third the size, Mars's white-coated toffee boffins have given us a Mars bar that we can devour at a gulp, thereby saving us precious moments in a busy working day – precious moments that can be used to eat even more Mars bars. Of course they're for kids, but that doesn't stop us testing them now and then, to make sure they're not poisoned or anything.

Marsh, Jodie

Jodie is apparently best known for wearing very revealing outfits to the openings of church fêtes and such. We've never noticed – we're too hypnotized by her teeth. Unlike her arch-rival Jordan, who has mastered the complicated pout-and-wink combination, Jodie has never knowingly been photographed without a grin so wide it threatens to bisect her head entirely. Why her teeth don't dry out is a major mystery. She accessorizes this rictus by outlining it with a red felt-tip pen. The overall effect is simultaneously hilarious and lovable.

Martin and Lewis See Lewis, Jerry.

Massage (at the Hairdresser's)

In the old days, they'd just wash your hair and then cut it. These days, your local snipper throws a head massage in for good measure. Are they still washing my scalp, you think as the digits dig in? Oh no, that's a massage. We say, resist the urge to ask 'Am I paying extra for this?' and enjoy.

Mastermind (The Board Game)

Mastermind the TV quiz is a simple concept. One chair, one quizmaster, one general knowledge round, one on your chosen specialist subject. So how could this popular idea be translated into a successful board game? How indeed, you might think, as one observes the box, resplendent with a photo of an ancient Chinese guru surrounded by not-so-ancient Chinese lovelies. The secret to such ancient wisdom, apparently, is to work out the secret sequence of four coloured pegs, armed only with a mystical code of black and white pegs: black for the right colour in the right place, white for the right colour in the wrong place. We may be showing our cultural ignorance at this point, but have a strong suspicion that the only connection the game has with China is where it was made. Magnus Magnusson not included.

Masturbation

According to a recent survey, 63 per cent of men and 42 per cent of women admitted to masturbating in the last year. This study revealed an important fact: that 37 per cent of men and 58 per cent of women are dirty, stinking liars. See also **Farrah Fawcett Poster, The**; *Penthouse Forum*; *Playboy*.

McClure, Doug (Films Featuring)

When we say 'Doug McClure films' we refer, of course, to the four Victorian-themed fantasy films he made in the second half of the 1970s which even now have the power to redeem a drizzly Bank Holiday afternoon. The series reached its peak in 1976 with the flawless *At the Earth's Core* in which Doug teams up with Peter Cushing's twitchy scientist and Caroline Munro's shapely cavegirl to defeat a race of somewhat clumsy ptero-dactyl men. Doug's ability to keep a straight face when wrestling with men who are wearing a variety of uncomfortable-looking rubber suits makes him the ideal choice as the hero of any low-budget dinosaur or giant squid-based drama.

McRib

The McDonald's menu is one long guilty pleasure, from the calorie-packed Big Mac to the deep-fried 'apple pie'. For years the only thing missing was a pork offering – an oversight the chain remedied with this 490-calorie, boneless, sauce-swathed, onion-topped creation. The creepy part about the McRib is that though it's shaped to look like a tiny rack of ribs, it's really an amalgam of fused pork pieces, à la Chicken McNuggets. Sadly, McDonald's only offers the McRib period-ically. Perhaps corporate headquarters thinks that demand won't support its year-round inclusion on the menu. But if that's the case, they need to spend more time on the Internet. We found several electronic petitions urging McDonald's to sell this sandwich year-round. See also **Big Mac**; **Chicken Nuggets**.

Meat in Tins See Spam.

Meat Loaf (The Food)

This dish, first mentioned in print in 1899, has gone from budget-stretching stopgap to cultural icon. The loaf was designed to make chopped or ground meat go farther, a feat accomplished by mixing whatever meat one had with crackers, rice, cornflakes, or some other starchy filler, then binding it all together with one raw egg. These days there are hundreds of recipes for this dish, incorporating everything from turkey to wine. But none, in our opinion, makes the grade unless it's topped with a paste of baked ketchup. See also **Ketchup**.

Meat Loaf (The Singer)

Like a bat out of hell – an overweight, very sweaty bat out of hell – Meat Loaf would do anything for love, with the exception of 'that'. No, we're not sure what 'that' is, either. See also *Rocky Horror Picture Show, The*; **Karaoke**.

Meat on a Stick

From the caveman roasting a rabbit on a branch to a waiter serving shish kebabs at a Greek restaurant, there's something about meat on a skewer that rivets the eye – especially if you're a red-blooded male. Even today, there's an inherent excitement about everything from chicken satay (Thai-style chicken on a stick with peanut sauce) to American corn dogs. Maybe it's just the wonderful convenience of a food that requires neither plate nor utensils.

'Members Only' Jackets

There was a time, back in the early Eighties, when a stylish man just didn't feel dressed until he'd pulled on his trusty black Members Only jacket – and then shoved the sleeves all the way up to his elbows, as if he was in *Miami Vice*, or a member of Spandau Ballet. These days anyone caught wearing one of these nylon, tab-collared wonders looks like a tool rather than a member. And yet, they're still out there. The line was recently reworked by fashion label Heatherette, but fear not for the traditional jacket. There are plenty for sale on eBay, waiting to make an inevitable comeback. See also **eBAY**.

Mentally Impaired (Films Whose Stars Pretend to Be)

For actors, playing a character with a mental impairment can be a quick ticket to critical praise, audience empathy, and even an Oscar. Closet fans of the genre (which ranges from Leonardo diCaprio in *Who's Eating Gilbert Grape?* to Dustin Hoffman's award-winning turn in *Rain Man*) get tear-jerking pleasure watching otherwise faculty-rich thespians play characters who rise above the cruel hand dealt them by fate. Yet mental disability, autism, or some other challenge doesn't guarantee a good performance. For every *Rain Man* there's a *The Other Sister*. And for every *Gilbert Grape* there's a *From Justin to Kelly* (Wait, you mean those characters weren't supposed to be mentally impaired?).

Michael, George See Urban Myths.

'Mickey'

Boasting nonsensical lyrics and a beat as infectious as typhoid, Toni Basil's 1982 No. 2 hit 'Mickey' was in 2001 named the greatest one-hit wonder of all time by no less an authority than VH1. Though it was Basil's only foray into the music charts, it capped a career that has spanned decades and brought her, Forrest Gump-like, into contact with some of the greatest guilty pleasures of the twentieth century. An actress and choreographer of considerable skill, she worked on the Elvis vehicle *Viva Las Vegas*; appeared on a *Baywatch* episode in 1992; and choreographed a Gap commercial for khaki trousers. See also **Baywatch**; **Gap Adverts**; **One-Hit Wonders**; **Presley, Elvis**; **Yankovic, Weird Al**.

Micro Chips

There's little argument that chips are the finest foodstuff available to man. Or woman. Tasty, comparatively nutritious, portable, sociable (when was the last time anyone asked you for a handful of mash?) and gloriously greasy. The only problem with chips is, they aren't instant. Well, not instant enough. Even the expert fryers at our local fish and chip shop (who always seem stunned that anyone wants either fish or chips and have to make some up for us specially) take an achingly long seven minutes to make a portion of chips. At last, however, technology has come to the rescue: whatever man can make, man can half-bake and then heat up unevenly in a microwave. All hail the advent of the micro chip: all of the satisfaction of real chips, without the wait, the flavour, or 73 per cent of the nutritional value. Wonderful.

Microwave Dinners

On the packaging, it looks like a gourmet meal. On the inside it looks like the school dinner from hell. But did you seriously think you were going to get a delicious taste sensation out of a prepackaged microwave dinner? Of course not. What you wanted – and what you got – is convenience. In this case, convenience being defined as a meal prepared in less than five minutes that can be devoured in another five minutes, and leaves behind nothing that needs to be washed, except for a fork. See also **TV Dinners**.

Mid-Season Sales

Mid-season sales bespeak certain desperation on the part of the retailer. If something isn't selling sufficiently in the season for which it was intended, it is either unfit for the purpose or was overpriced in the first instance. You don't tend to think of that when you see that tempting sale tag on an item. You don't tend to think so much about the product so much as the saving. Arriving home laden with carrier bags and proudly announcing how much you've saved seems all too often to elicit a disappointing reaction in the announcee, who tends to ask difficult questions like how much you actually spent, or whether you actually need water-skis.

Midsomer Murders

Just when we were finally managing to put the horror of *Bergerac* behind us and rebuilding our lives, along comes a new John Nettles vehicle – *Midsomer Murders*. It is set in an England that doesn't really exist, as opposed to *Bergerac*, which was of course set on an island that doesn't really exist. This time all the stories are set around a cluster of idyllic villages with names like Midsomer Plot, Midsomer Really, Midsomer Bloody and Midsomer Predictable. Here, in the heart of England, it is always sunny, the kettle is always on and people are always looking through slightly drawn-back lace curtains at two characters having an argument on a village green; but appearances are contractually deceptive, for, behind the hearty National Trust façade, murder lurks. Usually not content with just the one, the scriptwriters will throw in at least three a week. Luckily, DCI Barnaby and his sidekick Troy are on hand to make an arrest within fifty-eight minutes and, once the murderer is carted off with nothing more than a meaningful backward glance, the yokels can start tugging their forelocks again, John Nettles can ease out of his corset, the country squires can start driving around in their vintage cars and life can return to normal. Until next Sunday.

'Midgets'

Imagine having a rare, poorly understood genetic ailment – one that a certain segment of society found *absolutely hilarious*. Welcome to the world of the Little People, formerly known by the now-politically-incorrect term of 'midgets'. While speaking ill of literally any other disadvantaged group is uncouth if you're nobody and career suicide if you're famous (heard anything from Glen Hoddle be lately?), it's still perfectly okay to stage dwarf-throwing contests and for countless films to offer skits making fun of the height-impaired. Why do we laugh? Perhaps because we know the little people can't do anything about it. There are only about 200,000 in the entire world – not even enough for a decent march on Trafalgar Square.

Milk (Evaporated or Condensed)

 It's not a pleasure, it's a dilemma: evaporated milk, with its gift for seeking out every fold and crevice of your jelly? Or the more concentrated variant, condensed milk, spooned straight from the tin in an orgiastic flashback to breastfeeding? It's like choosing between morphine and heroin. Don't make us pick just one.

Milk (Straight from the Carton)

The dictionary definition of milk, of course, is simple. 'Milk,' the Oxford English Dictionary reads, 'it's what Ian Rush drinks.' And as we all know, people who don't drink the stuff are only good enough to play for Accrington Stanley. Accrington Stanley? Who are they? Exactly. We know you shouldn't gulp it straight from the carton. We know it's unhygienic. But we also know how nice it tastes straight from the fridge, particularly when it is gulped down quickly as our partner descends down the stairs, that white moustache wiped away as they open the kitchen door.

Mills & Boon Romances

The people who turn up their noses at bodice-ripping Mills & Boon romances most likely have never actually *read* one. Those Virginia Woolf worshippers have almost certainly never ploughed through five on a rainy day or binge-read a carrier bag full of them while recovering from a tonsillectomy. While no one will ever mistake the likes of *To Kiss a Sheikh* for great literature, that hasn't hurt sales of the paperback novels famous for displaying chiselled doctors on their covers and using words like 'throbbing', 'trembling', and 'drenched' in love scene after love scene after love scene. Richmond-based Mills & Boon was founded in 1908, but only moved towards specializing in the romance genre during the 1930s. The company releases 800 books a month and employs hundreds of writers. Mass production is a necessity, because loyal readers (average age: forty-four) can devour a book like *Prince's Passion* in roughly the same amount of time it takes to process a week's worth of dirty clothes at the launderette. The volumes are best when read in rapid succession, an experience as indulgently satisfying as eating an entire can of Pringles in one sitting.

Minesweeper

For reasons that have never quite been properly explained, whenever one purchases a computer, it always comes with a selection of games that, one can only assume, were considered too shit to try and get money for, and thus are given free. There's normally some version of Solitaire, and this evil little game that is probably responsible for the most time lost at work, well until the Internet and online poker came along. There are various 'mines' that have been 'laid' in a grid. The trick is to find them all without blowing yourself up. But you know how the game works. You've been suckered into that 'just one more go' routine. Even as we have been writing this entry, we must confess to having played the game seven times. Forget crack cocaine. This is real addiction. See also **Computer Games**.

Mini Cheddars

It's an established culinary truism that anything gets tastier if eaten by the handful. That's why chips are more popular than mash, prawn crackers are better than poppadoms, and Mini Cheddars are tastier than their full-sized cousins. We consulted a food scientist, who started going on about the amount of air in contact with the tastebuds or something, but we could barely hear him over the crunching sound as we demolished bag after delicious bag of the addictive little savouries.

Miniature Books

Calling these impulse buys 'volumes' is a stretch, since many contain only a few more words than an average comic. Yet the tiny tomes hawked at bookshop tills are big business for the handful of publishers cranking out such titles as *How To Hug*, *The Jordan Joke Book*, and *The Little Book of Calm*. However, minis aren't just a contemporary phenomenon. If you happen to have a copy of the 1628/1629 *Novum Testamentum Graecum* miniature Bible, for instance, you can look forward to a comfortable retirement.

Mini-Bars

The 'fully stocked' mini-bar is an evil femme fatale in any hotel room. On check-in you open it, marvel at the smallness of the bottles, the largeness of the prices and the inventiveness of the hotels, who all compete to add memorable 'extras' to the offering. Condoms are very passé, as are Chilli Nuts and mini Mars bars – these days you are just as likely to be offered CDs, DVDs, retro 'Kidult' sweeties and Dunkin' Donuts. As you unpack, you wonder out loud why people are happy to pay £3 for a mini Diet Coke and £15 for a quarter bottle of 'Champagne', but then eight hours later you are watching a pay-per-view film, dropping your fourth can into a waste bin full of empty wrappers and contemplating how you are going to explain all those extras to your accounts department when filing your expense claim. Twix anyone? See **Expenses (Putting It on)**.

Mirren, Helen

Have you seen *Caligula*? Yes, it's a right old load of tripe but it does offer Helen Mirren starkers by way of compensation. Have you seen *Excalibur*? Yes, it's a right old load of tripe too, but it does feature a similarly unattired Mirren (not to mention Cheri Lunghi), so who are we to complain? Have you see *The Cook, The Thief, His Wife and Her Lover*? *Hussy*? *Age of Consent*? We could go on. A cracking actress in every sense, Helen Mirren has graduated over the years from Shakespearian saucepot to the mythical status of Older Woman; the more mature she gets, the more of a prime suspect she becomes.

Miss World See **Beauty Contests**.

Monkeys (Films Featuring)

It really isn't a question of whether a film co-starring a monkey is a good one (*The Barefoot Executive*) or a bad one (all the rest). What matters is that there's a perverse pleasure in watching an actor – be he Matt LeBlanc (*Ed*), Jason Alexander (*Dunston Checks In*), Clint Eastwood (*Every Which Way but Loose*), or Ronald Reagan (*Bedtime for Bonzo*) – try to emote alongside a creature that expresses itself by throwing faeces. You can almost hear them (the humans, not the monkeys) cursing their agents as they struggle to escape the proceedings with their dignity. See also *Planet of the Apes* **Films**.

Morons (Entertaining, Untimely Deaths of)

Developed by scientist Wendy Northcutt, the web site www.darwinawards.com acts as a clearing-house for colourful tales about people who 'eliminate themselves in an extraordinarily idiotic manner, thereby improving the species' chances of long-term survival'. How shallow is the gene pool? Let's just say that Northcutt has produced three books (and counting) chronicling morons' ignominious ends. It proves the old adage that the last words out of an idiot's mouth before he dies are usually, 'Hey everybody, watch this!' See also *Jackass*; **Stunts (Insane, Televised)**; **Urban Myths**.

Morons (Venues That Feature the Antics of) See *Jackass*;
Springer, Jerry; *Sunday Sport*; *Trisha*; *Weekly World News*.

Most Haunted

The jewel in Living TV's almost entirely jewel-free crown, *Most Haunted* takes us into poorly-lit old houses to witness mysterious video breakdowns and inexplicable power failures. You could achieve these effects by the simple expedient of employing a singularly inept electrician. *Most Haunted* has adopted the more left-field approach of hiring footballer-turned-medium Derek Acorah. Derek's combination of glossy suits and mildly Keeganesque hair attracts tortured souls from all over the UK. Us included.

Motorway Service Stations (Food from)

You've been driving since 7 a.m. and have covered 224 miles with no break since Harlow, your partner is helpfully asleep and your four kids have been tapping out 'Are We Nearly There Yet' in morse code on the back of your seat for an hour and you finally snap. You lurch off the road at the next Services and find yourself in a world of '3 Polo Shirts For A Tenner', 'Your User Will Charge You £1.75 to Withdraw Your Own Money From Your Account' and where Jethro's 'Say Bull**ks

To Europe' is CD of the Week. Resisting all these temptations you head to the world-of-food-cafeteria-style-dining-experience-country-kitchen-food-hall and wrestle with the delights of Orange Juice as a Starter, a Full English Breakfast for afternoon tea or a Branston Pickle bap, onion rings and chips and a choc-ice for breakfast. For a useful rule of thumb allow approximately £16 per person for a light snack and £104 for a full meal for a family of four. And the added joy of this guilty pleasure (like marital infidelity) is that calorific overindulgence doesn't count away from home so, go on, have seconds.

Mr and Mrs

An ITV gameshow classic that is surely due another revival, complete with Graham Norton or Paul O'Grady hosting. The foolproof format was simple: spouses had to guess how their other half would answer a question. In the US version, one now-infamous moment had the host asking 'Where specifically is the weirdest place that you . . . have ever gotten the urge to make whoopee?' to which a bleeped bride answered, 'In the ass.' While zingers like that rarely happened, each episode usually featured at least one wife clunking her foolish husband over the head with an answer card. See also **Game Shows**.

Mr T

The man who launched a thousand lame 'I pity the fool' impressions was born Laurence Tureaud on Chicago's South Side in 1952. He started lifting weights so that he wouldn't get picked on, cultivated a Mohawk after seeing a similar style on a Mandinka warrior in *National Geographic* magazine, and worked as everything from a $3,000-a-day celebrity bodyguard to a gym teacher. Sylvester Stallone spotted him in 1982 and hired him to play his nemesis in *Rocky III*, after which he landed his signature role as B. A. Baracus on TV's *The A-Team*. Interestingly, though T looks like a seven-foot-tall juggernaut in *Rocky III*, in reality he's only five foot eleven. It's not that he's so big; it's just that Stallone is quite short. See also **Rocky Movies**; **Stallone, Sylvester**.

MTV

This all-music television network became an instant pop culture icon when it launched on 1 August 1981 (first song played: 'Video Killed the Radio Star'). But although it became famous for serving up wall-to-wall music videos, these days MTV offers almost none. Instead, its schedule is crowded with reality shows (*The Osbournes*, *The Real World*, *Road Rules*) and pretty-much-unclassifiable hits such as *Beavis and Butt-Head* and *Jackass*. Yet practically the entire human race, even people who last paid attention to pop music back when Duran Duran was king, still checks in occasionally. It's a great way to gauge one's age – not in calendar years, but on the maturity scale. When the tunes seem loud, pointless, and insipid, and the kids on the reality shows strike you as vapid, self-absorbed idiots, you've officially become your parents. See also **Beavis and Butt-head**; *Jackass*; **MTV Video Music Awards, The**; **Music Videos**; *Osbournes, The*; *Real World, The*; **Reality TV**.

MTV Cribs

Rap stars: they're richer than you'll ever be. Your nephew knows their birthdays, even though he's forgotten your name. *MTV Cribs* makes it all better. No matter how many platinum records he makes, 50 Cent will never have taste. It's something you just can't buy, not even from Ikea. We know. We tried.

MTV Video Music Awards, The

Though it likes to bill itself as the coolest of the major award nights, its audience tunes in mainly for the occasional oddball moments, gaffes, and world-class displays of T & A. OK, so 'You Might Think' by the Cars won Video of the Year during the programme's debut broadcast in 1984, but what we really remember is Madonna rolling all over the stage while singing 'Like a Virgin'. And the highlights that make the national news the next day don't concern the music, but the weird publicity stunts. Say, Michael Jackson playing face invaders with his soon-to-be-ex-wife Lisa Marie Presley, or Madonna (there she is again) swapping spit with Britney Spears and Christina Aguilera. See also **Jackson, Michael**; **Madonna (Non-music Projects)**; **MTV**; **Music Videos**.

Multi-Disc Music Compilations

If you are watching a particularly bad programme, you may find the entire advert break selling one of those multi-disc song compilations containing anything from specific decades (*'60s Gold*) to entire genres (*The Folk Years Collection*). More than one late-night viewer has sat through the pitch for *The Ultimate '70s Collection*, tapping his foot to sound bites from everything from 'Tears of a Clown' to 'Heart of Glass'. Quick question: if you're enough of a fan to buy this many discs, wouldn't you already have most of these songs in your collection? See also **Greatest Hits Albums**.

Muppet Show, The

By 1976, the variety show was already beginning to look like a tired old format. Yet nobody seems to have told Jim Henson and company, who launched *The Muppet Show* that same year. Spun off from *Sesame Street* – and ditching all that 'educational' baggage in the process – the programme was packed with bad puns, outrageous characters, and more bad puns. Although it took them a while to admit it, lots of adults loved the show, appreciating the absurdity of glorified puppets interacting – and singing and dancing – with such guest hosts as Rudolf Nureyev, Elton John, Sylvester Stallone and Peter Sellers. *The Muppet Show* was presided over by Kermit the Frog, a minor *Sesame Street* character who didn't host the original *Muppet Show* pilot (that honour went to a long-forgotten hippie Muppet named Wally). The series made stars out of such hand-up-their-rears new characters as Miss Piggy, Fozzie Bear and the Swedish Chef, all of whom made the leap to the big screen with varying degrees of success. See also **Royal Variety Performances**.

Murder, She Wrote

For twelve years, mystery writer Jessica Fletcher (Angela Lansbury) managed to solve a crime a week – often in tiny Cabot Cove, Maine, a picturesque seaside village with a per capita murder rate rivalling Detroit's. The only viewers who didn't feel a bit guilty watching this predictable series were those who had a little dish of boiled sweets on hand in case the grandchildren stopped by. See also **Mysteries, Cosy**.

Murphy, Eddie (The Stand-up Comedy of)

America loved him on *Saturday Night Live*. We didn't get a chance to form an opinion until the release of *Delirious*, a concert recorded in 1983 in which the comic, then only twenty-two, joked about sex, AIDS and drunken relatives in a show with more swear words per minute than Roy Chubby Brown assembling a flatpack wardrobe. There was more of the same in 1987's *Raw*, and the debate continued as to whether this man-who-would-be-*Shrek*'s-donkey was heir to Richard Pryor (of whom he does an impression), or just a potty-mouthed – albeit very funny – misogynist.

Museum Gift Shops

It's not that retail establishments tied to cultural institutions are inherently a bad thing. It's just that guilt can easily set in when you realize that you really want to spend more time in the shop than you do in the museum itself. See also **Pez**.

Mushy Peas

The apocryphal story about whichever politician you want to diss concerns a visit to a northern chip shop, an espying of the vat of mushy peas and a request for a side order of guacamole. Southerner. If any other vegetable was labelled mushy, it would be thrown away for being off, but for peas, their mushiness promotes them to the hallowed status of being the only vegetable allowed within the vicinity of a deep fat frier. There's something particularly gratifying about having them served in a polystyrene cup, ready for them to be poured over your fish supper the moment you get home.

Music Videos

The 'cutting edge' concept of putting pictures to music is actually more than a century old. As early as 1900, cinemas offered 'illustrated songs' in which a musician played a popular tune while glass slides illustrating the lyrics flashed on-screen. Later, performance clips were used as fillers at cinemas and, still later, on television. But it was the Beatles who truly pioneered music videos in the modern sense, producing conceptual films to go with some of their songs – mainly so they wouldn't have to perform those tunes in person on variety shows. By the early 1980s quite a few bands filmed clips to go with their music – all of which were gathered up by MTV when it launched in 1981 and then aired non-stop, twenty-four hours a day. Budding directors should remember the golden rule – the simpler the concept, the better the video. Just think of 'You Can Call Me Al', 'Addicted To Love' or 'Nothing Compares To You'. See also **MTV**; **MTV Video Music Awards, The**; **Royal Variety Performances**.

My Little Pony

Girls like horses. Girls like hair. So why not put the two together, some bright spark thought in the Eighties, and thus created My Little Pony: a five-inch high piece of Day-Glo equinery that needs brushing, is all but begging for plaits and (hey!) ponytails to be made from its bright pink hair. Little girls learnt, early on, that mentioning their collection in their playground was just asking for them to be teased . . . even though every girl had such a collection at home. We're unaware of any nasty injuries involving little girls being drop-kicked while trying to dress up a proper horse. But then we're also unaware of any horse being bright blue, though, so what do we know?

Mysteries, Cosy

Also known as Whodunits Featuring Recurring Amateur Sleuth Protagonists. The first adventure can be okay, because it's not too difficult to believe that just about any of us could one day stumble on a murder and maybe even help solve it. Somehow there's supposed to be something comforting about the idea that trained law enforcement professionals bumble around on the sidelines while an assortment of Philadelphia schoolteachers (the 'Amanda Pepper' series), semi-retired Cotswold PR executives (the 'Agatha Raisin' series) and Ancient Roman private detectives (really! The 'Falco' series!) identify the maker of the poisoned quiche. See also **'Postcard' TV**.

N

Nachos
One day Ignacio 'Nacho' Anaya was working as maitre d' at a restaurant in the tiny Mexican border town of Piedras Negras when a large party of women arrived, looking for lunch. The cook was absent, so Anaya took matters into his own hands. He headed for the kitchen, put some tostadas on a plate, covered them with grated cheese, slipped them under a grill for a couple of minutes and then added a jalapeño garnish. Needless to say, there's now a bronze plaque in Piedras Negras commemorating this accomplishment, which has surely had more impact on the average person's life (and certainly, waistline) than, say, the space programme.

Naked Celebrities (Photographs of)
You would think, considering how many paparazzi earn their livings hounding them, that famous people would be extra careful about stripping off outdoors or near open windows. Yet such is not the case. For whatever reason, everyone from Prince Charles to Brad Pitt has been caught standing on a hotel balcony or lounging on a yacht in the altogether. Of course anyone who's ever darted down their front steps in their pants to grab the morning paper at 5 a.m. can sympathize with their plight (while at the same time ogling the pictures). However, celebrities who willingly posed nude when they were nobody, only to have the photos resurface later, have no right to complain.

Neither do actors and actresses whose nude scenes – however important to the plot – end up as Internet downloads. If you plan to flash your bum, be prepared to be bitten on the bum. See also **Royal Family, The**.

Name-Dropping
We were discussing this category at a party given in our honour by Robbie Williams and the Pope at Madonna's London home and were fascinated to hear that opinion differed – Angelina felt name-dropping was out of the question but Brad and Eminem felt it was acceptable under extreme circumstances. But their opinion doesn't really count because we are mates and go way back.

Nethouseprices.com
One of the problems with buying a house is getting accurate information on other houses in the same area, in order to make a judgement as to whether a price is fair. At Nethouseprices.com, someone has logged in all sales for the last five years, thus allowing you to see what other houses went for in the same street, and to work out roughly how much things have gone up over the last few years. But as useful as the site is for buying, its real joy is when you have no intention of moving, and just want to be nosy about your neighbours. They paid how much? For that shitheap? How to feel smug and superior with one click of the mouse.

Newspapers (Local Free)
In a world of 24/7 global newsfeeds, there is something refreshingly parochial about those freesheets that land on your doormat once a week. Nothing is too trivial for the crack news team of your local NewsShopper or Advertiser. In a quiet news week we rejoice in headlines such as, 'Dead Flies Found On Windshield – End This Carnage', 'Bypass Setback As Rare Squirrels Discovered' and the classic 'Child Molester Lynching – Win Tickets'. The heady news agenda is topped off beautifully by 196 pages of car and property adverts and small ads offering the likes of 'Wedding Dress – Unused. £25 o.n.o', 'Flared Trousers – 58 inch waist. £5. Buyer to collect' and

'Work From Home – No Cold Calling. Estimated annual earnings £150,000 or more if full time. P.O.Box 18061993'. Remember – if you have a news story please call our news desk now. PLEASE.

Newton-John, Olivia

No self-respecting Seventies or Eighties hard rock fan could bring himself to say he liked this Aussie import's music. And the truth is, they didn't. But that doesn't mean they didn't like her. Many was the hardcore Led Zeppelin, Van Halen, and/or Kiss devotee who secretly dreamed of saying 'I Honestly Love You' to the singer of such immortal classics as 'Let Me Be There' and 'Have You Never Been Mellow'. But though she flirted with a harder image, first slutting it up as Sandy in 1978's *Grease* and then releasing the No. 1 hit 'Physical' in 1981, Newton-John seems hell-bent on remaining an angel. In recent years she's written a children's book and become involved in animal rights. See also **Kiss**; *Xanadu*.

Nicks, Stevie See Urban Myths.

Nielsen, Leslie

There was a time when the star of such films as *The Poseidon Adventure* was known for playing stone-faced, humourless authority figures. But all that changed in 1980 when he played an inept doctor in the disaster film parody *Airplane!* From then on, Nielsen became, of all things, a slapstick comedian and an indispensable part of any film that takes the piss out of other films. So if you get out, say, *Repossessed* (makes fun of devil movies), *Spy Hard* (makes fun of spy movies), or any of the *Naked Gun* films (makes fun of police shows), it's only a matter of time before Nielsen wanders into the scene – and trips over something. See also **Films That Parody Other Films**.

Nodding Dogs

Adverts for Churchill car insurance boast one of the road industry's finest contributions to cultural life: the nodding dog.

In the advert, this back-seat monstrosity ('Oh yes!') was originally voiced by Vic Reeves, but then Vic was done for drunk driving and now a Vic-soundalike is employed instead. In real life, the dog is equally dangerous – either mesmerizing the driver behind, or infuriating them so much that they feel impelled to overtake immediately. Yes, they're cute and funny. But only for about three seconds, not in a twenty-mile tailback on the M6. Why are furry dice naff and nodding dogs acceptable? No, we're not sure either.

Norris, Chuck

After battling with the legendary Bruce Lee in *Fury of the Dragon* (a.k.a. *Return of the Dragon*, *Revenge of the Dragon*, and *Way of the Dragon*), this real-life martial arts instructor – who trained Steve McQueen, Priscilla Presley, and the Osmonds – became a star in his own right in a series of films beginning with *Good Guys Wear Black* in 1978, in which he played a sort of cut-price Rambo. His run of hits stretched into the Eighties, culminating in the *Missing in Action* trilogy. Quite an accomplishment for a man with an acting range only slightly broader than one of those boards martial artists are forever chopping in half. See also **Kung Fu Films**; **Rambo Films**.

Not Waking Someone Up on the Train

It's 11.27 p.m. on the last train home, and all human life is there – the lovers, the losers and the man so pissed that he stumbles onboard, slumps into a cosy warm seat and is asleep before the doors have swished shut. Where he is going, no one knows. He can sleep peacefully though, safe in the knowledge that he is surrounded by socially responsible individuals and that one of us is obviously going to wake him at St Albans just before the train becomes the non-stop express service to Birmingham. Not.

Novelizations

With the prose largely serving to fill the space around eight or so pages of photos, novelizations – which take a television programme or film and put it between covers – are a godsend to hack writers . . . and to people for whom two hours of film time just isn't enough to spend with *Jaws 2*.

Nuns (Media Representations of)

Julie Andrews baffles her fellow nuns and becomes a cinematic icon. A nun with a guitar sings 'The Lord's Prayer' and the result is perhaps history's unlikeliest pop hit. What is it about these penguin-like creatures of habit that fascinates us so? Why have actors as diverse as Audrey Hepburn, Whoopi Goldberg, Mary Tyler Moore and Eric Idle donned habits on screen? Our guess: even if we didn't suffer the indignities of an old-fashioned parochial school education, we've heard enough tales of stern sisters and knuckle-cracking rulers so that we feel as if we had. Thus, these films – as much as we hate to confess it – serve as a form of therapy.

OC, The

It's difficult to explain why, as we gird our loins for another week at the gritty coalface of book-writing, we find solace in a television show about young, impossibly attractive Americans with no real problems to speak of. Perhaps it's just calming to look at so many well-toned bodies surmounted by perfectly symmetrical faces. Perhaps it's the scenery. Perhaps we're being vicariously sybaritic. The best explanation offered to date is that we're so thoroughly weakened by the weekend's activities that we can't be bothered to hunt down the remote.

Office Parties

Yes the drinks are free, but the real fun to be had at an office party is to pretend you're the designated driver. That way you notice the details that a tipsy attendee might overlook: The Team Leader that you never liked getting slapped for goosing a tequila girl . . . The chap in Sales that always seems to have a cold emerging from the gents . . . Lorraine from Reception engaging in some distinctly transgenerational osculation with the gawky office junior . . . It's all there for the perceptive viewer. Plus, if you're very lucky, that girl from accounts that you've always had your eye on might let you hold her hair while she throws up. Christmas can't come soon enough.

Office Politics

Office politics are so much fun these days. Gone are the days when you had to whisper backstabbing remarks in the ladies' loo about Beryl from Accounts and Tony from Dispatch – now you can spend the whole day on MSN Messenger or email exchanging up-to-the-minute gossip with Carol and generally mixing it with Deborah. Now what Gavin said to Marjorie in that North-Eastern reps meeting can be filtered through to Anthony before Gavin gets back to his Mondeo and you can even wreak havoc if you spot an unattended computer terminal by adopting someone's identity and sending 'All' emails asking if anyone has a good cure for thrush.

Officer and a Gentleman, An See **Chick Flicks (Cinderella Fantasies)**.

Old Love Letters (Discovering)

In the search for somewhere to secrete some clutter, you come across an old battered shoe box at the back of a cupboard. It looks vaguely familiar but as soon as the lid comes off you are sucked back into a former time – a time when love was something you aspired to rather than something you took for granted and a time when Charlie was a sophisticated perfume. Time stands still and out comes letter after letter you didn't know you had kept, documenting that first poignant holiday romance. Memories flood back of that first look across a dance floor to the strains of Boney M, that first tentative conversation and that first glorious kiss followed by an early-morning walk on the beach. Memories, too, of the tearful parting at the airport and the subsequent exchange of photos, plans for meeting up and soppy song lyrics. But then you reach the last few letters and the tone changes, and terms of endearment become a cry for help and you realize that after a while you stopped replying, and life moved on.

Old Spice

A more appropriate name for this long-lived aftershave might be Old Man. But you can enjoy the memory of Old Spice without opening the bottle – just put Classic FM on and you won't have to wait long for Carl Orff's masterpiece *Carmina Burana* to come belting through and soon you will be on your surfboard, conquering extraordinary waves with a beautiful woman waiting for you in the surf. See also **Cheap Perfumes (From the Chemist's)**.

Olsen Twins, The

Mary-Kate and Ashley Olsen first became famous in the US playing, in turns, Michelle Tanner on *Full House* (1987–1995). Their careers could have gone the way of other wisecracking TV kids but instead, they became a marketing empire through the magic of such made-for-video extravaganzas as *You're Invited to Mary-Kate and Ashley's Mall of America Party*. The twins are so popular they've even received a star on the Hollywood Walk of Fame. Women guiltily pretended that these films were enjoyable only in an ironic way. Men hid the fact that they counted down the days to the Olsens' 18th birthday. See also **Hollywood Walk of Fame**.

One-Hit Wonders

One-Hit Wonders are the lifeblood of the download charts and the soundtrack of any school playground, and actually they are usually impossible to get out of your head and sometimes, just sometimes, bloody good songs. How can you NOT like at least three of the following: 'There She Goes' by the Las, 'I'm The Urban Spaceman' by Bonzo Dog Doo-Dah Band, 'Fire' by Crazy World of Arthur Brown, 'Make Luv' by Room 5 (featuring Oliver Cheatham) and Chesney Hawkes' 'The One And Only'. We bet you are humming at least one of these right now and that you will be shortly searching for that box of vinyl somewhere in the cellar. Or there's always iTunes . . . See also **Death Songs**; **'Mickey'**.

'One Night in Bangkok'

Reaching No. 12 in the charts in 1984 this walk on the Thai wild side holds the distinction of being the only pop song to utilize the words 'cloister', 'cerebral', and 'Somerset Maugham'. A disco staple sung to a pulsating beat by Murray Head, 'One Night in Bangkok' emerged from the Cold War musical *Chess*, written by the gentlemen of ABBA. 'One Night in Bangkok' had little to do with the action, but did get the show away from the game for a little while and into the realm of writhing prostitutes. See also **ABBA**.

One-Night Stands

If you believe such shows as *Friends* and *Sex and the City*, one-night stands are as common a form of social interaction as exchanging business cards. So why are people still reticent to discuss them? Perhaps because, while just about everyone has a couple of these on their sexual CV, making a habit of them can still hurt one's marketability. Setting aside the whole disease thing, people who spend Sunday mornings stumbling around dark bedrooms, looking for their shoes, risk being pegged as either minor sexual predators or (even worse) having their names written on public-toilet walls, usually in association with the phrase, 'For a good time . . .' See also **Sex (In Unusual and/or Inappropriate Places)**.

Online Gambling

The average casino gambler, even when going solo, encounters a series of people – doormen, cashiers, fellow big spenders, croupiers – on the way to losing his money. Online gamblers dispense with these undesirable interactions and can focus entirely on deciding whether or not to stick or twist. Technically, the games are the same when you play online. But it takes a seriously focused player to avoid thinking about the fact that you're a long way from Monte Carlo. In fact, you're sitting in front of the same computer you've used for online porn and e-mailing your mum. See also **Online Games**.

Online Games

Perhaps we just naturally lose interest in games as we get older. But more likely we give them up because we can't talk our friends into playing any more. That theory is supported by the thousands of players who can be found at any one time at pogo.com, Yahoo!Games and many other online sites. Here, there's always someone willing to sit down for a round of backgammon, chess, draughts or bridge, with ongoing scores and/or the possibility of cash prizes to keep players playing. See also **Online Gambling**.

Only Fools and Horses

If there were a shark to jump, this show would have jumped it way back in 1983, when Grandad died. Luckily, like most British situation comedies, the budget for *Only Fools and Horses* didn't run to sharks, so we just had Uncle Albert instead. The collision of (mainly artificial) rhyming slang and faux-continental malapropisms that comprised most of the dialogue shouldn't have been funny, at least past the first few episodes. But the show managed to tap into the spirit of thumbfingered capitalism and inept pretension that typified the Thatcher years and it's no surprise that it was so popular in its day. What merits its inclusion here is the inexplicable popularity of *Only Fools and Horses* repeats, which routinely trounce rival shows in the ratings and the genuine sense of anticipation which heralds the annual Christmas special. It may be predictable and repetitive, it may have run out of credible situations for the characters, but it's still the best we have.

Organic Produce (Bought from Farmers' Markets)

It started in a small way with farmers delivering small, organic food boxes on a subscription service. You never knew what you were having for supper until the horny-handed son of the soil rang the doorbell, grabbed your £25 and handed over a small bag of non-chemically enhanced goodies. Goodness me – we never knew there were quite so many ways to cook with celeriac until that moment. Now we have moved on and love the whole farmers' market experience. We love it because the food tastes so much better; we justify the sky-high prices by thinking that we are paying for health and quality; we love the authentic manure smell, the preponderance of mud everywhere and the characterful bales of straw upon which it is all displayed. We also love the feeling that we are putting something back into the sustainability of the countryside and that we are helping the farmers keep their heads above water. It is only later, when you hear the farmers arranging to meet at the Ivy for dinner and watch them packing their produce into a gleaming fleet of top of the range 4x4s that you remind yourself that where there is muck there's brass.

Orlando

This central Florida town was just a mosquito-infested dot on the map until the arrival of Walt Disney World in 1971. Now it serves as the front porch for the world's biggest collection of amusement parks, including Universal Studios Florida and SeaWorld. But it's also something else: a tourist trap that's a long way from the relentless, U-rated fun of Disney. For one thing, Orlando seems to have more (and more aggressively promoted) strip clubs than any other city its size. For another, its environs still offer the kinds of off-kilter 'attractions' that characterized Florida in its pre-Disney days. Oddities include Gatorland (an alligator park featuring a politically incorrect gift shop filled with scorpion key chains and stuffed frogs playing saxophones); the palatial Tupperware World Headquarters (yes, there's a museum); and Splendid China (sixty famous Chinese landmarks, including a half-mile long facsimile of the Great Wall, recreated at scale model size). It's great to know the Magic Kingdom hasn't cornered the market on all things dopey and goofy. See also **Theme Parks (Not Owned by Disney)**.

Osbournes, The

Why were we so interested in the antics of a former heavy metal god turned doting (and doddering) father? The reason was as obvious as the numerous piles of dog pooh on the Osbourne family's living room floor. Watching them cursing and flailing through what passed for a typical day put our own troubled lives into perspective. We might not be model mates or parents, but compared to the Osbournes we're f——ing Mary Poppins. See also **MTV**; **Reality TV**.

Oscar Acceptance Speeches (Embarrassing)

Just as a certain sick segment of the motor racing community attends races primarily to see crashes, so a hefty portion of the billion-or-so humans who watch each Oscar broadcast wait breathlessly for someone to deliver a truly humiliating acceptance speech. Seeing a major performer reduced to a blubbering mess is interesting (Sally Field's 'You like me, right now, you like me!' comes to mind), as are overlong speeches eventually drowned out by 'wrap it up' music from the studio orchestra. (Oscar hint: the more insignificant the category, the longer the speech. So when Best Dubbed Film with Out-of-sync Dialogue is announced, that's a good time to put the kettle on.) See also **Award Shows**.

Other People's Hair (Laughing at)

You are walking down the street minding your own business when on the horizon you spot a man with a very long grey beard sporting what looks like a rather handsome jet black fur hat. You like the look and make a mental note to ask him where he bought it as it is cold and you quite fancy masquerading as a Cossack for a bit. Then he gets nearer and your admiration turns to pity and then seconds later to almost undisguisable joy as you realize that what you have spotted is a man of a certain age trying to look younger by dipping his head in a bucket of Dulux blackboard paint. Not even Count Dracula has hair that black. A few questions go through your mind: Don't these people have mirrors? Don't they have partners? Don't they have any visual sense at all? When men get old they should go grey gracefully and when women get old they should obviously dye their hair blue (à la Marge Simpson) or purple (à la Mrs Slocombe). Simple as that. And as for men who wear wigs, we have no sympathy at all. Not even Elton John can make them look good and he is a multi-millionaire, so what chance have you with a National Health standard issue combover 'natural wig weave'? None at all.

Outdated Fair Rides

They visit a new town each week, transported on old lorries and set up in no time flat in locations ranging from shopping centre car parks to the local patch of wasteland. We *know* those old, obsolete-looking fair rides don't hold a candle to exciting, state-of-the-art theme park attractions. However, they do offer thrills that are uniquely their own. Instead of screaming through half a dozen 5-g barrel rolls, you can wonder if the rust spots you spied as you boarded indicate structural damage; or if the facially tattooed, hungover fair person who took your ticket is the same man who put the ride together. See also **Fairs**; **Roller coasters (Enormous)**.

Out-Of-Office Auto-Response (Faking an)

You are having a low-energy day and sit slumped at your desk safe in the knowledge that there is nothing in the diary that should get in the way of messing around on the Internet pretending to work, having a long long lunch and then sloping off at about 4pm for an 'urgent off-site client meeting'. Until disaster strikes and into your inbox pops an email from someone you arranged lunch with ages ago. It says 'I may be a little late as the train from Edinburgh has been delayed at York but I should be at the restaurant by 1.15pm'. You pause for a moment, type OUT-OF-OFFICE AUTO-RESPONSE in the subject line and then in the text: 'Thank you for your email – due to a personal tragedy I am out of the office until further notice. I have tried to contact all people in my diary to rearrange appointments but in the circumstances some people may have been overlooked and for that you have my sincerest apologies'.

P-Q

Pac-Man

Developed in Japan and originally called Puckman (the name was changed to prevent vandals from substituting an 'F' for the 'P' on arcade machines), this 1980 game swallowed up oceans of discretionary income, one coin at a time. Everything from a breakfast cereal to a Saturday-morning cartoon was trotted out to feed our insatiable desire for more information about its minimalist protagonist – a little yellow circle with a wedge chopped out of it. Pac-Man was also the first computer game to become popular with women – perhaps because it was pretty much the only one that didn't feature a gun-toting character ejaculating – oops, we mean shooting – at everything in sight. To hammer home this deeply Freudian point, Ms Pac-Man was offered in 1982. See also *Doom*; **Computer Games**.

Page 3

Ever since Stephanie Rahn went topless in the *Sun* for the first time on 17 November 1970, the Page 3 girl has been a mainstay of British culture and although there have been many attempts to outlaw them, they seem pretty lame these days given what is available at the click of a mouse, on a few shelves above the papers in WHSmith and the 'services' advertised on chatline pages. The real pleasure from Page 3 doesn't come from the breasts or the stars who have emerged and built real 'careers' (whether Linda Lusardi, Sam Fox or Melinda Messenger) but from watching people trying to pretend they are reading the news section on page 2 instead.

Paintball

Take the most mild-mannered office drone, dress him up in camo gear and place an automatic weapon in his hand: irrespective of the raw material, you will have created a deadly Special Forces operative, capable of besmirching the most stain-resistant garment with brightly-coloured goo. Something happens to men when they go paintballing: suddenly, talk of caravanning in France with the wife and kids gives way to eager discussions of fields of fire, flanking positions and enfilades. The fact that none of the participants quite knows what they're talking about in no way detracts from the enthusiasm of the debate. Afterwards, in the pub, the warrior bond enables combatants to show each other, without censure, bruises in intimate spots that even their wives rarely see.

Paint-by-Numbers Paintings

Artist and designer Dan Robbins earned the eternal thanks of hobbyists and inmates of mental wards everywhere when in 1949 he developed the concept for paint-by-numbers paintings. Figuring that anyone could make a masterpiece if they were provided with an outline of the finished product, a set of paints and numbers on the template to show where each shade went, the first Craft Master Paint-by-Numbers kits soon hit the shops. Within a year or two they were as popular as ration cards. See also **Plastic Model Kits**.

Pajama Bottoms (Wearing Instead of Trousers)

Worn around the house on a chilly Saturday morning, a comfy pair of jim-jams is the only attire of choice for anyone nursing a Friday-night hangover. Wear those same drawstringed britches to a pub lunch later that day, on the other hand, and you're playing a dangerous game of chicken with the fashion police. See also **Sweatpants**.

Pan's People

Any British man watching television between 1968 and 1976 knew Pan's People as well as he knew that woman on the cardboard Big-D peanuts dispenser in his local pub. Unattainable fantasy and yet wholesome 'girl next door', every one was somebody's favourite; statuesque Babs, exotic Ruth, playful Cherry and well-laundered Sue all had their admirers. Whether holding teddy bears or lecturing Labradors, they always maintained a ladylike demeanour which not even the most literal choreography could undermine. Ruby Flipper and Legs and Co. may have replaced them – some of them might have even been *in* Legs and Co. – but that's hardly the point. Pan's People stood for something in an age when British society was in uproar. The three-day week, the miners' strike, the end of flared trousers – all these tribulations came and went but Pan's People danced about on Top of the Pops every Thursday. We thanked them for it. They were one still, sweet voice of mildly fruity calm in a world of upheaval and conflict. If they were dancing today we'd be watching them still. Although some of them might be a bit old now . . .

Parton, Dolly

From her first appearance on American television with country legend Porter Wagoner in the late sixties, this big-hearted blonde has been in the public eye. After storming the hats-and-boots circuit, she crossed over into mainstream pop success in the mid-Seventies with a string of hits including 'I Will Always Love You' and 'Here You Come Again'. She also founded an amusement park, Dollywood, and put Pigeon Forge, Tennessee, on the map. Did we miss anything? Oh, yes, there's the reason why she gets an entry here: she's got big, big breasts. We're talking getting-stopped-at-customs-because-it-looks-like-she's-smuggling-two-bald-men-across-the-border bazooms. So overwhelming are her endowments that American talk-show host Jay Leno, in explaining his hosting style to a reporter, said, 'I don't do wife jokes and I don't do Dolly Parton jokes', a statement that clearly shows the hold these twin peaks have on the world's consciousness. See also **Chick Flicks (Female Bonding)**; **Chick Flicks (In Which Someone Dies)**; **Reynolds, Burt**; **Stallone, Sylvester**; **Theme Parks (Not Owned by Disney)**.

Peel-off Masks

Long before SPF, UVA, and UVB were part of the vernacular, we got sunburnt – blisteringly, skin-singeingly sunburnt. But as consolation for all that pain and itching, we enjoyed the guilty pleasure of peeling dead skin off our faces. Don't pretend you didn't do it. Who can forget the twisted fascination of carefully picking off onion-skin-thin sheets of, well . . . skin? The trick was to see just how big a piece you could lift without tearing into live tissue. For adults who are clever enough to come in out of the sun, peel-off masks provide that same moulting merriment, without the threat of skin cancer.

Penthouse Forum

Whereas *Playboy* touted its high-class articles, lifestyle advice, and, oh yeah, pictures of naked women, *Penthouse* did away with the preaching and offered a double serving of baps. One of its most interesting non-pictorial staples is the 'Forum' section, in which readers describe their own sexual experiences. And what sexual experiences they are. Some sound so much like porn film set pieces (three-ways in university halls of residence; getting it on with taxi drivers; sex in public places) that it's tempting to believe they contain about as much truth as the typical *Sunday Sport* cover story. And yet, decade in and decade out, the *Penthouse* editors swear these missives are real. See also **One-night Stands**; *Sunday Sport*; *Playboy*.

People's Court (UK)

Carol Smillie hosts this low-rent *Crown Court* meets *Neighbours From Hell* thirty-minute daytime mock-justice show with a QC masquerading as a judge and real people in the dock. Honestly – Essex must be empty on the days it is broadcast. A typical dispute involves Mum, Dawn, trying to get £500 from her 'door-ah' Meeee-shell, to pay for all the phone calls she has made ('But Mum, you told me it was free calls after six' – 'Yeah 'Shell, but not to mobiles – you muppet') or Big Ron from

Romford telling his ex-business partner Fletch that he is a 'lying little slag who deserves a slap' for knicking his car radio – whose only line of defence (repeated ad nauseum) is, 'I'd never do that to you, Ron – I look after my own and you're like a bruvver to me.' 'Judge' Jerome Lynch – Errol Brown meets Jeremy Paxman – treats them all like naughty, rather stupid schoolkids and almost every case ends with a guilty verdict, leaving the Lynchster looking mildly annoyed that the death penalty is outside his jurisdiction. All mindless twaddle, but impossible not to stay the distance with. TAKE HIM DOWN!

Pepperami

'A little bit of an animal' is the strapline for this meaty snack that is so deliciously dirty it is advisable not to be seen eating it in decent society, but instead devoured at home when everyone is out. A little bit of which animal? The playground story about donkeys is just an urban myth, sadly. Though probably not that sadly for the donkey. The snack itself enjoys a spirited animated advertising campaign, the highlight of which remains the TV ad in which a pepperami watches a pepperami style 'horror movie': a pepperami head-banging a cheese-grater to turn itself into slices. The advert was taken off real television when small children nationwide began imitating the head-banging pepperami and doing themselves serious cheese-grater damage. It makes you worry for the future, it really does. Hee-haw!

Petrol Stations (Flowers From)

You're going round to someone's house for dinner. You're in a rush. As you drive down the road, you realize with horror that you haven't bought a bottle of wine, a box of chocolates or indeed anything to offer the host. Then, with a flush of relief, you see the neon sign of a petrol station ahead. Of course, you think, pulling into the forecourt: I'll get them some flowers from the garage. It may not seem like it at first, but buying flowers from a garage is one of the most satisfying purchases it is possible to make in life. Firstly, they offer instant relief from that sense of panic and guilt that is rising up inside you. Secondly, they're cheap. So cheap in fact, that even if the roses are covered in exhaust fumes and smell of petrol, the assumption is still that you wouldn't be so insulting to your host as to offer up Esso in Bloom. For being a forgetful cheapskate, you get a grateful 'Oh, you shouldn't have'. If you get a 'These must have cost you a fortune', it is all but compulsory to smile at the thought of the £2.99 price tag in your pocket.

Petrol Stations (Food From)
Until comparatively recently, people went to garages to buy petrol. If they were feeling particularly adventurous, and Halfords was shut, they'd get some oil too. During the summer of 1988 there was an inexplicable upsurge of late-night confectionery trade, which in turn led the shadowy powers behind Britain's forecourts to wonder how much more lucrative their franchises might be if they sold even more goods targeted at the late-night marijuana abuser. Within weeks, microwaves dispensing superheated pies, vast stacks of no-brand biscuits, and even barricades of charcoal briquettes for ecstasy-crazed barbecue chefs were all available in the fortified bunkers sited at every petrol station. For those of us with more pedestrian tastes, wandering onto the forecourt at closing time represented an opportunity to try a tasty alternative to self-destructing kebabs. Sausages, pies, and even soup – all hotter than the surface of the sun, and all available for an undifferentiated handful of change that happened to be in our pockets anyway.

Pez
Developed in the 1920s by an Austrian sweet maker (and named Pez because it was short for Pfefferminz, the German word for peppermint), this rather infantile sweet was originally marketed as a sophisticated breath mint for grown-ups. The first Pez dispenser was a sleek-looking contraption (without a novelty  head) but in time, it branched out into fruit flavours and acquired colourful Pez dispensers originally topped with cartoon characters such as Popeye and Mickey Mouse. Of course the line-up has since expanded to include well over 1,000 characters, and collectors have created a robust market for old dispensers.

Phillips, Leslie

I say. Hel lo.

Phillips, Zara

Posh totty has been a staple of male fantasies ever since Antony copped a load of Cleopatra in her bath of asses' milk, and they don't come much posher than the blue blood of the House of Windsor. But, let's be frank, centuries of marrying from suitable stock have left the royals with a dash of equine beauty. Quite how the gene pool threw up the blonde glory of Zara Phillips we're not sure, but we say hurrah for the royal who has the sense to ride horses rather than look like one. We say hurrah, too, for the sheer audacity of having her tongue pierced (and Lord only knows what else), and showing it off in public. We say hurrah, three . . . actually, we won't say that because her boyfriend plays rugby and looks enormous.

Phone Sex

The unknown person who invented this 'service' is a genius for getting men to shell out £2.50 a minute for the privilege of flogging their fun puppets while balancing a phone on their shoulder. Think about it – you're paying to masturbate! And that woman on the other end of the line who sounds like Anna Kournikova could just as easily look like Anne Widdecombe or Mollie Sugden. Surely there are less costly ways to let your fingers do the walking. Haven't these people heard of Yellow Pages? See also **Kournikova, Anna**; **Masturbation**.

Pic 'n' Mix (Stealing Your Child's at the Cinema)

We've all done it: reluctantly given in to our children's demands at the local multiplex for a huge plastic bag full of luminous jelly-snakes, mini cola bottles, milk chocolate mice, sweetie fried eggs, sweet 'n' sour stars and liquorice shoelaces, 'helped' to carry the E-number love-in to Screen 9 for our little darlings . . . and then quietly scoffed the lot under the cover of dim lights and Surround Sound entertainment. Modesty prohibits describing in too much X-rated detail the guilty pleasure of licking one's fingers, dipping them into the remaining sugar stash right in the bottom corner of the waxed bag . . . and then sucking every last bit off in a moment of pure retro heaven.

Pickled Onions, Eggs and Gherkins

Is there any foodstuff that cannot be improved by immersion in a weak acid solution? The strange alchemy which transforms a noxious fresh onion, capable of inducing tears in the hardiest of cooks, into a delicacy fit to be popped into the mouth whole must be one of the most inspired innovations in food preparation ever. (Except perhaps yoghurt, that's always impressed us too. Oh, and beer – who thought of *that*?) The tiny silverskin onions which magically appear around a turkey sandwich on Boxing Day are so delicious it's unclear why we don't eat them constantly as part of our 'way to five' – they *are* a vegetable after all! Rounded out with a gherkin, which after all is just a cucumber which is on some sort of witness protection programme, and a pickled egg for protein purposes, you have the makings of a healthy balanced diet. It's a shame that they tend to have a more deleterious effect on the breath than a sustained application to the Atkins diet.

Pictionary

Created by a twenty-four-year-old Seattle waiter called Rob Angel and launched in 1986, this game (an iteration of charades in which participants try to guess a word or phrase based on pictures their partners draw) became a brief phenomenon – as well as the cop-out entertainment of choice for parties that are going stale. The game even made it into the 1989 comedy *When Harry Met Sally . . .* , which gave us the immortal phrase, 'Baby fish mouth! Baby fish mouth!' See also *When Harry Met Sally . . .*

Pinball Machines

Pinball machines have been around since 1931, but in their original incarnation were about as exciting as, well, being around in 1931. Early versions lacked tilt control, and flippers didn't arrive until 1947. Yet prior to the creation of mass market computer games, arcades were full of Tommy wannabes, who played not to win prizes, but merely for a free game – and, perhaps, to ogle the artwork on the machine itself. See also **Computer Games**.

Pink Flamingos See **Waters, John**.

Piper, Billie
What is the source of the monkey-faced siren's appeal? It certainly isn't the seminal *Smash Hits* TV ad in which we first saw her sexily simian features, nor is it likely to be her long-forgotten string of bubblegum hits – even though she is still the youngest performer to début in the number one spot. No, her charm seems more centred in her willingness to be squired around town, at least for a while, by a somewhat unkempt man sixteen years her senior. It suggests that Ms Piper is something of a sport, albeit maintaining a residual air of purity, and as such she possesses a powerful attraction for poorly-groomed men of a certain age who, lacking a partner of their own, spend much of their time reading periodicals such as *FHM* or watching *Doctor Who*. Probably while eating sausages and beans.

Pipes
Not very long after Sir Ralph Lane brought clay tobacco pipes back to England from the New World, Queen Elizabeth impressed her court by blowing smoke rings. Such was the addictive appeal of this in-your-face nicotine delivery system. These days, pipe smoking is an affectation best savoured privately, where your friends won't notice that you look like a parody of a Harold Wilson portrait – or that your favourite 'blend' smells like a fire at a syrup factory. See also **Cigarettes**.

Pit Bulls
Why are these vicious dogs so popular? Blame a foible of male character. Many men think they can absorb the traits of objects simply by possessing them. For instance, a cool car will make *me* cool. A sophisticated mobile phone will make *me* sophisticated. Likewise, a tough, intimidating dog will make *me* tough and intimidating. Sadly, nothing could be further from the truth. If you're a nineteen-year-old dropout living with your

parents, getting a big, strong, well-nigh uncontrollable fighting dog simply confirms your status as someone with very poor judgement. It's the pet equivalent of walking around with a pistol in your belt with the safety off. Plus, owning one *won't make your penis one bit bigger*. See also **Morons (Entertaining, Untimely Deaths of)**; **Rampaging Animals (TV Specials About)**.

Pitt, Ingrid (Appearances in Horror Films of)

Although not to the same heroic extent as *Only Fools and Horses* star Buster Merryfield, Ingrid Pitt was a comparative latecomer to the old acting caper, first coming to our notice as an extra in *Doctor Zhivago* at the venerable age of twenty-seven. At least Ingrid had an excuse, having been held in a Nazi concentration camp during her teens. She exacted at least some measure of revenge with her breakthrough film, *Where Eagles Dare*, in which a quite gratifying quantity of goose-stepping Teutons met satisfyingly unpleasant ends. It was in her next screen outing, however, that she found her *métier*: from 1970 onwards she appeared in over twenty films, nearly always as a saucy vampiric vixen, frequently Sapphic, invariably a countess. It's an established fact that any red-blooded man would be happy to give up a half-pint or so of said blood if such a loss were to lead to a bit of a roll-about with a lady as frankly fruity as Ingrid. All right, we accept that Ingrid isn't really a lesbian, and probably isn't even a vampire, but she's exactly what a Transylvanian hottie should be and we love her for it.

Pizza (Last Night's)

Pizza. For that, Italy, we thank you. Melted cheese, pepperoni, onions and chilli beef – man, we're getting hungry just thinking about it. But as delicious as pizza is when it has just been cooked, those four cheeses just gooey to perfection, nothing beats a chilled slice for breakfast the following morning. Just imagine it: you wake up feeling the worse for wear, crawl down to the kitchen, open the refrigerator door and there, sliced and ready to eat, is your manna from fast-food heaven. As hang-over food goes, it just can't be bettered.

Pizza Express (Getting Money Off Pizza at)

We like Pizza Express. We're going to turn our noses up at that silly argument about whether the pizzas have got smaller or not. But it would be churlish of us not to point out the money saving flaw in their menu. One of the Pizza Express staples is the American, described on the menu as 'Nothing but a big helping of pepperoni for those who like their flavours strong and simple.' The price of this pepperoni feast? £7.35. But hang on; what if we ordered a Margherita (£5.25) with an added helping of pepperoni (£1.45)? That's an American pizza by any other name, but at £6.70 rather than £7.35 – a saving of 65p. Go to the 'Express twice, and you've got enough for a cup of coffee afterwards. You heard it here first.

Pizza, Frozen

During the Second World War, an Italian-American marine on Iwo Jima wrote to his brother back home in America saying how much he'd love to have a pizza like mama made. So his brother set to work creating the first frozen (and, thus, shippable) pizza. When the happy and well-fed marine returned home, he and his family started the frozen food company Nino Foods. But regardless of whether the brothers actually froze the very *first* pizza, one fact remains: the stuff you get in a box from your supermarket freezer is never quite as tasty as the stuff delivered from your local pizzeria.

Placemats, Interactive

Grab a pen, it's puzzle time – at least, until the waitress turns up. Used by restaurateurs to help keep hyperactive children from building sugar packet houses and hanging spoons from their noses, preprinted interactive placemats, filled with not-too-hard crossword puzzles, fairly simple mazes and absurdly easy word search puzzles, are also a favourite of bored solo diners, drunks, and couples with nothing to say to each other.

Planet Hollywood See Theme Restaurants.

Planet of the Apes (Films)

Yes, you can make a case that it's sharp social satire. Or you could argue that it's one of the headier pieces of big-screen science fiction. But in your heart of hearts you know that there's perverse pleasure in seeing Charlton Heston get chased by armed monkeys on horseback. See also **Heston, Charlton**; **Monkeys (Films Featuring)**.

Plasma Screens

Colossal objects too wide to fit into almost any British home, and too expensive to fit into any British budget, plasma screen TVs are no more than a pipedream for most British telly addicts. Still, it's easy to see that the lure of watching *EastEnders* on a screen so wide that you can see the pores on Dot Cotton's nose is almost unbearably powerful. The fact that this potent piece of technology is so simple that anyone except Ozzy Osbourne can work it only sharpens its appeal. Convincing your long-suffering spouse that it's a worthwhile investment to buy a vast telly that will be obsolete before it leaves the shop, that's the difficult part.

Plastic Model Kits

There was a time when model aeroplane kits were excruciatingly complicated affairs made of balsa wood. To build one, you had to cut out dozens of individual wing struts and fuselage supports, glue everything together, then coat it all with a paper skin held in place by a foul-smelling shellac called dope. These days children (or, more likely, middle-aged men with time on their hands) use less messy, less complex plastic models made by such companies as Airfix. The models are still difficult enough to give one a sense of accomplishment, but nowhere near as demanding as the old balsa wood nightmares. None of which answers the age-old question of what to do with the model once you finish it.

Plates, Collectible See **Franklin Mint, The**.

Platform (Knowing Where to Stand on the, So That the Train Door Will Stop Right Opposite You)

If you get it right the smug sense of satisfaction as your personal carriage arrives and you sweep through the double doors to your seat is empowering, but if you get it wrong and you are facing a grubby window then the day gets off to a somewhat sadder start.

Playboy

Yes, it contains lots of pseudo-academic articles and information on the latest in consumer electronics and cars, but most hot-blooded adults never bought into Hugh Hefner's assertion that *Playboy* is a lifestyle publication rather than a grot mag. Since its inception in 1953 (centrefold No. 1: Marilyn Monroe), Hef has pitched the idea (extremely novel in the Fifties, but passé today) that sex is fun and healthy and part of the everyday man's swinging, sophisticated lifestyle. But as the years passed, his competitors (chief among them, *Penthouse* and *Hustler*) beat him at his own game by offering saucier pictures and a 'streamlined' philosophy that could be summed up as 'Me like sex'. Although most men would like an invitation to the Playboy Mansion and the chance to hang out with the bunnies, these days *Playboy* is rated somewhere alongside a Channel 5 late-night movie on the erotic scale. Useful in an emergency, but only just.

Playgirl

A funny thing about naked men: the harder they try to look sexy, with their clean-shaven pecs and intense come-hither stares, the harder women laugh when they see pictures of them. This doesn't seem to inhibit the seductive efforts of *Playgirl*, the New York-based magazine that has featured a new batch of steamy nude models every month since its 1973 debut. *Playgirl*'s inaugural centrefold, a certain Lyle Waggoner, stopped just short of full frontal nudity. Readers complained. So the featured model in issue No. 2 left nothing to the imagination. When Burt Reynolds appeared as a centrefold in the Seventies, the hirsute actor concealed his private parts with a strategically placed hand (or 'Arm!' as he contended on a TV chat show shortly after publication). See also *Playboy*, **Reynolds, Burt**.

Plot Spoiling

What's better than enjoying a really good plot? Knowing what happens in a really good plot in advance. Knowledge, after all, is power, and is there any greater power than knowing that Bruce Willis is a ghost before you settle down to watch *The Sixth Sense*? Revel in the glory of pissing off a packed theatre settling down to watch *The Mousetrap* by declaring loudly 'Is there anyone left who doesn't know it's the policeman?' Impress your date with cunning foresight as you declare during the opening scenes of *The Crying Game*, 'Is it just me, or does she look like a bloke?' We are forever grateful for fan sites of American dramas running well in advance of their British showing. There's just no way we can be expected to wait patiently for twenty-two episodes to find out what's going on. Not when we can log onto the Internet and discover that it's nothing worth writing home about. And then tell everyone else as well, of course.

Police Academy Films

Suffice to say that enough people saw *Police Academy 5: Assignment: Miami Beach* (one of the few films in film history whose title included two colons) to justify the making not only of *Police Academy 6: City Under Siege*, but also *Police Academy 7: Mission to Moscow*. Which isn't bad going, considering the 'shark' was jumped ten minutes into *Police Academy 2*. Starring Steve Guttenberg for the first four instalments and American football great Bubba Smith for the first six, the series about wacky police recruits also featured visits from *Sex and the City*'s Kim Cattrall in the original film and Sharon Stone in the fourth. See also **Happy Days**.

Political Soundbites

It's not until you stumble across one of the rolling news channels that you realize just how dull politics really is. On the one hand we all accept that Gordon Brown is a very clever man and that his opinions on Third World debt or the European

Currency are likely to be very informative. On the other, have you ever heard him speak for more than ten seconds? That lilting Scottish burr will have you asleep in minutes – and he's the best of them: Tony Blair's persuasive estate agent doubletalk is all very punchy and inspiring when edited down to a couple of catchy sentence on the ten o'clock news, but any more than a minute of it will give you a headache that will last all day. We know we're not getting the whole story by just getting a 'best of' compilation, but it's like classical music: no one can stay awake for the whole show.

Pong

Released in 1972, Pong was the world's first commercially successful computer game. It was popular for a couple of reasons, neither of which reflected well on the people who played it. Firstly, it was simple enough even for half-drunk people in pubs to quickly grasp; secondly (and perhaps most importantly), it was the first and only computer game that the average bloke could not only get good at, but master. That's right, youngsters. This simple game, based on ping-pong (its maker, Atari, couldn't call it that because the word was copyrighted), didn't churn out ever-more-complicated challenges until players screamed for mercy. At a certain point its tiny CPU simply gave up the ghost, and you won. That's why veteran gamers occasionally miss its lame graphics and glacial pace, in the same way retired playground bullies sometimes miss the fat kid with glasses. See also **Doom**; **Pac-Man**; **Computer Games**.

Pop Idol

It's natural for people to want to better themselves. It's also natural, therefore, when an opportunity to achieve fame (and possibly fortune) which is open to all comers presents itself, that there is a sizeable rush to the auditions. Regrettably, only a small percentage of the world's population are natural performers. Most people are merely indifferent entertainers, but there is a small 'special' percentage of the auditionees who are genuinely demented. It is from this demographic that 100 per cent of the entertainment of the *Pop Idol* franchise derives. Once the engine of evolution (represented by the sepulchural Darth Cowell) kicks in the show rapidly becomes unwatchable, because there are far too many people on it that are more talented than us. Those first few magical episodes of each series, though, are the sheerest delight: dozens of simple-minded burger-flippers cavort briefly before our eyes in the forlorn hope of being lifted from the Sisyphean futility of their pointless lives. Of course it's not going to happen, but there's nothing quite so funny as watching them try.

Pop Idols (Failing to Become Pop Stars)

Here's the curious thing about winners of *Pop Idol* and *Popstars* and *The X Factor*: while they're on the show, they look great. The minute they step onto *CD:UK*, their terrible ordinariness becomes immediately apparent. Maybe its because they've been up against such terrible singers that they sound OK. Actually that's not true, is it: Hear'say somehow beat Liberty X, while David Sneddon was chosen over Lemarr. Maybe it's more that we don't like winners (or in the case of Sam and Mark, losers). By being beaten, Liberty X had that shred of credibility that Hear'say never managed. Michelle McManus? Steve Brookstein? It's panto with Gary Wilmot for you.

Popbitch

For the uninitiated, Popbitch is an incisive, publish-and-be-damned, free email scandal sheet circulated on a Thursday to hundreds of thousands of subscribers every week. Put together in anonymity by two journalists at one of the larger magazine groups, it culls its material from tip-offs from pissed-off record company PRs who are fed up with papering over the cracks, from roadies who can't wait to share the latest excess-all-areas exploits of the stadium rockers, and a plethora of other industry insiders. The really near the knuckle stories are presented as questions such as 'Which star recently dropped by their label has such a big gak habit that their spouse is making worrying noises about divorce?' A typical week might include gossip, tip-offs, animal tips ('Vervet monkeys have blue testicles and the ones with the bluest balls are dominant'), and info on what is likely to be charting in the weeks ahead. There is even a chat forum on the Popbitch web site which famously got shut down one afternoon when rumours abounded about two England footballers and an affair one was supposedly having with the other one's wife. Happily untrue, and happily, Popbitch is back online. It is so admired by the industry that you are likely to see the majority of the printable stories appear as hot stories (or even exclusives!) the next day in the tabloid pop pages.

Popex

The original and the best of the Internet trading games, Popex is a great way of wasting hour upon hour buying and selling shares in pop stars. With dividends based on chart positions and column inches, it combines the cruel world of supply, demand and the stock market with the ability to actually use that completely useless information you've got about what the midweek position of the new Coldplay single is. Who said pop trivia couldn't make you (pretend) money?

Pop-Tarts

Designed to expand the range of items that could be cooked in a toaster, Kellogg's Pop-Tarts first appeared in 1964 with a name inspired by the pop-art movement. The original treat was a rectangular pastry with filling and (later) an optional sweet exterior coating on one side. In the mid-Nineties experimenters discovered that the strawberry variety caught fire if left in the toaster too long. (American comedian Dave Barry later corroborated – and popularized – these tests, which are said to have generated flames up to eighteen inches in height.) Note to Lynne Truss: Pop-Tarts, like overalls and (eye)glasses, are always plural.

Popworld

The best music show on the planet, *Popworld* is 1980s *Smash Hits* writ large on twenty-first-century television screens: rude, cheeky and passionate about pop. The principal culprit for its excellence was original Simon Amstell, a curly-mopped pop pundit with just enough wit and swagger to send pop up as it deserves to be, while still getting the stars to come back on the show again. In a world of anodyne PR-ed to death interviews, a welcome breath of fresh air. Why is it a guilty pleasure? Well, it's on at 9.30 on a Sunday morning and aimed at children . . .

Pork Scratchings

Few food products have a less appetizing name. Fewer still have less appetizing ingredients: consisting mainly of deep-fried pigskin and the occasional bristly hair, they are sold exclusively to the drunk and those aspiring to be drunk. Still inexplicably legal under EC law, pork scratchings occupy a special place behind the bar of all but the snootiest drinking establishments, between the cardboard sheet with the bags of peanuts on and the hook for Wayne's tankard. It's an unusually restrained pub patron that doesn't at least consider buying a bag during that magical period between realizing they still haven't had their tea and Last Orders.

Porky's See **Teenage Boys Losing Their Virginity (Films About)**.

Post-Pub Food

Despite their high calorific content, alcoholic drinks have a disappointingly low nutritional value. Even anaesthetized by multiple rum and cokes, the canny drinker will be aware of this disparity on some cellular level and will, zombie-like, seek out late-night nutrients. The kebab is of course the king of the tipsy snacks, a casually assembled meat sandwich with conscience-salving salad adornment, which has everything the night bus passenger needs to satisfy their bodily needs while simultaneously irradiating the immediate environment with a lethal vapour which destroys 103 per cent of known germs. The no-brand burger is a worthy rival to the kebab, but lacks its ability to fragment. Mysterious boxes of chicken are a comparative newcomer to the post-pub catering environment, but the chicken – being a flightless bird – is more affected by gravity than most other animals and consequently a disproportionate amount of fried chicken falls to the ground part eaten. Good news for the urban rat population, bad news for the hungry socialite. See also **Kebabs**.

Post-Turkey Coma

This is the true meaning of Christmas: senses dulled by a combination of Baileys Irish Cream and the deepest blood-sugar crash you've experienced in exactly 365 days, you slump on a sofa at the epicentre of a noxious fug of your own making while allowing piss-poor, lowest common denominator bland-u-tainment to invade your optic nerve and numb your already crippled synapses into submission. Forget all that Scrooge rubbish; peering over a painfully distended, poultry-packed belly at a thirty-two inch cathode ray tube full of leering idiots is what yuletide is all about.

'Postcard' TV

In order to anaesthetize us against the ineluctable drudgery of the working week, the shadowy conspiracy that controls our world has devised the exclusively weekend phenomena known as Postcard TV. The recipe for a Postcard show is simple, and inflexible: most importantly there should be countryside to distract the vast majority of urban-dwelling viewers from the entirely unnatural nature of our existence. There should also be a period setting (the Second World War is always a winner) or a social fabric which still has rigid class structures. The third element of the Postcard formula is of course the cast of elderly, preferably northern, characters portrayed by actors who have been thrown on the scrapheap by the producers of *Coronation Street* or *Emmerdale*. These rules sound simple, but they have given us television programmes as diverse as *Heartbeat*, *Where the Heart is*, *Born and Bred*, *Monarch of the Glen* and a host of other shows that do a grand job of dulling the pain of the impending week's toil. The funny thing is, we love 'em.

Pot Noodles

Ramen is a Chinese-style wheat noodle that's as popular in Japan (indeed, perhaps more so) as in the rest of the world. The big difference is that while the Japanese enjoy freshly

prepared noodles served in restaurants, we eat them in plastic pots whose chief advantages are speed of preparation (add boiling water to your 'tub' and you're dining in seconds), flavour (anything containing approximately 8 grams of fat per serving and 900 milligrams of salt can't taste bad), and low, low price (Pot Noodles can keep a student alive for a week on change scrounged from the Union's pub sofas). Living on a diet of these during college is like drinking yourself blind every weekend: it's a rite of passage. See also **Salt (Excessive Application to Food of)**.

Potter, Harry

At first sight, the recipe for the magic potion is pretty simple: 'One part Enid Blyton to one part *Bedknobs and Broomsticks*, shake vigorously, then add some nice kids, some scary wizards and a man in a white beard and garnish with a portion of Quidditch, several owls and some muggles. Serve with a light frosting of epic pretension.' Hey presto, the world waits up till midnight for bookshops to open, the film world goes into overdrive and the merchandise boys have multiple orgasms. Meanwhile, ex-teacher J. K. Rowling becomes richer than the Queen. You may think you can resist but you can't. 'You know who' won't let you . . .

Pound Shops

Veritable Aladdin's Caves of tat, Pound Shops offer an intoxicatingly tempting mix of no-brand toys, terrifying glass clowns and mysterious cleaning products. Even the most cynical consumers can be seen wandering the narrow aisles goggling in wonder at the cornucopia of bargains that they'll never use and wondering how any establishment offering such extraordinary deals could remain solvent. The only explanation is that somebody, somewhere, is buying armfuls of junk from these places when no one else is looking. OK. We admit it. It's us.

Practical Jokes

Though no one particularly enjoys being the victim of a practical joke, almost everyone loves pulling them. That's why, inexplicably, joke shops still exist, keeping the world knee-deep in fart powder and fake vomit. Lately, however, stitching people up has become an industry of sorts, with a new crop of *Candid Camera*-like shows (only more mean-spirited) taking to the airwaves. These days, with programmes like MTV's *Punk'd* seeking to turn celebrities' lives upside down; *Trigger Happy TV* flummoxing tourists by staging fights between grown men in giant squirrel costumes; and the American Sci Fi Channel's *Scare Tactics* staging fake alien abductions, landing in the crosshairs of Jeremy Beadle is the least of your worries. See also **Vomit (Fake)**; **Whoopee Cushions**.

Prescott, John
The wonderful thing about Prezza, is a Prezza's a wonderful thing. That's why New New Labor [sic] can never, despite his prodigious appetites and innumerable gaffes, quite let him go. He's like a Toby Jug in the window of Heals, he's a croquet-playing totemistic reminder of Labour's noble roots, he's *our* Two Jags, he's *our* Two Shags, he's our Guilty Prezza.

Presley, Elvis
During his forty-two years of life, the King of Rock and Roll was both the coolest and un-coolest person on Earth. At the start of his career, his rockabilly attitude, rockin' tunes and swinging hips challenged the establishment and made him a hero to teenagers. The trouble was he didn't grow older gracefully. By the 1960s Elvis was squandering his street cred by making terrible films, playing Vegas, dressing in ever-more-outlandish stage costumes, and changing his physical appearance almost beyond recognition through over-eating. If only he'd seen *Super Size Me*. See also **Elvis Impersonators**; **Prison Films Featuring Men**.

Pre-*Star Wars* 1970s Sci-Fi Films
The release of *Star Wars* in 1977, with its state-of-the-art special effects, made it easy for the masses to like science fiction. But it also made it difficult for diehard fans to admit they enjoyed the cinematic offerings of the pre-*Wars* Seventies. This was an era of dark, special effects-starved apocalyptic and

post-apocalyptic visions such as *Soylent Green*, *A Boy and His Dog*, *Death Race 2000*, *Westworld*, *The Omega Man*, and *Logan's Run*. True, the production values could be patchy and the effects awful, but these films often had something many a CGI-laden twenty-first-century space opera lacks: a script. See also **Death Race 2000**; **Heston, Charlton**; *Planet of the Apes* **Films**; **Star Wars**.

Pretty Woman See **Chick Flicks (Cinderella Fantasies)**.

Price is Right, The

If you know the phrase 'Come on Down!' you must be one of the millions who were addicted to *The Price is Right*. Leslie Crowther, a host of lovelies and over-excited members of the general public guessing the prices of various consumer items; what more could you want from your evening entertainment? No one ever seemed to work it out, but like poker, the person who goes last has the best chance of winning. All you need to do is to bet one pound higher or lower than the rival sugges-tion (depending on whether they're being cautious or silly) and the booty is yours.

Prince (Films of)

Of these there are three: 1984's *Purple Rain* (which ruled, in a dance-intensive, big-haired, 1984 sort of way), followed by 1986's *Under the Cherry Moon* (which stank), and 1990's *Graffiti Bridge* (a sequel to *Purple Rain*, but without hit songs, production values, or a believable plot). All three are guilty pleasures, though for different reasons. *Purple Rain* because it's a delicious slice of Eighties nos-talgia that is absolutely indecipherable to anyone who wasn't actu-ally there. For a laugh try making your children watch it with you. As for *Moon* and *Bridge* (both of which were directed by Prince, which explains a lot), there's the sheer, cruel joy of watching an egotistical celebrity wander, Nero-like, through mon-strous, flaming disasters of his own making. See also **Prince (Girlfriends of)**.

Prince (Girlfriends of)

Say what you will about the music and fashion sense of His Purpleness. What cannot be debated is his fabulous taste in sidekicks. Starting in the early Eighties, a seemingly never-ending series of women clung tightly to his coat-tails (and, perhaps, other parts of his anatomy). The only requirements to be a Prince protégée (besides a fit body) seemed to be big hair, the fashion sense of a prostitute, and, of course, a daft name. The all-time favourites include lingerie-wearing Vanity (now an evangelist, of all things), Apollonia, drummer Sheila E. and dancer Cat. What were all these women being groomed for? Who knows. All we can say is that whatever they were getting ready for, they certainly looked good doing it. See also **Prince (Films of)**.

Prince Philip

When he dies, he will be as much remembered for his gaffes and his alleged affairs as he will be for his fifty-plus years of loyal service to the Queen and the nation. Philip symbolizes an era that is long gone, but his human-izing gaffes will live on – we are spoilt for choice . . . During a state visit to China in 1986, he famously told a group of British students, 'If you stay here much longer, you'll all be slitty-eyed!'; he asked an Australian Aborigine, during a visit in March 2002, if he was 'still throwing spears?'; he shared a joke with a blind, wheelchair-bound girl with a guide-dog, asking her if she knew that 'they have eating dogs for the anorexic now?'; he responded to calls for a firearm ban after the Dunblane shooting, saying, 'If a cricketer, for instance, suddenly decided to go into a school and batter a lot of people to death with a cricket bat, which he could do very easily, I mean, are you going to ban cricket bats?'; and refer-ring to an old-fashioned fusebox in a factory near Edinburgh in 1999, said that, 'It looks as if it was put in by an Indian.' If Kofi Annan ever fancies a sabbatical, we know where to turn . . .

Pringles

One of the beauties of the Pringles package is that it can be so simply resealed in order to keep the suspiciously regular-shaped crisps fresh for another day. Just one more though, just *one* more . . .

Prison Films Featuring Men

As with gladiator epics, films about men in prison offer an undeniably dramatic situation (surviving in a harsh environment filled with caged desperados) fraught with homoerotic overtones. But while prison films featuring women usually go out of their way to exploit those overtones, flicks about men's prison for the most part ignore the gay subtext in favour of chaste camaraderie – along with plenty of danger and violence. The limited choice of locales (the exercise yard, the chain gang, the laundry, the cell block, the warden's office, and, of course, The Hole) helps create taut storytelling. That might explain why this relatively small sub-genre has produced a relatively large number of very good films, including *Cool Hand Luke*, *The Shawshank Redemption*, *The Birdman of Alcatraz*, *Papillon*, *Midnight Express*, and *Kiss of the Spider Woman*. There are even prison comedies (*Ernest Goes to Jail*, *Stir Crazy*) and a prison musical, *Jailhouse Rock*. However, should you ever find yourself in a real prison, we recommend you refrain from dancing around like Elvis. See also **Gladiators (Films Featuring)**; **Presley, Elvis**; **Prison Films Featuring Women**.

Prison Films Featuring Women

We're sure someone, somewhere, has made a film that examines the lives of incarcerated women in a realistic manner. Good luck finding it. Ask at your local video shop for flicks on the subject and you'll likely be steered to *Caged Heat*, *Chained Heat*, *Girls in Chains*, *Naked Cage*, *Women Unchained*, or any number of other X-rated films, almost all of which include the words *Caged*, *Chained*, *Naked* and/or *Heat* in their titles. See also **Blair, Linda**; **Lesbians (Film Scenes Featuring)**; **Masturbation**; **Prison Films Featuring Men**.

Private Lessons See Emmanuelle (Films Featuring the Character of); Teenage Boys Losing Their Virginity (Films About).

Private Members' Clubs

Obviously we are all socialists and anti anything that smacks of elitism in the depersonalized, homogenous society we all live in . . . but there is no finer experience than to be greeted by name and being asked if one wants 'your usual?' – it means that you have arrived and that you belong. Even better is to hear those words uttered in an exclusive private members club where there is a long waiting list for membership and a galaxy of media stars hoving into vision – hopefully just as your friends are arriving. Sitting there sipping a perfect Martini and trying not to look smug is a challenge (especially if your company is paying the huge annual fees) but it is well worth the effort. Garçon!

Prizes (Cereal Box)

Though it shames us to think about it now, few among us haven't rushed home with a box of cereal, ripped it open, then stuck our arm in down to the elbow in search of the prize inside – usually a plastic figurine that is even more fragile and poorly made than the crap sold in a supermarket's toy aisle. And yet, cereal-box prizes have been around almost as long as cereal. Bowls made with the new miracle product 'plastic' were big in the 1930s, while tiny metal license plates caught on in the 1950s. Today the cereal companies are very interested in software, dropping CDs loaded with computer games or music tracks into their Crispies and Flakes. What's next, iPods in boxes of Shredded Wheat? See also **Chocolate (Breakfast Cereals Featuring)**.

Professional Wrestling

As the century turned, the Connecticut-based World Wrestling Federation finally admitted (mostly for tax reasons) what everyone with an age above five and an IQ above 70 already knew – pro wrestling is fake. As if to drive the point home, the WWF even changed its name to the WWE (World Wrestling *Entertainment*). This after half a century of telling fans that daft personas from Gorgeous George to Rowdy Roddy Piper and Hulk Hogan were on the level, and that all those sleeper holds and body slams were legit. But the truly shameful part is that we keep watching, just as we have since the invention of television. Believe it or not, before television, this was actually a real, semi-unrigged sport. The funny business started when early wrestling broadcasts drew dismal ratings. Figuring they needed more than just a group of big, sweaty men in tights to keep drawing crowds, producers soon added storylines, garish personas and costumes, and 'good' wrestlers facing 'bad' wrestlers. Enter Big Daddy and Giant Haystacks. Exit reality. See also **Mr T**.

Property Shows

It's a wonder sometimes that the TV schedule doesn't collapse under the weight of all the house programmes it has on. *Location Location Location. Relocation Relocation. Property Ladder.* The funny thing is, though, that despite this wall to wall schedule carpeting, the people who appear on these programmes never seem to have watched them. We don't know much about trying to sell a house, but having seen endless programmes, we do know this: don't try to stamp your personality on the place! No one ever likes it! Paint the walls white and take the cash! Honestly, it's so simple and yet every week, some numbskull ignores Sarah Beeney's advice and paints the bedroom bright purple. A nation sits smugly and waits for the 'I told you so' moment.

Pulp Novels

The name comes from the fact that these tomes were printed on the cheapest available paper – the kind the folks at Andrex wouldn't touch. The guilt came from the fact that the sleazy cover art and attention-grabbing titles made them not quite proper for, say, your local book club. These days, some masters of the genre, including James M. Cain (*Double Indemnity*), Jim Thompson (*The Grifters*), and Mickey Spillane (the Mike Hammer series) have been welcomed into the pantheon of great American writers. But though the pulps produced a handful of diamonds, most were simply fit to be, well, pulped.

Remember *Marijuana Girl* or *The Oversexed Astronauts*? Neither do we.

Pussy (Jokes about Mrs Slocombe's)

Ground Floor Perfumery, Gents Ready Made Suits . . . going up. For thirteen years *Are You Being Served?* was a flagship BBC comedy and is still on every week on satellite. Its success on one level is baffling – it had a wobbly set, a boring premise ('people working in a shop, customers come in and funny things happen') and the plots are paint-by-numbers predictable. But actually it is a work of pure genius with exquisite performances from the likes of John 'I'm Free' Inman, Trevor Bannister, Wendy Richards, Arthur English and Frank Thornton. But it was the weekly double (actually, almost single) entendre jokes about Mrs Slocombe's cat Tiddles that made the nation's parents tut as they stifled giggles and the nation's kids laugh but in a slightly not-sure-why-this-is-funny way. How we chortled at her remark to Miss Brahms, 'I'm very worried about the funny rash I've found on my pussy,' not to mention her announcing to the nation that, 'It's a wonder I got here at all – my pussy got soaking wet and I had to dry it out in front of the fire,' or her simple statement about next door's dog, that 'The mere sight of my pussy drives him mad.' A glorious series appealing to the schoolboy in us all.

Queen Elizabeth II, Her Majesty

You can't help but get misty eyed about our dear Queen, who has sat on the throne since 1952 accompanied by Phil the Greek. Maybe it's because Elizabeth Alexandra Mary Windsor sort of reminds us of our own grandmother – if our own grandmother rode around in a gilded carriage and never left the castle without putting on a pair of full-length white gloves. And let's not think too deeply about the fact that we probably know more about Her Majesty's royal likes and dislikes than we do about those of our own grannies. Sure, she's had some bad press – her sister and most of her children got divorced, she had a very public annus horribilis and maybe she wasn't the best mother-in-law – but after more than fifty years on the throne, she still has a hat to match every outfit, knows all the words to 'God Save Me', savours her gin and tonics, and speaks perfect Queen's English. But then, how could she not? See also **Royal Family, The**; **Prince Philip**.

Quiz Shows (Intended for a Younger Audience)

It's natural to be bitter when some show-off answers a question about opera on *University Challenge*. How on earth is anyone supposed to know that? There always seems to be one question that stumps us even on simpleton-fodder like *Millionaire*. It's just annoying. The only way we've found to preserve our self-esteem and prevent ourselves from ending up with an eating disorder or something is to find an episode of *Blockbusters* (it wanders the channels like the Flying Dutchman, but it's always on somewhere) where the questions are pitched at a more sensible level. Completing a Gold Run from your well-worn sofa is a guaranteed path to inner peace and fulfilment.

QVC

Begun in 1986, created by Joseph Segel (founder of the Franklin Mint), today it employs some 12,000 people, selling direct-to-you-with-no-middleman, live on television, everything from garden furniture to scary-looking, high-priced dolls. The station is fronted by people who have that vague whiff of ex-celebrity neatly obscured by a splash-it-all-over reek of failure. It is worth watching simply for that pathos-filled look behind the eyes when they are having to convince an audience of sad losers that immediate action is needed to secure a valuable family heirloom that looks, to us ironic viewers, remarkably like a piece of 'Made In China' tat. Have your credit cards ready and call now.

Radio 2

Not so long ago, Radio 2 was what your aunt listened to. It was all Jimmy Young telling an imaginary chipmunk what the recipe was, followed by 'Sing Something Simple'. We stopped paying attention for a little while and when we looked back, everything had changed: now Jonathan Ross sets the tone on Saturday mornings with his engaging mix of ineptitude and cheek. His show seems so much like the kind of show we'd all make ourselves, if only we had the gall, the contacts and the ability. Add to that the roll-call of presenters that were the soundtrack to every essay you ever wrote: Steve Wright, Janice Long, Mark Radcliffe . . . it's like you never left school. Therein, we suspect, lies the appeal. Let the kids fill Radio 1 with grime and breakbeat. *We* have retreated to the safer shores of Radio 2, where we feel secure.

Radio Competitions (Winning)

Want to win a competition on radio? Well, whatever you do, don't ring up with the right answer to the question. Radio stations like to pad their competitions out. Before they get to the caller with the winning answer, they like to rip the Michael out of a couple of morons with completely the wrong response. The trick is to ring in with a ridiculously wrong answer, so bad that you get on air, but then, when they say, 'So, Tom, who said, "We will fight them on the beaches"?' rather than your expected response of 'Wasn't it that Geordie guy off *Club Reps*?' you say, 'It was Winston Churchill.' Cue stunned radio silence. Cue two tickets to England versus France.

Railway Stations (Food)

You're not hungry but you've bought your ticket and spent the requisite £7.50 or so in WHSmith on magazines and newspapers and there are fifteen minutes until your train is due. Do you a) sit quietly on a bench and do the Sudoku puzzle? b) board the train early and get a good seat or c) stand in front of a bewildering array of food franchises such as Upper Crust, Burger King and The Bagel Factory and, although you had breakfast an hour ago, load your self up with irresistible but gratuitously unnecessary snacks? For the answer to this conundrum see the title of this book.

Rambo Films

Sylvester Stallone captured a less endearing aspect of America's character in 1982's *First Blood*, which introduced the character of John Rambo. An embittered Vietnam vet, Rambo seemed less interested in getting respect than in getting payback. As anyone familiar with this film, or any of a hundred other films just like it, already knows, the plot goes like this: a) Hero is introduced; b) bad people repeatedly vex the hero; c) rat-tat-tat-tat! Whoosh! Boom!

The difference with Rambo was that, unlike earlier vigilantes such as Charles Bronson in *Death Wish*, who usually kept their revenge killings in the low double digits, these films featured body counts rivalling those of First World War battles. Nevertheless, the public ate it up. *First Blood* was followed by two sequels, one set in Vietnam and the other in Afghanistan, both of which were denuded of buildings, bridges and men of military age by the time the credits rolled. These vestiges of the late Cold War blazed the trail for that other pumped-up action-hero-turned-action-figure, Arnold Schwarzenegger. See also **Rocky Films**; **Schwarzenegger, Arnold**; **Stallone, Sylvester**; **War Films**; *Death Wish*.

Rampaging Animals (Films About)

Before *Jaws*, there had already been plenty of films about animals consuming humans, but this 1975 megahit about a great white shark depopulating a New England town one swimmer at a time is the *Citizen Kane* of its kind. It deftly exploited humanity's fears about the primal creatures lurking on the edges of civilization, causing thousands of terrorized filmgoers to cancel their holiday to Bognor. The near-numberless post-*Jaws* releases include *Grizzly*, *Orca*, *The Swarm*, *Lake Placid*, which starred a giant crocodile and *Anaconda* which saw J-Lo do battle with a giant Amazonian snake. Though that last one wasn't scary – just frighteningly bad. See also **Allen, Irwin**; *Halloween* (**The Film Series**); **Sharks**.

Rampaging Animals (TV Specials About)

The thing about a show with a title such as *When Good Pets Go Bad* is that the title tells you everything that is going to happen in the next thirty minutes. Yet we hang around anyway, in the hope of decent footage of Tiddles turning into a killer cat. See also *Crocodile Hunter*; **Pit Bulls**; **Rampaging Animals (Films About)**.

Ramsay, Gordon

The satisfyingly sweary sultan of the skillet, Gordon Ramsay is one of the most welcome sights on British TV. His sandblasted cheeks flank a winning smile, his great beefy hands are capable of squirting a gobbet of *coulis* across the most unpromising dish, and his fertile mind can generate some of the foulest language permissible on our famously liberal broadcast media. He has a craggy charm which his great rival Jamie Oliver lacks, and his steadfast refusal to court the *Guardian*-reader vote by sullying his hands with the petty politics of school dinners only adds to his monumental charm. He's a one man Mount Rushmore of cookery, and we love him for it.

'Rapper's Delight'

The Sugarhill Gang's 1980 hit that brought rap – albeit in a sugar-coated, neutered form – out of the ghetto and into the mainstream. All the essential elements (except for anger) were there: lyrics spoken, not sung, with a background melody lifted from another tune (in this case, Chic's 'Good Times'). It was danceable, and who cared if the words (sample: 'I said a hip-hop the hippie the hippie / to the hip hip-hop, a you don't stop') were a bit vapid? Later adapted for Las Ketchup's holiday smash, the 'Ketchup Song'. Seriously.

Razzies, The

Some films have Oscar winner written all over them. One only has to take a glance at *Shakespeare in Love* and think, Better get the hankies in for Gwyneth. Other films, however, find the seasoned filmgoer reaching a different conclusion. When Jennifer Lopez uttered the immortal words, 'Gobble gobble, it's turkey time' in *Gigli*, there was only ever going to be one winner in that year's Raspberries, the alternative film awards for very bad movies committed to celluloid. The turn out of A-list stars tends to be slightly less than those attending the Academy Award show, but occasionally the stars will turn up to accept their award and show they have a sense of humour. Paul Verhoeven famously took it on the chin to claim the award for worst film for *Showgirls*. And more recently Halle Berry turned up to pointedly thank her agent for securing her the title role in *Catwoman*. Miaow.

Reader's Digest

A magazine that first appeared in 1921 and whose first office was in a basement under a Greenwich Village speakeasy has become one of the most staid institutions in journalism. The Reader's Digest Association publishes both the *Digest* and its myriad foreign editions, along with those famous compendiums of condensed books in hand-tooled plastic and a slew of other magazines – all destined to be a mainstay of Oxfam shops all over the UK. Lately, however, in the face of falling readership, it has taken steps to 'jazz up' the pocket-sized pamphlet with diet stories and more celebrities. That's fine, but there was a certain weirdness about the old *Digest* that we miss, and trips to the dentist will never be the same again. Who can forget their 'classic' Humour In Uniform section, not to mention features like 'Eat Your Way To A Healthier Planet' and 'Knit Your Own Orgasm'. Some things should be sacrosanct.

Reader's Digest **Condensed Books**

Forget the 'If a tree falls in the forest' query. The more relevant philosophical question is: 'If you've read the Reader's Digest Condensed Book version of Tom Clancy, David Baldacci, or Michael Crichton, have you really read the book?' See also **Cliffs Notes**; **Crichton, Michael**; **Clancy, Tom**.

Reader's Digest **Prize Draws (Being in the Final Round of)**

When you hear a heavy plop through your letterbox, it can mean only one thing: you have BEATEN THE ODDS and YOUR NAME has been SPECIALLY SELECTED to GO FORWARD from YOUR POSTCODE to the FINAL ROUND of the MILLION POUND FREE PRIZE DRAW. Make sure you have uncovered your THREE TREASURE CHESTS on the ENCLOSED SCRATCHCARD and chosen an ADDITIONAL PRIZE GIFT should you choose to REPLY WITHIN TWENTY-FIVE DAYS, applied the appropriate sticker to the 'YES' ENVELOPE and read the EXCITED MESSAGE from MR A of CROYDON who has just taken delivery of a BRAND-NEW JAGUAR and has just returned from a ROUND-THE-WORLD CRUISE exhorting you to SAY YES and POP YOUR ENVELOPE IN THE POST TODAY! How can anyone refuse or, worse still, doubt the veracity of any of these claims – especially when the prize draw manager has a really down-to-earth name such as TOM CHAMPAGNE. See you at the Hilton Hotel Hounslow for the PRESENTATION BY A TOP SOAP STAR. Alternatively you could just read the magazine next time you go to the dentist.

Real World, The

One of the first reality shows, MTV's *The Real World* launched in 1992 by following a group of 'typical' young adults living together in a New York City flat. Every room was bugged, the phones were tapped, and camera crews lurked 24/7 to capture every moment of their lives. The results, condensed into 30-minute shows, featured twenty-somethings whining about their interpersonal relationships and dating quandaries as if the fate of the world hung in the balance. Sort of if *Friends* wasn't funny and had no sympathetic characters. See also **MTV**; **Reality TV**.

Reality TV

When we first heard the words, 'This is the true story of seven strangers picked to live in a house . . .' during the opening credits of MTV's inaugural season of *The Real World* in 1992, the idea of watching ordinary people caught in the act of being themselves seemed novel – even a bit naughty. But that was nothing compared to when *Big Brother* hit town. 'It's only a gameshow,' sang the contestants, but we the viewers knew better, as Nick Bateman became Nasty Nick and the most loathed man in Britain. From then on, the list of horror shows just grows and grows: *I'm a Celebrity, Get Me Out of Here!*, *Fame Academy*, *Celebrity Love Island*, *The Farm* . . . And when critics write scathing reviews practically blaming Rebecca Loos wanking off a pig for the fall of civilization, all it proves is that they watch too. OK, so it's crap, but it's entertaining crap. See also *Celebrity Love Island*; **COPS**; *Real World, The*.

Rear of the Year See Kendall, Felicity.

Red Bull

Red Bull gets its name from one of its active ingredients: 1,000 milligrams of the amino acid taurine. The taurine is supposedly a natural pick-me-up, but it gets help from a couple of tried-and-tested stimulants: 27 grams of sugar, plus 80 mg of good old caffeine in each slim blue-and-silver can. As if to emphasize the air of misplaced invincibility that imbibing so much sugar/caffeine/taurine can create, Red Bull sponsors an annual event at the Serpentine in Hyde Park, London, called Flugtag (or 'flying day' in German). Participants, no doubt fuelled with the sponsor's drink, are invited to try to fly human-powered machines. This is the nearest Red Bull gets to giving you wings.

Red Shoe Diaries (a.k.a. Zalman King's Red Shoe Diaries)

Followed by his dog, *X-Files* star David Duchovny wanders around reading a letter. Dissolve to a dramatic retelling of the contents of the letter – a retelling in which the protagonists, inevitably, shag. Such was the formula for Showtime's softcore hit series that ran for sixty-seven episodes from 1992 to 1999 and which found its natural home on late night Channel 5. Somehow, they managed to lure a pack of Hollywood middleweights onto the show, including a young Matt LeBlanc as a bike messenger who, ahem, goes down in a lift.

Reeves, Keanu

A man of few words and even fewer facial expressions, Reeves first piqued the interest of filmgoers in the 1989 hit *Bill & Ted's Excellent Adventure*, surfing through time as the classic Everydude, Ted. While the actor's chiselled good looks haven't exactly hurt his career (which has included such blockbusters as *Speed*, *Bram Stoker's Dracula* and, of course, the *Matrix* trilogy), we believe it is Reeves's economy of emotion – his flat, stoic delivery of lines like 'Trinity? *The* Trinity?' – that keeps us going back for more.

Regional News

National news is great. Guns and bombs and politicians and stuff. Regional news however, particularly outside London, really pushes the trade descriptions act. A car accident in which two people were slightly hurt? A supposed sighting of a large cat? The opening of a new playground? Wouldn't it be great if, just once, they said, 'You know, nothing's really happened in the South today. So instead we're going to play you a song'. That in itself would be more newsworthy than the non-events they waste five minutes of our evening with.

Regional Weather

You know what? We might not have a degree in Geography, but we can just about read a map. So why do TV executives decide to show us the national weather, and then the regional weather as well. It's OK! We can work out from the map of the UK roughly where we live. We don't need a second, identical forecast thirty seconds later, particularly when it is bookended, as on ITV, by some long and tedious sponsor's advert. Why not just make the national weather a bit longer? Give us a bit more info? Hurry up and get back to the film that you've cut in half to give us this vital rubbish.

Repeats See **UK Gold**.

Revenge Fantasies See *Death Wish*; *Incredible Hulk, The*; **Norris, Chuck**; **Rambo Films**; **Rampaging Animals (TV Specials About)**; **Schwarzenegger, Arnold**; **Superheroes**.

Reynolds, Burt

A Florida State University American football player, Burt Reynolds was scouted by the Baltimore Colts but had to stop playing due to injuries, so ended up acting. Reynolds rode the success rocket throughout the Seventies, appearing in such hits as *Starting Over*, *The Longest Yard*, *The Cannonball Run*, and his masterpiece, 1975's *Smokey and the Bandit* (his co-star was nominally Sally Field, but we preferred his souped-up Trans Am). Since then his star has dimmed, though he seems to be positioning himself for some sort of elder statesman role in films, à la Sean Connery. He even earned a Golden Globe and a Best Supporting Actor Oscar nomination for his role as a pornographer in the 1997 film *Boogie Nights* (a film he thought would ruin his career). See also **Unbelievable Sporting Comebacks (Films About)**.

Rice, Anne

Born Howard Allen O'Brien (!), this New Orleans native bumped around the literary world for years before hitting on a unique formula for success. Beginning with *Interview with the Vampire* in 1976, Rice's 'vampire chronicles' tell the story of impeccably dressed bloodsuckers who make their way through time, draining the bodily fluids from unlucky humans. The books are popular with teenage goths and with people who want something undemanding to read on long plane flights. See also **Vampire Novels**.

Richard and Judy

As Richard edges ever closer to adolescence and Judy comes increasingly to resemble Dame Margaret Rutherford, it becomes more and more tempting to suspect that some sort of Dorian Gray-style bargain has been made. Their onscreen banter, once a duel of equals, now the chidings of an exasperated mother to her giddy schoolboy of a son, only serves to confirm the conjecture that some kind of Faustian funnies have occurred. Despite the whiff of the occult, Richard and Judy are still massively popular. They only need to be vaguely connected with a book for it to become a best seller, although we're not all that optimistic about our one, and the sight of Judy's bra at that awards show prompted the biggest nationwide brouhaha since the repeal of the Corn Laws. Moving their hugely successful morning show to another station and a later timeslot, a suicidal move for most presenters, merely extended the lie-ins of their core student and malingerer audience and therefore boosted their popularity. Frankly, we see no obstacle to their domination of British daytime TV until Richard is in nappies. Long may they continue!

Richards, Denise

Two words: *Wild Things*. Yes, there was *Scream*, and yes there was the risible Dr Christmas Jones in that James Bond film, but Denise's reputation rests solely on a three-way scene from *Wild Things* with Neve Campbell and Matt 'I can't believe this is happening' Dillon. Neve Campbell's contract ruled out nudity; Denise Richards's didn't. Thus the champagne went on her. Of course, it's all puerile soppy-soft porn for men who haven't got the guts to buy the proper stuff. Even so, the number of men who would swear blind never to have seen this film is bigger than you might think.

Ricicles

Given the current concern for the nation's children eating crap, the writing might seem on the wall for some of our favourite unhealthy cereals. Take the humble Ricicle, for example. The problem with Rice Krispies is that, without that final touch of sugar, they are a little bit dull. Fortunately, someone at Kellogg's had the bright idea of coating the Rice Krispie from head to toe in sugar. The result? A breakfast fave that no one over ten has any excuse to eat. Kellogg's tried the formula again by coating the Krispie in chocolate, thus creating the Coco Pop, but really, it just wasn't in the same league.

Ringo

It took a spine of steel (something rare among teenage groupies) to admit that Mr Starr was your favourite Beatle. It takes an even stronger spine to say that you like his post-Fab Four music (remember 'Wrack My Brain'?). Don't weep for Ringo, though. He did, after all, bag the finest Beatle wife, Barbara Bach – agent Triple X from *The Spy Who Loved Me*.

Ringwald, Molly See *Breakfast Club, The*.

Riverdance

This *Cats* of dance revues originated in 1984 as a seven-minute intermission performance at a song contest in Dublin. That's probably how long it should have stayed, but the standing ovation it received gave troupe member Michael Flatley delusions of grandeur. Was there, perhaps, a vast, untapped demand for Irish step dancing? Apparently so. Flatley and company turned their intermission bauble into a two-hour travelling stage production loaded with traditional Irish dancing and featuring a bare-chested, baby-oiled Flatley tapping, twirling and sweating amidst a clogging army of lycra-swathed step-dancing men, and wig-wearing, mini-skirted, step-dancing lassies. Flatley, who choreographed the show, tapped his way through fifteen weeks of *Riverdance* before being ditched for 'artistic differences' in October of 1995. Unfazed, the world's fastest tapper (according to the *Guinness Book of World Records*) went on to create and star in *Lord of the Dance*, which has grossed more than £300 million. Yes, that's £300 million. See also **Guinness World Records**.

Road Runner

No witty repartee. No wordplay. No social satire. Just a bipedal coyote chasing a really fast bird through a stylized American Southwest landscape. The first Road Runner cartoon was made by Warner Brothers in 1949 and the last in 1966, with nary a plot difference from episode to episode. Why do we keep sitting still for them? The shameful truth is that everyone who ever watched Road Runner cartoons secretly longed for Wile E. Coyote to *wring that bird's beep-beeping neck*.

Rock School (Not to be Confused with Gene Simmons' Teaching Efforts)

Struggling to interest beginners and cocky intermediates alike, *Rock School* failed to fully engage anyone. Thousands tuned in though, every week, to see if anyone famous was going to come on to talk about how to choose a drum stool or something. The show's drummer, Geoff Nichols, had evidently bought a Roland Octopad drum synth with the money from the first show, because he pulled it out at every possible opportunity. Deirdre the guitarist had squandered her wages on the most geometrically perfect mullet available outside Paul Young's backing band. We think they had a keyboard player as well, but no one can remember him; the real star of the show was Henry 'King Thumb' Thomas, who seemed to be able to squeak a little bit of slap bass showing-off into any musical genre. Long vanished from our screens, the Betamax tapes are highly prized at car-boot sales up and down the country.

Rocky Films

Over the last couple of decades, filmgoers have watched Sylvester Stallone slowly drain every last ounce of life out of his original 1976 blockbuster, *Rocky*. So far there have been four sequels, each with the same recycled story. First we meet a new boxing villain; then Rocky doubts his ability to whup the new guy; then he decides to fight; then he trains while 'Gonna Fly Now' (or one of its clones) thunders in the background; then he fights and wins, but not before getting pounded like a piece of veal scaloppine. And yet, even though the proceedings are as formulaic as a Thai temple dance, we still buy tickets in the millions – except for *Rocky V*, that didn't do so well. See also **Rambo Films; Stallone, Sylvester**.

Rocky Horror Picture Show, The

The Rocky Horror Picture Show bombed when it was first released. But the film was no ordinary Tim Curry dud. Unlike *Clue* and *Annie* and *Oscar*, this outrageous musical science-fiction horror spoof got a second chance. A gutsy advertising executive called Tim Deegan convinced his bosses at Twentieth Century Fox to book the show for a midnight run at the Waverly Theater in New York on April Fools' Day 1976, and the rest is cult flick history. If you've never done the 'Time Warp', you're a liar. See also **Meat Loaf (The Singer)**.

Roller coasters (Enormous)

Anyone who screams on a roller coaster feels slightly embarrassed afterwards, because the sense of danger they inspire is just an illusion. But *what* an illusion. Modern designs can be more than 300 feet high, and experts insist that there's no reason why these thrill rides couldn't go 200 mph and tower 600 feet high. Loops are another matter. Physiologists report that the average human can take only about seven or eight of these before bringing up his chips and gravy. Which is why you'll never see 'coasters with more than seven or eight loops. See also **Theme Parks (Not Owned by Disney)**.

Rome

Essentially *The Sopranos* in togas, *Rome* takes the basic Veni, Vidi, Violence template of *Gladiator* and ladles on extra layers of Latin and lechery. All right, it's little more than a post-watershed confection of moderate sex and violence but because it's *history* that makes it essentially *educational* and therefore OK with us.

Romy and Michele's High School Reunion

This 1997 film starred Mira Sorvino and Lisa Kudrow as two dumb-as-dishwater blondes attending their ten-year high school reunion in Arizona. In spite of sometimes-scathing reviews, the film (based on characters from the Robin Schiff play, *The Ladies' Room*) has built a *Rocky Horror*-like cult following. And why wouldn't it, with such immortal dialogue as, 'I was so lucky getting mono. That was like the best diet ever', and 'Let's fold scarves!' It also contains one of the funniest three-person dance scenes ever filmed. See also **Chick Flicks (Female Bonding)**; ***Rocky Horror Picture Show, The***.

Ronco, K-Tel and JML

Ron Popeil, who founded Ronco, was the originator of the entire 'insane gizmo' industry which has given us such pleasure over the years. Even now, although over seventy, he still comes up with occasional inventions which are a boon to anyone who needs to shred root vegetables quickly, cleanly, and in a wildly over-engineered manner. Ronco and K-Tel also branched out into the soundalike compilation album – a genre consigned to history now but one which not only gave low-budget musical pleasure for thousands but also provided employment and valuable studio experience to rock legends like David Bowie and Elton John. JML are a more recent addition to this proud tradition, but anyone who has searched in vain for a specialized pancake-flipping device or a bag to make toast in will know instantly that they can find an innovative, useless, or downright baffling solution in the JML range.

Room Service

This is your chance to be rock-star picky and to really put the staff through their paces. There is something irresistible about ordering a club sandwich ('Please make sure the bread is medium-rare toasted buckwheat and that the mayonnaise is on the side') and a caesar salad ('with extra anchovies') at three in the morning, knowing that a poor, underpaid night manager has to trek all the way from reception to the kitchen to prepare it, serve it on a silver platter, trundle up to your room and then deliver it with panache and style. Irresistible, despite the fact that this is costing you the best part of £20. John Lennon once took things to extremes by ordering a 24-track mixing deck from the front desk (it arrived and he then proceeded to record 'Give Peace A Chance' on it), and several knowing businessmen can tell you the meaning of ringing down and asking for 'an extra pillow'.

Rourke, Mickey

John Waters released his film *Polyster* in Odorama – which meant that scratch-and-sniff cards were issued to the audience for use at key points in the film. No such gimmick was necessary when watching Mickey Rourke films – you could smell the stink all the way from the back row. The former boxer, known for his difficult on-set behaviour (he's said to have walked off a set because the director wouldn't give a part to his pet Chihuahua) snagged a string of leading roles in such films as *Angel Heart* and *Nine ½ Weeks*. The quintessential Rourke experience, though, remains 1987's have-a-shower-afterward epic *Barfly*, which was written by the equally nutty Charles Bukowski. See also **Gimmicks, Film**; *Red Shoe Diaries*; **Waters, John**.

Royal Family, The

What is it about the House of Windsor that stirs so many inquiring minds? Is it the way their freakishly large ears pink up so nicely when they tromp around Balmoral in giant rubber boots? Is it the fairy-tale accoutrements of castles and horse-drawn carriages? Perhaps. But more likely it's all the juicy revelations suggesting that HM the Queen and her kin are just as human as the rest of us. Rumours of infidelity, same-sex liaisons, addiction, topless sunbathing, toesucking and other royal shenanigans make for fascinating tabloid reading – the grainier the accompanying photo, the better. And that's not even mentioning *It's A Royal Knockout* or the 'hilarious' heir-to-the-throne wardrobe malfunction summed up so succinctly by the *Sun* headline as 'Prince Harry Is A Nazi'. Even ancient scandals have an undeniable allure, whether they involve Queen Victoria's possible love affair with her Scottish servant John Brown, Elizabeth the First's questionable virginity or the sensational antics of King Edward VIII. *I'm A (Royal) Celebrity – Get Me Out Of Here!* anyone? See also **Dianamania**; **Queen Elizabeth II, Her Majesty**; **Prince Philip**.

Royal Society Christmas Lectures, The

Michael Faraday, one of the pioneers of electricity, gave the first 'Christmas Lecture for Juveniles' in 1826. Due to technical difficulties it wasn't until the early 1970s that they were shown on television for the first time, introducing a new audience of semi-comatose adults to the world of easily-understood science and entertaining experiments. As much a part of the Christmas break as *The World's Strongest Man* and family arguments, the lectures are at their most entertaining when presented by a comedy science maverick like 'The Reading Terminator' Professor Kevin Warwick, or a nerd pin-up like Helen Sharman. As educational standards plummet and the BBC progressively dumbs down its output, it's only a matter of time before we see a discussion of whether a dinosaur could beat Spiderman in a fight, probably chaired by the Chuckle Brothers.

Royal Variety Performances

It is very rare we feel sorry for the Queen, but the annual Royal Variety Performance is certainly one of those occasions – an evening of saccharine obsequiousness with the latest glitzy number from the West End interspersed with 'will-they-won't-they swear' cheeky comedians, newsreaders 'doing turns', *Pop Idol* winners singing 'acceptable' cover versions and someone like Stephen Fry poking gentle fun at the inhabitants of the Royal Box like a flirtatious gargoyle. This is all followed by the ubiquitous 'line-up', where the joy is in seeing who is going to bow the lowest and crawl the fastest up the royal fundament.

Royal Weddings

You've got to admire the organizers of these things; they certainly know how to put on a show: thousands of men on horseback, gold carriages, trumpets, cathedrals, palaces, loads of OAPs sleeping out all night, waving flags and repeating well-worn anecdotes about Lady Di and the Queen Mum in the East End during the Blitz to eager breakfast TV reporters, and chaste kisses on balconies as millions cheer. You even get a public holiday and extended licensing hours. Great stuff. Obviously, the wedding ends in a public tabloid-driven divorce but, in a sense, the horrible inevitability of this crash-and-burn fairy-tale ending heightens the whole god-damn experience. Mark and Anne, Charles and Di, Margaret and Lord Snowdon, Fergie and Andrew, Harry and Paris Hilton etc. etc. etc. (ad lib to fade).

Rubbernecking

Flashing lights ahead, traffic reduced to a snail's pace – it can mean one of only two things: either John Prescott is being escorted to the airport, or there has been a crash on the opposite side of the central reservation. There is of course no reason whatsoever why this should affect traffic flow on our lane, save for the fact that we all want to gawk at some other poor driver's misfortune, maybe catch a bit of real-life *Casualty*-as-it-happens and then mentally thank God it didn't happen to us. But of course if you get to see some blood, some corpses under blankets and a couple of heads being removed from electricity pylons by firemen with sticks then the delay will have been almost worth it and one can always put your foot down a bit to make up the lost time.

S

Salad Bars (Unlimited Visits to)

It's all a question of architecture, really. Extensive research has shown that a soft bed of coleslaw and cottage cheese provide ample foundation for a wall of vertically inserted crispbreads. Into the resultant void (now a handy 100 per cent higher than the dish itself) you can pile in the cherry tomatoes, grated carrot, pasta twirls in an indeterminate spicy sauce, cold meats, chicken wings, cheesy mayonnaise stuff and three colours of sliced peppers whilst still leaving room for the Thousand Island dressing and the crispy bacon bits. And the joy is that you can always go back for more. See also **Thousand Island Dressing**.

Salad Cream

On the Continent, mayonnaise is in such plentiful supply that some people even smear it on their chips instead of tomato sauce. Not so in austerity-hit Britain; during World War Two the nation's mayo supply was needed to lubricate vital components on Spitfires, so the Ministry of Salads and Picnics devised a mayo substitute which combined the adhesive qualities of mayonnaise with the vile taste of cheap vinegar. Unfortunately even in the darkest days of the Blitz no one could be persuaded to eat the stuff, so the wartime stockpile still exists, slowly metamorphosing into its more deadly form, sandwich spread, as it matures on supermarket shelves.

Sales Conferences

Sales conferences are school trips for grown-ups, except with alcohol and shagging thrown in for good measure. We're not sure why being in a hotel just off the M25 is any different from being in the office, but suddenly any number of things you'd never consider in your normal life become strangely compelling. Like that assistant in marketing, for instance. There's a golden rule about rock bands when on the road: what goes on tour, stays on tour. Do not, under any circumstances, think this rule applies to sales conferences. You are not a rock star, you are an accountant. By the time you sit down for breakfast, everyone in the entire company will know about the strange noises Sue heard from the other side of the wall. Fact.

Salt (Excessive Application to Food of)

Waiters and waitresses wilfully wave their magical wooden wands over your salad, cranking out clouds of peppery pixie dust. However, you never see one haul out a giant salt cellar and ask if you'd like some extra sodium. That's because salting an entrée, like putting tomato ketchup on a steak, is considered an insult to the chef. You should be satisfied with the savoury zest of lime or the bouquet of fresh herbs seasoning on your fish, beef or fowl. Yet everyone knows that some foods (pastas and potatoes in particular) benefit from a blast of salt. The same goes for tomatoes, turkey, fried fish and chicken. Is that so wrong?

Sandler, Adam

If you'd been asked in 1991 to pick the two *Saturday Night Live* regulars who would become Hollywood stars, the chances are you'd have guessed Mike Myers and Dana Carvey. But while Myers has certainly done well for himself (at least when he plays Austin Powers) and Carvey also did okay (though only when playing opposite Myers in the *Wayne's World* films), their lesser co-star Adam Sandler became the unlikeliest A-lister since Burt Reynolds. Why? Because he makes blokes laugh, whether they admit it or not. Say what you will about Sandler's range. It takes skill to make a golf comedy (*Happy Gilmore*) that's now quoted almost as often as the leader of the genre, *Caddyshack*. Another secret of Sandler's success: he never tried to turn one of his *SNL* characters into a feature film. See also **Caddyshack**.

Sarpong, June
Two words: That laugh.

Sat Nav
The brilliant simplicity of the in-car portable TomTom Satellite Navigation device has benefits far beyond the car. With its TFT screen, live-streaming traffic news and pin-sharp maps, it will not only get us where we want to go in a trouble-free manner, but will probably save marriages as well. Say goodbye to arguing with your loved one at 83 miles an hour or going the wrong way round the M25. Just type in the postcode or house number of where you are going and, with a rather sexy soothing voice, it leads you every step of the way right to the doorstep of your destination. Future models will probably give you an in-car massage, a pedicure and an optional Brazilian wax.

Satellite TV
Despite the very best efforts of those quixotic underdogs behind Freeview, in the UK satellite TV really means Sky. No matter how awful the programme you're watching may be, with Sky there's always the knowledge that something even more dreadful can be beamed to you from Murdoch's Death Star at the push of a squidgy rubber button. Can't sleep? Get ready to embrace your hitherto undiscovered enthusiasm for Canadian high school curling. Think the quality of TV shows is on an irrevocably downward spiral? Flick to UK Gold for some jaw-droppingly bad *Mind Your Language* repeats. It's all out there, and if you've missed it, it's all out there again an hour later on the 'Plus One' channel. Eventually, though, you will settle for warming your hands in front of low-volume MTV, which flickers hypnotically much as a cave fire once fascinated our brutish forebears. The only real progress is that the people of Lascaux only had mammoth to eat. We've got pizza *or* Pringles.

Saturday Morning TV

Once upon a time, when there were only four TV channels, Saturday morning became, by common consent, the ghetto into which kiddie programming was consigned. Thus, between the hours of, say, seven a.m. and noon, children could dig into a bowl of Sugar Puffs while watching everything from *Noel Edmond's Multi-Coloured Swap Shop* to Chris Tarrant's *Tiswas*, Mike Read's *Saturday Superstore* and Philip Schofield's *Live and Kicking*. Ant and Dec reignited the flame in the late 1990s with their *SM:TV*, but now that they like a lie-in and there are enough children's and music channels to keep everyone entertained, crowding round the telly to watch Keith Chegwin is just a distant memory.

Saturday Night Fever

Like *Rocky*, this 1977 blockbuster is about a local loser who tries to make good. Except that instead of punching his way out of obscurity, Tony Manero (John Travolta) tries to dance his way out. OK, so the clothes and the dancing are dated (sometimes hilariously so), but it's touching to watch Tony try to wrap his pretty, muddled head around the idea of doing something with his life. Also, the Bee Gees-intensive soundtrack remains as crisp and colourful as a new polyester shirt. See also **Rocky Films**.

Saturday Night TV

The Saturday night TV schedules have long been a dumping ground of second-rate TV aimed principally at dull-eyed simpletons who are slumped before their plasma screen in shellsuits, repetitively masticating savoury pancakes while dimly planning their own humiliation on a forthcoming episode of *Trisha*.

It was not always thus: broadcasters would once hoard blockbuster movies which they would unleash on a Saturday night, immediately after an all-star variety show which offered something for all the family. These days, if you're in watching television on a Saturday night, you have failed as a person and that's all there is to it. You can't knock *Millionaire* though.

Saved by the Bell

Running for four years, *Saved by The Bell* grew out of the Disney Channel's show about an American high school called *Good Morning, Miss Bliss*. In hindsight, one of the reasons we liked this Saturday-morning, pre *T4* filter was the eye-candy casting. For girls, there was Mario Lopez and Mark-Paul Gosselaar. For the boys, there was Tiffani Thiessen, Elizabeth Berkley (of *Showgirls* in-famy), and Lark Voorhies. For everyone else, there was Dustin Diamond. See also *Showgirls*.

Scalextric

Scalextric is the brilliant game that brings all the excitement of grand prix racing right to your front room. Two cars ping round on silver strips, while their two 'drivers' fail to resist the temptation of offering the world their Murray Walker impersonation. And it's Simon's Formula One car that has disappeared under the table while Michael's TR-7 continues to forge ahead, except wait! Simon's foot is covering Michael's track, as he continues to look for his car. I'm not sure this is in the rules . . . The game enjoys a renaissance at various points in a man's life, in an all-boys' house at university, and later as a 'present' for Junior.

Schwarzenegger, Arnold

A dirt-poor (albeit well-built) Austrian export, Arnie became a bodybuilding superstar, then transformed his fame into a film career studded with hits ranging from *Conan the Barbarian* in 1982 to *True Lies* in 1994. Mostly by playing monosyllabic killer cyborgs and monosyllabic killer mercenaries, he became one of Hollywood's hottest box office draws. Though many of his most recent films have been disappointments (primarily because, in flicks such as *End of Days* and *Collateral Damage*, Schwarzenegger actually tried to *act*), he's far from a has-been. In October 2003, through a controversial 'recall' election that made headlines around the world, 'Ah-nold' became the governor of California.

Scooby-Doo

Most classic, long-lived cartoons earn their success by serving two audiences. They provide slapstick for the kids, plus sly puns aimed squarely at the old-enough-to-drive crowd. Not so, *Scooby-Doo*. This longest-running of all cartoons caters to small children and no one else. The animation is crude, the dialogue lame, and the premise downright bizarre. Four teenagers – beatnik Shaggy, debutante Daphne, brainy Velma and hunky Freddy – plus a talking Great Dane (the aforementioned Scooby-Doo) drive around in a heap of junk called the Mystery Machine, investigating spooky occurrences. Kind of like an *X-Files* for CBeebies. In the summer of 2002 came the big-budget Hollywood film that, although only slightly more sophisticated than the cartoon, nevertheless earned more than $100 million in America alone. That buys a lot of Scooby Snacks. See also **Hanna-Barbera Cartoons**; **Saturday Morning TV**.

Scooby-Doo (Daphne)

There are undoubtedly ethical, not to mention psychological questions, about experiencing urges towards a cartoon character. But in the case of Daphne from *Scooby-Doo*, we do feel that there are grounds for justification. While Scooby and Shaggy kept the janitor with the ghost costume busy, Daphne, Fred and Thelma kept themselves otherwise occupied. Ahem. Our theory is that the whole thing was meant to be some sort of double date, but Fred was feeling greedy and Shaggy was sent packing with the dog. Personality-wise, Daphne strikes us as perhaps a little two-dimensional for any sort of long-term relationship, but for a short burst of animated action, she remains a bit of a draw.

Scraps (Chip-Shop)

Go into a Southern chip shop and they don't know what you're talking about. Go into a Northern chip shop and if you don't ask for them, they'll know you're not from round here. Scraps are the bits of batter that have flaked off the fish during frying. They are ostensibly, actually, let's not go into what they ostensibly are. Just remember they go great with chips and they're free.

Screen Savers, Comedy

Years ago, leaving the same image on a computer monitor for long periods could cause a problem called 'burn-in'. The screen's glass surface would actually become discoloured, creating a ghost image that never went away. Screen savers prevented this problem. Modern monitors are immune to burn-in, but people still love personalizing their computers with screen savers: the odder the better. Almost anything is available (often for free) on the Internet, from tropical fish, to pretty much any sex act you would care to name. We don't recommend that last category for office use.

Screening Calls

We all love that Emperor Nero moment when the phone rings and the 'Call Accept?' message appears, and our thumb hovers over YES or NO. There is something wonderfully empowering about deciding whether you are at home to the mother-in-law, the boss or the bank, or actually just 'in a meeting', 'going into a tunnel' or 'switched off'. And the joys increase tenfold when you are at home with the answerphone volume up and you can let your callers ramble on and on and on before switching the TV volume up and pulling the phone out of the socket.

Sea Monkeys

A staple of adverts in the back of comics, the Sea Monkeys of real life shocked millions of children by not holding hands, not having big smiles and not wearing bows or crowns. They were – and are – saltwater shrimp eggs that hatch when thrown into water laced with a secret solution (mostly salt) that comes with the Sea Monkeys kit. Their Dr Frankenstein was inventor Harold von Braunhut, who 'created' them in 1957. He first slapped the hapless eggs with the name Instant Life, but then modified it because the creatures sort of had something that looked like a monkey's tail – if you looked really, really hard. And most children did look at them really, really hard – for about an hour, after which they flushed the 'monkeys' down the loo and got on with their lives.

Selection Boxes

Every Christmas, there's always one tipsy uncle who turns up at the family festive gathering with a load of stuff that they've bought that morning. Female relative? Cheap perfume from the all-night chemist's. Male relative? A CD that's first been copied to the uncle's iPod for quality control purposes. Anyone under fifteen gets a selection box. Consisting of half a dozen standard chocolate bars mounted on the world's most expensive piece of cardboard, the selection box has been at the root of every late December sugar-fuelled tantrum since records began. Depending on how many tipsy uncles a child might have, these cocoa-based cluster bombs can continue their disruptive work in said infant's bloodstream until late January. The only peacekeeping tactic available to the beleaguered parents is to store the offending articles in the fridge and hope the child forgets about them. The easiest way to ensure that is to covertly eat them during that magical couple of hours after the kids have gone to bed. Not that any of us would resort to such subterfuge.

Self-Publicists (Blatant) See Branson, Richard; Archer, Jeffrey; Dickinson, David.

Serial Killers (Films About)

From Fritz Lang's 1931 *M* to Alfred Hitchcock's *Psycho* to such modern 'masterpieces' as *The Silence of the Lambs* and *Henry: Portrait of a Serial Killer*, serial killer movies not only win critical acclaim, but also sell tickets by the millions. The best of these productions try to analyze the inner workings of the criminal mind. But things get creepy when these human chainsaws become stock characters, à la *The Bone Collector*, *Seven*, and *Manhunter*. The bottom line is, no matter how nasty traditional horror films get, we can always tell ourselves that we're watching outlandish fiction. Serial killers, on the other hand, are real. Which means the man sitting next to you in the cinema could be watching the screen, thinking, 'Hey, they stole my bit'. See also *Halloween* (The Film Series).

Sex (In Unusual and/or Inappropriate Places)

For some, discreetly doing the no-pants dance in public (be it on a plane, in a pub toilet, a lift, the sea, or even a moving car) provides the ultimate sexual thrill. Unfortunately, the presence of Inspector Gadget-like mobile phones with digital cameras means these semi-private trysts can sometimes be made public (thanks to Internet porn sites) in a big way. Of course, since the danger of discovery is what makes this so exciting, perhaps the threat of lurking cameras will only make it *more* enticing. See also **Naked Celebrities (Photographs of)**.

Sex (Things Losers Waste Their Time On Instead of Having)
See *Battlestar Galactica*; *Doctor Who*; *Dungeons and Dragons*; *Lord of the Rings, The*; Shatner, William; *Star Trek*; *Star Wars*.

Sex (Watching Other People Have)
See Lesbians (Film Scenes Featuring); Masturbation; Films (Pornographic); Penthouse and Sex (In Unusual and/or Inappropriate Places).

'Shagger' Norris

In the early 1990s, then Prime Minister John Major made his famous 'Back to Basics' speech about personal morality – a speech that, given his taste for a spot of late-night Currie, was perhaps a tad rich. It also sank any government minister who was similarly playing away: Tim Yeo, David Mellor and many, many more. All, that is, except one. Stephen 'Shagger' Norris was a minister with a whole handful of lady friends. But unlike his errant colleagues, 'Shagger' was always upfront about his extra-curricular activities. Somehow, he got away with it. Jammy git.

Sharks

Ever since the film *Jaws* appeared in 1975, the world has been fascinated by these marine predators. Books on the subject fly off the shelves, and documentaries get top ratings on the Discovery Channel. Everyone, it seems, is interested in, and more than a little afraid of, sharks.

Well, 'everyone' is an idiot. The truth is, dreading an

encounter with these creatures is like fearing a UFO abduction. It just isn't going to happen. According to the Florida Museum of Natural History's International Shark Attack File, there were only sixty unprovoked shark attacks worldwide in 2002. Each year elephants, hippos, and even *bees* claim more lives. You have a far better chance of choking to death on those crab sticks you bought on the sea front in Grimsby than of falling victim to a great white. See also **Rampaging Animals (Films About)**; **Rampaging Animals (TV Specials About)**.

Sharpener

A sharpener is, of course, that much maligned, and sadly disappearing guilty pleasure: the lunchtime pint. While a loosener 'loosens' you up for a long evening ahead, a sharpener 'focuses' the mind for the afternoon's work ahead. Order it at five to two. Sink it by the time the clock strikes. Re-enter the office feeling bloody marvellous. See also **Loosener**.

Shatner, William

It's hard to think of another actor whose personality contains such an entertaining mix of arrogance, cluelessness, and bizarre likeability. Canadian-born Shatner knocked around Hollywood during the late Fifties and early Sixties, mostly doing bit parts. Then came *Star Trek*. The programme only ran from 1966 to 1969 and was never a hit in its initial run, but for years it typecast Shatner as Captain Kirk. Not that Shatner didn't do everything (including some very ill-advised things) to break that mould. Though he can't sing a note, he nevertheless released an album, which includes his immortal, proto-rap rendition of 'Lucy in the Sky with Diamonds'. Finally he managed to break out of 'set phasers on stun' mode, landing the TV series *T.J. Hooker* in 1982 and then filling the Michael Buerk *999* role in *Rescue 911* – all while appearing in a seemingly never-ending stream of *Star Trek* films. See also *Iron Chef*; **Nielsen, Leslie**; *Star Trek*; *Twilight Zone, The*.

Shields, Brooke See *Blue Lagoon, The*.

Shoes (Buying Them if You Are a Girl)

In a recent shoe amnesty carried out by this publication it was discovered that the number of shoes in most girls' wardrobe (x) is equivalent to their age (y) multiplied by (z) where z is a constant figure of 75 per cent. Therefore $x = yz$. This is fact. Thus your average Bridget Jones will have approximately forty-two pairs of shoes but that may or may not include espadrilles depending on the polling method being employed. A woman's relationship with shoes dates back to playing with Barbie and Sindy who had a whole welter of shoe choices whereas little boy's Action Men had a choice of combat boots or, um, bare feet. We can't remember about Ken but that's not important here. Those formative nursery room years have produced a generation of Carrie Bradshaws with enough Manolos, Jimmy Choos and Christian to open a shoe shop managed by Imelda Marcos safe in the knowledge that the foot is the only part of the body that doesn't change as you get older. I mean have you ever heard a women saying 'Do my shoes look fat in this?'

Shoes (Not Buying Them if You Are a Bloke)

Ask most men (except for Laurence Llewelyn-Bowen and Elton John) and they will profess to owning three, maybe four, pairs of shoes (if you include Wellington boots) and no cajoling is ever going to change that. Men wear shoes until they fall apart and then they probably buy the same pair again but carefully refusing all offers of cleaning products or spare laces. And you know what? They like this lack of choice, it makes them a little smug and able to utter those immortal 'putting out the fire with gasoline' lines: 'I'm ready – I'll wait downstairs' just at the moment when their partner is having her 'I'm fat, ugly and have nothing to wear' moment.

Shopping See **Bid TV**; **QVC**; **Shopping While Drunk**.

Shopping (While Drunk)

One of the greatest dangers to face white-collar workers in recent years has been the increasing prevalence of late-opening music and video shops. Combined with a well-lubricated leaving party after work, it's a recipe for disaster. Sometimes, if you're lucky, you'll come to your senses amid a queue of gently-swaying office drones and realize that you've got five terrible DVDs in your hand and you're about to pay £30 for them. Sometimes, if you're very lucky, you'll realize that you've already got two of them anyway. More often than not, though, the first thing you'll know about it is the next morning when you'll peer over the side of your bed, already sick with self-loathing, and see amongst your scattered clothes and loose change the makings of a full-fledged John Hughes retrospective. The danger doesn't even end when you've made it home: eBay runs all night and has yet to refuse a bid due to evident drunkenness. What you're going to do with a tea chest full of old Commando Picture Library comics is anyone's guess, but there's an email in your inbox congratulating you on having bid £27 more than anyone else on earth for the privilege of owning them. See also **eBay**; **Hughes John (The Films of)**.

Shops That Sell Smelly Things for Your Bathing Pleasure

There's so much promise stacked on the vanilla-scented shelves of a shop with 'Bath', 'Body', or 'Beauty' in its name. Choose a physical imperfection (be it as small as a blackhead or as large as a cellulite-dimpled backside), and you'll find a remedial goo among the orderly rows of bottles and tubes. A pioneer in the business of self-service beauty, the Body Shop sold its first product in 1976, before anyone even knew that tea trees had oil or that avocados could make body butter. The Body Shop now sells a product every 0.4 seconds, while its rapidly-growing competitor, Lush, is busy coming up with clever new scents like Youki-Hi and Tisty Tosty which you can smell from absolutely bloody *miles* away. Of course when people drop £50 on cosmetics at Aveda, they're bringing home not just a bagful of plant-based tonics, but a whole new lifestyle attractively packaged to suit a wood nymph's mood. And when that mood changes, there are plenty of other testers to sniff at Virgin Vie, Origins, and all the other modern apothecaries that have saturated the market – or at least made it smell like calendula.

Showgirls

An absolutely terrible film that everyone makes fun of, yet everyone seems to have seen. *Saved by the Bell* alumna Elizabeth

Berkley plays a stripper who wants to become a Las Vegas show-girl and will do anything and anyone to make it. Unlike most high-profile train-wreck films (*Ishtar*, *Howard the Duck*, *Heaven's Gate*), *Showgirls* offers something to compensate for the bad acting and bad script: legions of naked and almost-naked women (which explains why the copy at your local video shop is never available). *Showgirls* is like having a drink with a beautiful, sexy girl with a horrible personality; you have to bite your lip and stay focused to get to the good stuff. Try watching it with the sound off. See also *Saved by the Bell*.

Sideburns

Daft sideburns are a coming-of-age statement for young men who finally achieve the hormone levels necessary to sprout them. Imagine their embarrassment when, years later, spouses or children stumble across old college photos of Dad looking like a Dickensian cabbie. Apparently, the world owes this dubious fashion statement to an officer from the American Civil War, General Ambrose Burnside. He was so famous for his jaw hair that the look became known as burnsides – and then, for reasons unknown, got switched to 'sideburns'. The rest is hair history. See also **Humperdinck, Engelbert**.

Siegfried and Roy

Let's face it: it's doubtful that anyone ever paid to see these guys for their lame conjuring tricks. Certainly no one ever paid good money to witness their curiously German idea of a good haircut. No, the real pull at an S&R show was the danger inherent in working with untameable jungle beasts. Sooner or later someone was going to get their mullet chewed off. Eventually, one of them did. The witnesses to that horrifying spectacle came away from Las Vegas burdened with the same dilemma that afflicts everyone that's seen a Formula One crash or a boxing knockout; on the one hand, how deeply traumatic. On the other hand . . . result!

Silly String

A plastic-like compound that hardens when exposed to air (the exact formula is a trade secret), Silly String has found its way into everything from weddings (where it rivals rice and confetti as the missile of choice to aim at the departing bride and groom) to boozy New Year's Eve parties. The only problem is, while blasting it all over the place is fun, getting it out of your hair and off your living room walls is not.

Singers (Who Must Have Made Deals with Satan in Order to Gain Fame) See 'Agadoo'; Awful Records; Soap Actors (Attempting to 'Make it' as Pop Stars); *X-Factor*.

Six Million Dollar Man, The

An astronaut who suffered a calamitous flight test accident, Colonel Steve Austin was the inspiration for ten-stone weaklings everywhere. Who, after all, wouldn't want a limb or an organ (in Austin's case, an eye, an arm, and both legs) enhanced by the wonders of science? And what bionic boy wouldn't want a sidekick like Jaime Sommers (a.k.a. the Bionic Woman) to fight crime with? Towards the end there was even a bionic boy and a bionic dog, and Austin, instead of fighting the commies as he originally did, was facing off against Bigfoot. No doubt about it – they pulled the plug just in time. See also **Lunch Boxes**.

Ski Sunday

The sublime grace of the ladies' downhill? Or the knockabout frolics of the luge? Be honest, you only watch it because someone's bound to fall over at some point. It's like Formula One on ice.

Sky Sports News

Imagine a place where nothing exists but sport, where breaking news is Jermaine Defoe stubbing his toe and you can watch people watching football matches all night long. In the 1970s, *World of Sport* was just three hours on a Saturday afternoon with Dickie Davies. In the twenty-first century, that world is twenty-four-hour reality thanks to *Sky Sports News*. Be sucked in by the split-screen delights of league tables and rolling results. Be unable to move as the anchorman says, 'Coming up . . . why Lee Hendrie believes Aston Villa can beat Portsmouth this weekend.' Be woken up by the sound of your girlfriend slamming the front door as she leaves you for someone marginally less lobotomized.

Sledging

Not spinning down a snowy hill on your Gran's best tea tray, but the cricketer's art of passing the time of day with his opposite number. We say passing the time of day: we mean jovial banter in order to put them off. The all-time classic is perhaps the Glenn McGrath–Eddo Brandes twosome. 'Why are you so fat?' Glenn asked Eddo. 'Because every time I shag your wife, she gives me a biscuit,' was his response. But there are many ways to unsettle a batsman. The wicket-keeper talking just loud enough for the batsman to hear is another favourite. 'Oh dear, he's not moving his feet at all. Hey Freddie! Bowl him the inswinger . . .'

Slim-Fast

A diet regime that lets you drink milkshakes *and* lose weight sounds a little too good to be true. But at roughly 200 calories and one gram of fat per serving, this gritty chocolate libation has plenty of before-and-after pictures to back up its claims. The trick is to drink Slim-Fast exactly as directed (a shake for breakfast, a shake for lunch, and a sensible meal in the evening). Not as a post-lasagna chaser, or as part of an ice cream float. See also **Before and After Photos**.

Slush Drinks

This beverage, like youth is wasted on the young – which is why you see so many adults hurriedly filling huge cups with this semi-frozen concoction. Slurpees or Slush Puppies got their start in 1959, when the technology for chilling beverages to 28 degrees and turning them into slush was developed by a Texas company. Today some 11 million 'Slurpees' are sold monthly, in flavours such as Memphis Melon, Banana Split, Crystal Light Pineapple Orange, and Sausage Dog. Sorry, there's still no cure for brain freeze. And we may have made up the bit about sausage dogs. See also **Soft Drinks (Giant Plastic Cups Filled with)**.

Smith, Anna Nicole

If you take sick pleasure in watching a gone-to-seed celebrity self-destruct before your eyes, here's your gal. Smith (real name Vickie Lynn Hogan) was born in the small Texas town of Mexia. In a sense, she never left. Early on she put her pneumatic figure to work at a strip club, where she was spotted by a photographer, started modelling, and in 1993 became *Playboy*'s Playmate of the Year. Then the weirdness started. In 1994 Smith married eighty-nine-year-old oil magnate J. Howard Marshall II. The very next year Marshall died, igniting a huge inheritance fight with his heirs that saw Smith walk away with a cool $450 million – more than enough to pay the court costs from a 1994 sexual harassment suit filed by a female former assistant. Since then she's devoted herself to what seems to have become her life's work: bloating up to the size of a hot-air balloon. See also **Anderson Pamela**; *Osbournes, The*; **Reality TV**.

Smokey and the Bandit See **Reynolds, Burt**.

Snickers

Long before anyone thought of Slim-Fast, this chocolate bar became the meal replacement of choice for harassed office workers. And why not? Crammed with 14 grams of fat, 35 grams of carbs, and 30 grams of sugar (not to mention 280 calories), it packs enough punch to carry a cubicle drone through even the toughest afternoon. Could its creator, Mars founder Frank C. Mars, have foreseen its utility as a clandestine pick-me-up for drones when he launched it in 1930? Perhaps. Why else would he name it after his family's horse? Though why it was called Marathon in the UK for so long, God knows. See also **Slim-Fast**.

Snooker/Darts

Somehow, not only have Fatty and Porky convinced the powers that be that the game they play down the pub is actually a 'sport', but they've only gone and got it on the telly as well. Unlike say football or cricket, snooker and darts players's sheer lack of physical prowess allows us all to believe that we, too, could be stepping up to the oche. And however dismissive we might be about the coverage – God, snooker is so boring – we all know that a mere five minutes' viewing will lead us to staying up until 2 a.m. to find out who wins the match.

Soap Actors (Attempting to 'Make It' as Pop Stars)
See also **Awful Records (Pretending to Like in an Ironic Way)**; **Soap Actors (Attempting to 'Make It' in Hollywood)**; *Strictly Come Dancing*.

Soap Actors (Attempting to 'Make It' in Hollywood)
There's only one place soap actors should be seen beyond Albert Square and that's on the boards of the local theatre during the Christmas season. But, occasionally, some stars get ideas beyond their station (that's Walford East, by the way) and think that shouting 'Leave it out!' for a living guarantees them a free pass to Tinseltown. Sorry Martine. But at least she could sing: Jack Ryder's Hollywood ambitions ended with not a single role and no return to the day job as his character had been killed off. Next!

Soap Operas (Glamorous)
No matter where our day took us, the approach of evening in the Eighties always brought us back to familiar territory: *Dallas* or *Dynasty*. These days, we have *Footballers Wives*. In such parallel universes, the beautiful people don't mind us staring at them while we slouch around in tracky bottoms eating peanut M&Ms from a one-pound bag. You know you have it bad when you still care about the characters' lives long after they cease to bear any resemblance even to a plasticized version of reality. Why else would we have obsessively watched *Dallas* for so long, even when the plot grew so thin that a dead Bobby Ewing appeared in the shower and the whole previous series was dismissed as a dream?

Soft Drinks (Giant Plastic Cups Filled with)
The loathsome trend of 'super sizing' food portions is at its most grotesque and shameful when applied to drinks. These days most fast-food outlets offer a half-gallon-sized plastic cup from which patrons can consume an entire day's supply (or

what, in a sane world, *should* serve as a day's supply) of their favourite soft drink. If the drink of choice happens to be sweetened with sugar, that's about 620 calories in one go. Yet we happily plump for the big bucket, knowing that for, say, an extra 20p, we can nearly double the size of our drink.

Solitaire

Despite the fact that Napoleon Bonaparte, Franklin Roosevelt and Leo Tolstoy all played it, solitaire is still a red flag to the rest of the world that you have too much time on your hands. Dating back to the sixteenth century, this game (and its countless variations) seems important only when you're in the middle of it. Afterwards comes the inevitable 'What was I thinking?' guilt.

Someone Else's Paper on the Train (Reading)

Stuck on a crowded commuter train you can often see up to three people unintentionally reading the same paper. Often, when it is inches from your nose, you have no option – but there is a real skill to doing this on purpose, and it needs to be honed. Our advice is to start with tabloids and work your way up to broadsheets. The trick is to cultivate a nonchalant middle-distance daydreaming expression which will fool any tabloid-brandishing accuser, or to carry a pair of dark glasses for added camouflage. Giveaway signs one should avoid include comments such as, 'Sorry – I haven't finished reading that yet', '1 Across is "bullfrog" not "darkness"' and 'Why are you hiding the *Daily Sport* behind the *FT*?'.

Sopranos, The

The jewel in HBO's already impressive crown, the *Sopranos* is essentially a (marginally) less comedic take on the turn-of-the-century gangsters-and-shrinks chucklefest *Analyze This*. What makes it better than its cinematic progenitor is the strong language, scenes of a sexual nature, drug references, and graphically depicted lampings that are guaranteed every week. Whenever there's a lot of talking to be done it's done in a strip club, and there's plenty of shots of Tony Soprano's big sweaty back to prevent you from getting too carried away during the frequent sex scenes. Best of all, every now and then a cast member is locked up for getting a little bit *too* method and knocking over a liquor store in Poughkeepsie or something. Our only complaint is it's always on so late. Excuse, if excuse were needed, to buy the whole thing on DVD.

South Park

Everything about this cartoon is crude, from the language to the animation. Yet you've got to admire the pluck of its creators, former University of Colorado film students Matt Stone and Trey Parker. Their saga began when they created a holiday cartoon called *Jesus vs. Frosty*, in which a homicidal snowman battled the Saviour, who eventually cut the snowman's head off by throwing his halo at him. This novel take on the festive season caught the attention of executives at the Fox network, who commissioned Stone and Parker to create a video Christmas card called *The Spirit of Christmas* (in which Jesus battles Santa Claus). The video made it onto the Internet, and the duo soon had a deal to do a cartoon series, which became *South Park*. A masterpiece of envelope-pushing comedy that mines everything from Presbyterianism to paedophilia for laughs, it once featured the voice of George Clooney (who was instrumental in getting the duo noticed) as a gay dog.

Spam

Invented in 1937 (it was originally called Hormel Spiced Ham) Spam has been the meat of last resort for everyone from soldiers (Soviet leader Nikita Khrushchev said it kept Russian troops from starving during the Second World War) to hungry stoners searching for something to stop the munchies. So far, more than 5 billion tins have been sold. What's in it? Even the official Spam Web page leaves room for speculation. 'Pork shoulder and ham, mostly', it says. What exactly does 'mostly' mean? See also **Beans and Sausages**.

Spam (Replying to)

Every so often, the media run stories about how the ever-growing volume of junk emails is threatening to grind the Internet to a halt. What they never mention are the people replying to them: those who want their P.E.N.1.5. enlarged, and those, like us, who have no need for such services (ahem) but feel duty bound to do their bit and fight spam with spam. If you've never replied to an African dictator desperate for funds to save his country from itself, you've missed out. Go on, write back. Tell him you'll think about it. Discuss your childcare problems with him. Send him some photos. Forward him the P.E.N.1.5. enlargement email. It's puerile, yes, but wasting his time as much as he's wasting yours is seriously spamtastic.

Spandau Ballet

From their first, bekilted appearance on Janet Street Porter's LWT show in the early Eighties, the Spands established themselves as a force to be reckoned with. Somehow Gary Kemp's clunky lyrics (more awkward by far than anything in the Oasis canon) sung by Tony Hadley's musical-comedy voice became the voice of a generation tired of the unremitting drabness of the 1970s and ready to embrace glamour once more. The group's willingness to dress up like metrosexual Scottish bikers (with text-book footballers' mullets) was so enchanting that we were willing to overlook the lumpen posturings of 'Musclebound' and Gary's toe-curling rap in the otherwise excellent 'Chant No.1'. Something went wrong soon after Live Aid, and the happy band that were given to winking at each other on *Top of the Pops* (as if unable to believe that they were getting away with such a hilarious caper) sued their record company because they weren't as popular as Duran Duran, fell to infighting and dissolved.

Spears, Britney (Videos Featuring)

No adult has any excuse for voluntarily listening to this borderline jailbait's music. Why, then, are men so transfixed by videos such as 'Oops! . . . I Did It Again' and '. . . Baby One More Time'? Think of it as pining for lost youth. Or, perhaps, a certain unobtainable youth. See also **Music Videos**; **Olsen Twins, The**.

Speed Cameras (Watching Other Motorists Being Flashed by)

Pick a stretch of road leading up to a poorly-positioned speed camera (three miles long should do it) and wait in a lay-by until a likely looking vehicle driven by two law-abiding citizens comes over the horizon. Slip out ahead of it and then drive really erratically for approximately 2.5 miles. Slow down when there is nothing ahead; speed up when rounding a blind corner only to pull up fast shortly afterwards, causing much braking from behind. When you are within striking distance of the speed camera pull over sharply onto a conveniently placed grass verge. At this point your poor no-claims bonus people will have had enough and will speed past at about fifty miles an hour in total rage – straight into the path of a flashing speed camera. Repeat till bored.

Spelling, Aaron

It's not the man himself who we guiltily care about. It's the creations that bear his name (usually as some sort of producer). His glory days included *Charlie's Angels*, *The Boy in the Plastic Bubble*, *The Love Boat*, *Fantasy Island*, *Friends* (sorry, not that *Friends*, this is the one that lasted five episodes in 1979), *Hart to Hart*, *Dynasty*, *T.J. Hooker*, *Glitter*, *Beverly Hills 90210*, *Melrose Place*, and *7th Heaven*. Without him, this book might not exist. See also **Beverly Hills 90210**; **Charlie's Angels**; **Dynasty**, Spelling, Tori.

Spelling, Tori

We knew she got her *Beverly Hills 90210* gig because her dad, Aaron, was the producer. We knew after watching a few episodes that she couldn't act to save her pampered life. But we watched, and we inexplicably cared about what the show's writers had in store for her character, Donna Martin. And we knew – don't ask how, we just knew – that Shannen and Jason and Luke and even Gabrielle would leave the show at some point but that Tori would endure to the end. And we were right. After all, where else did she have to go? See also **Beverly Hills 90210**; Spelling, Aaron.

Spin-Off TV Series

Joey will never be *Friends*. It just won't. Similarly, *Frasier* was never *Cheers*. It was funny in parts, yes – but that whole Dick van Dyke accent thing that Jane Leeves was rockin' kept distracting people from the actual jokes. Great comedy is like a good cup of tea, or like really good sex: if you try to make it again it'll never be quite as nice. Especially if you don't wash your cup. Don't think that British TV is above such barrel-scraping either: we feel obliged to remind you of some sequel-shows that you may have managed to forget: *Going Straight* (*Porridge*), *George and Mildred* (*Man About the House*) and *Murder Investigation Team* (*The Bill*). Not forgetting *Holby City*, even though we'd like to.

Spirits (Miniatures of)

The miniature bottle is a fun-sized treat that lets you feel like a giant. A giant who, inexplicably, is fond of Drambuie. Once the preserve of international airline travellers these diminutive drinks would seem to serve little purpose in the corner shop, where more substantial treats are readily available. Nevertheless, some subtle market forces are at work which pressure the canny shopkeeper into giving up valuable shelf space to the contents of an Oompa Loompa's cocktail cabinet.

SpongeBob SquarePants

You can imagine the pitch for this at Nikelodeon – 'Hey guys, we want you to buy a series about a really upbeat sponge called . . . er Bob, who lives in the undersea town called . . . wait for it . . . Bikini Bottom, who has adventures with his friends . . . and he wears pants that are square.' There is something worryingly comforting about this *Finding Nemo* meets *Trumpton* acquatic experience, with Bob frolicking with his slightly dim friend Patrick, the athletic acquatic squirrel Sandy and the annoyingly perfect neighbour Squidward. SpongeBob is employed as a chef at the local burger place, The Krusty Krab, which is operated by a mean old crustacean named Mr Krabs. Only in TV land would you willingly buy food from someone with that name.

Spreadable Butter

In 1970 Dr Robert Norris and Mr David Illingworth from the New Zealand Dairy Research Institute sat down to share breakfast and one of them suffered the humiliation of 'Torn Bread Misery'. So began a quest that was at the cutting edge of butter technology, the search for the Holy Grail – a butter that spreads like margarine straight from the fridge. Twenty-seven years later (that's about 8,500 breakfasts) Torn Bread Misery has been banished for ever, to be replaced by pure, advert-quality, butter spreading joy. Spreadable butter must rank among the top three products for lazy people (alongside pre-grated cheese and pitted olives) but annoyingly it is fantastically useful. Rumours that they are now turning their great intellectual weight to developing pre-buttered toasted bread – 'tastes like toast straight from the bread bin' – are sadly greatly exaggerated. See also **Grated Cheese (Pre-Packed)**.

Springer, Jerry

He was a campaign aid to Robert Kennedy and mayor of Cincinnati. But his day of infamy arrived when his issues-oriented talkfest *The Jerry Springer Show*, on the brink of cancellation, was re-imagined by a new producer hired from the *Weekly World News*. The result: Jerrymania. These days researchers troll the trailer parks to bring us such programmes as 'My Boyfriend Is a Girl', 'My Brother Is My Lover', and 'Brawlin' Broads' (all offered in the same week), followed by Springer's too little, too late moralizing at the end. It's no surprise that Springer became daytime TV's No. 1 programme and spawned his own opera.

Squeezing Spots

We were all told by our parents not to squeeze spots, as it encouraged and spread infection. But can anyone honestly say they can stand in front of the bathroom mirror and see a white-headed monster clinging to the side of their nose without wanting to give it the old double-forefinger pressure poke? For added enjoyment why not step six feet backwards, angle your head slightly and see if you can get the pus projectile to splatter the mirror? You can even mark out a basic dartboard format on the mirror using toothpaste, keep score and get a league going with your nearest and dearest. Apparently, you can also tell what a person has been eating from the smell of their pus, so why not incorporate this into any head-to-head confrontations as a tie-breaker?

Stallone, Sylvester

It just isn't cool to say that you love the Italian Stallion. It's okay to enjoy *Rocky* or even *Rambo*, but not the man who brought both characters to life. Why? Perhaps it's because the Manhattan-born muscleman has made so many questionable cinematic decisions, including starring in some of the daftest Bombs ever committed to celluloid. His personal Hall of Shame includes *Rhinestone* (in which Sly plays a country music singer), *Cobra* (one of the most over-the-top vigilante movies ever made), and *Stop! Or My Mom Will Shoot* (which won Stallone the 1992 Golden Raspberry Award for Worst Actor). And yet, the man still gets leading roles – perhaps in the forlorn hope that this proven heavy hitter will one day smack another one over the fence. See also **Flops (Big-budget Films That Turn Out to Be)**; **Rambo Films**; **Rocky Films**; *Saturday Night Fever*, *Escape to Victory*.

Star Trek

In this age of big-budget science-fiction productions, it's hard to remember why so many children (and so many nerds) found

the old *Star Trek* television series interesting. The special effects were only marginally better than those in black and white Flash Gordon adventures. But it did have one important advantage. The programme actually took science fiction sort of seriously. Instead of rolling around the galaxy blowing up planets, Kirk, Spock and the rest of the crew philosophized about racial intolerance, war, and pretty much every other burning issue of 1960s America. There was even Nichelle Nichols, a black woman, as part of the bridge crew. She was just a glorified switchboard operator, but she was *there*.

After its undistinguished, low-rated three-year run, the show vanished from the airwaves. But when the original seventy-nine episodes aired as repeats, something unprecedented happened. Ratings soared. Fans started gathering to hold conventions.

And *Star Trek* became The Programme That Wouldn't Die. Today, after four follow-on series, almost a dozen big-screen films, and numberless other commercial tie-ins, it's The Media Franchise That Wouldn't Die. Which still doesn't mean you can wear your Star Trek tunic to the office Christmas party. See also **Shatner, William**.

Star Wars

Why did this 1977 space opera come out of nowhere to become one of the biggest films of all time? Perhaps because its creator, George Lucas, thought so carefully about the plot. He'd studied the works of scholar Joseph Campbell, who believed certain myths, and mythic types, are universal throughout human history. Calculating that anything that could hold the attention of neolithic cave dwellers would also appeal to twentieth-century filmgoers, Lucas tried to insert as many archetypes as possible into his film. There was the Lovable Rogue (Han Solo); the Reluctant Hero (Luke Skywalker); the Princess in Distress (Danish-pastry-coiffured Leia); and many more. So there's lots more going on than meets the eye (as any hardcore fan will explain, usually at great length, unless you tell him to go and play in the road with his lightsaber and leave you alone).

Which leads to a delicate question many an aficionado has faced. Are you just a *Star Wars* fan or a *Star Wars* geek? Here's how to find out: if you know what a Wookie is, you're okay. But if you know what a Bantha is, you've got a problem.

Star Wars: Clone Wars Cartoons

Animated in the crude style that typified Genndy Tartakovsky's previous best known work, *Dexter's Laboratory*, SW:CW ran as two series of blink-and-you'll-miss-them episodes on the Cartoon Network. There was no effort to schedule the series for adult viewers on the grounds that anyone over eighteen who wanted to see them would buy them (probably while drunk) on DVD, thereby maximising the profit margin for cash-strapped independent filmmaker George Lucas. The sketchy characterisation and languid narrative drive of the 'real' movies are ditched in favour of an aspartame-fuelled kineticism which baffles as it boggles as it bewitches. Watched after a night of cold drinks it creates a roller-coaster intoxication known otherwise only to connoisseurs of class-A drugs. And all for only £14.99! See **Shopping While Drunk**.

Stars in their Eyes

Honestly, it is a slippery slope – it starts with singing in the shower or even, in extremis, in the bath, but before you know it there is a whiff of karaoke on the horizon and then the whole 'Tonight, Cat, I'm going to be . . .' look-at-me-look-at-me experience is looming on the horizon. The pleasure of seeing Gary, a slightly plump certified accountant from Droitwich, being given a bad wig, large earrings, big glasses and a suspiciously generously cut jacket and then emerging through the smoke-filled tunnel as Elton John to play 'Candle In the Wind' is immeasurable – matched only by Beverly's amazing transformation from slightly dull-looking shop girl into Dido. Erm . . .

Stars' Homes

With all due respect to Robin Leach, presenter of iconic American programme *Lifestyles of the Rich and Famous*, the real reason why we can't get enough of shows like MTV's *Cribs* and *Through the Keyhole* has nothing to do with 'champagne wishes and caviar dreams'. No, what we really want is a glimpse at stardom's dark, embarrassing 'ugly-tile work wishes and shoddy-crown-moulding dreams'. Biscuit crumbs on the sofa. Paintings of dogs dressed as historical characters. Now *that's* good stuff. After all, MTV's hit *The Osbournes* was only supposed to be an episode of *Cribs*. See also *InStyle Magazine*; *Osbournes, The*.

Status Quo

'Roll over, lay down and let me in.' So sing Francis Rossi and Rick Parfitt on 'Roll Over Lay Down', and like the musical slags we are, we're not about to refuse. Is there any better driving album than *12 Gold Bars*? We think not. 'Down Down', 'Whatever You Want', 'Paper Plane' – the nuggets of top-drawer back-room boogie just keep on coming. The Quo are like that pair of jeans you went through years ago, but can't quite bring yourself to throw away. Familiarity breeds content.

Steel Magnolias See **Chick Flicks (In which Someone Dies)**.

Steptoe and Son

If you watch Sky often enough you will soon come across reruns of Galton and Simpson's unmissable drama-as-comedy *Steptoe and Son*. This total classic charts the love-hate relationship of a widower father and his unmarried son, who between them run a shabby rag-and-bone business from Oil Drum Lane in Shepherd's Bush, London. Pathos-rich performances to die for from Harry H. Corbett and Wilfrid Brambell owe as much to the theatrical traditions of Pinter and to the Theatre Royal Stratford East as they do to the creators of *Hancock's Half Hour*. Best watched whilst 'working at home' from the office and wearing a pair of scruffy old pyjamas. You dirrrrty old man.

Stick Cricket

Computer games are great. And when they're free, it's even better. Stick Cricket, found at www.stickcricket.com, is perhaps one of the most fiendishly addictive we've seen. We're not sure why: the game is pretty much what it says on the Web address. You go into bat against various attacks, and try and score as many runs as possible. Hooking the fast bowlers for six soon becomes a doddle. Staying in against the spin bowlers remains a mystery. Now comes in a two-player version, so you can waste time with a co-worker.

Streisand, Barbra (as Actress)

In order to watch a Barbra Streisand film, you must enter into a make-believe world where EVERYTHING IS ALL ABOUT BABS. That's true for her Hollywood debut, 1968's *Funny Girl*, true for her latest work, 1996's *The Mirror Has Two Faces*, and also true for everything in between. What closet Streisand fans (both gay and straight) understand is that it's just that me-me-me egomania that makes her so compellingly watchable. And you can't beat the guilty pleasure of watching a forty-something Streisand playing a young girl trying to pass herself off as a young boy in *Yentl*. Need evidence of an inflated ego? In that 1983 musical, producer/director Streisand allows no one in the cast other than herself to sing. See also **Streisand, Barbra (as Singer)**.

Streisand, Barbra (as Singer)

Selling a phenomenal number of albums, charting a phenomenal number of hit singles and charging phenomenal prices for her phenomenally rare concerts, Barbra Streisand has been an entertainment force for four decades. With an appeal initially derived from her unattractive-girl-who-rises-to-the-top-on-chutzpah persona (and amazing voice), Streisand became a gay icon – which is one of the reasons why straight men are hesitant to call themselves fans. And even if the discs within them are winners, there's also the embarrassing album cover factor. Just try deciding which is more cringeworthy, the picture of Babs on *Streisand Superman* or the one on Barry Gibb-era *Guilty*. See also **Streisand, Barbra (as Actress)**.

Strictly Come Dancing

Strictly Come Dancing is the silly dancing bit of *The Generation Game* grown drunk on its own power and inflated to massive size. With Bruce Forsyth. Every one of the 'celebrities' featured appears in the vain hope of becoming a camp national treasure like Reg Holdsworth or Jim Bowen. It'll never happen, you can't do that kind of thing on purpose. The contestants' transparent longing for a daytime chat show or even just a supermarket to open makes *Strictly Come Dancing* a worthy alternative to the ad breaks in *Pop Idol*.

Strip Clubs

Red lights are not intrinsically sexy. But they do a good job of hiding blemishes and imperfections. Handily, they also provide equally good camouflage for customers who don't want to be seen by friends and neighbours. (Although being spotted isn't necessarily a disaster, because the standard reply to a self-righteous 'What are you doing here?' is an even louder 'What are *you* doing here?') In recent years these 'gentlemen's clubs' have worked valiantly to shake this stigma by positioning themselves as classy places for adult entertainment. Dream on. The day polite society accepts ogling naked women in a bar is the same day ordinary people start referring to pole-straddlers as 'dancers'. See also *Showgirls*; **Smith, Anna Nicole**.

Stunts (Insane, Televised)

In 1974, when stunt king Evel Knievel tried to jump Idaho's Snake River Canyon on a rocket-powered motorbike, television viewers around the world were transfixed. But that bit of insanity was just a hint of the madness to come. Over the last quarter of a century, we've been privy to a parade of *World's Most Dangerous Stunts* specials, David Blaine encasing himself in a block of ice, and even Knievel's own son, Robbie, jumping a motorbike from the roof of one Las Vegas hotel tower to another. But perhaps the most interesting development has been the entry of minor celebrities and the common man into the world of loony stunts. Whereas playing dice with death was once the stuff of professional mentallists, now we can watch fallen soap stars on *I'm a Celebrity* . . . lying in pits of snakes, eating animal penises, and collecting dead rats from pitch-black tunnels. See also *Knievel, Evel*; **Morons (Entertaining, Untimely Deaths of)**.

Sudoku

How ancient is the ancient Japanese number puzzle sudoku? Truth be told, it's got about as much history as a ploughman's lunch. That was invented by the pub trade in the Seventies to persuade people to go to the local for lunch; sudoku was invented in the Eighties and is these days used to sell newspapers in large quantities. In spring 2005, Britain went officially sudoku crazy: Carol Vorderman even got her own live sudoku programme on Sky One. We say, don't worry about specifics such as getting the numbers 1 to 9 in each square. Far better to fill the boxes in as quickly as possible, thus impressing your fellow commuters no end. They are young, but they will learn.

Sugar (Excessive Application to Food of) See Alcopops;
Bubble Yum; Candy Floss; Chocolate (Breakfast Cereals
Featuring); Cinema Food; Doughnuts; Dunkin' Donuts;
Garcia, Cherry; Gobstopper Machines; Ice Magic; Ice Pops;
Jelly; Jiffy Pop Popcorn; Mars Bar (Fun-Size), Pez;
Pic'n'Mix; Pop-Tarts; Ricicles; Snickers.

Sugar Cubes

For centuries mankind had to make do with sugar in its
naturally-occurring form: bags of white stuff. Then Mr Tate
(or Mr Lyle, it's never been entirely clear) thought to himself, 'What if we could produce sugar that you could construct
tiny buildings out of during boring presentations?' From that
apparently simple idea one of life's greatest pleasures was born.
Horses like them too, apparently.

Sugarcraft

There's a big difference between simple cake decoration and
the complex art of sugarcraft. So what better way to spend your
hard-earned leisure time than crafting tiny three-dimensional
little flowers and teddies from fondant and then sticking them
on the top of cakes? It is apparently rewarding both for the
artist and the recipients and not only do you get to enjoy doing
the 'craft' (as the thousands of aficionados worldwide call it)
but you can eat them too.

Summer, Donna

In the private sanctum of many a car stereo,
the former Ladonna Gaines still reigns as the
queen of disco – even though it's been a
couple of decades since her prime (1975's
'Love to Love You Baby', consisting of an
infectious beat melded with Summer's
orgasmic moans, followed in 1978–79 by
four No. 1 hits in the US, including 'MacArthur Park' and the
roller disco standard 'Hot Stuff'). Around 1980 Summer
became a born-again Christian, which put a damper on her
club credibility, to say the least. Still, even now, the first notes
of 'Bad Girls' can send a horde of unrepentant fans stampeding

towards the dance floor. Disco may be dead, but Summer never ends. See also **Disco (Dancing)**; **Disco (Fashions)**.

Sunday Night Costume Dramas

They're like a tin of Quality Street made flesh. The current fashion is for plenty of Austen and Brontë: for the womenfolk they're as comforting as a Mills & Boon but somehow have an air of GCSE set-book quality – and men can always be guaranteed enough firm young bosoms yearning to be free of their Empire-line confinement to keep their twitching hand from the remote control. All the comfort of that other Sunday night staple, the Postcard TV show, and with enough underlying sexual *frisson* to send us all to bed with a little more enthusiasm than 'The Night Before Monday' might reasonably be expected to hold.

Sunday Sport

World War Two bomber found on Moon. Upskirt pics of Girls Aloud star. Five solid pages of sex chatlines. Every week. In a *national newspaper*. It defies understanding, doesn't it? It's ridiculous, but it's a lot more fun than the bloody *Observer*.

Super Soakers

Does it come as a surprise that the man who invented the Super Soaker water pistol worked at a Jet Propulsion Laboratory? An engineer on the Galileo Jupiter space mission, Lonnie Johnson started tinkering in 1982 but didn't launch his creation, first dubbed the Pneumatic Water Gun, until 1989. Its hand-pumped, high-pressure water delivery system revolutionized the water pistol industry, with recent versions able to shoot a stream of water forty feet. Technically, of course, they're designed for children, but much pleasure has also been had by adults retaliating against a munchkin onslaught or exercising a pre-emptive strike on a battalion of unsuspecting brats. Besides which, it's more dignified than running through a sprinkler.

Superheroes

When superhero comics first appeared in the mid-1930s (the very first was *The Phantom* in 1936, followed in 1938 by *Superman* in *Action Comics* No. 1), they tapped into something powerful and primal in the human psyche. For whatever reason, drawings of men in brightly coloured skintight outfits and flamboyant capes who wore their underwear over their clothes became incredibly popular. So popular that the biggest names from the early days of DC Comics – Batman, Green Lantern, Wonder Woman (who started out as *secretary* for the Justice Society of America), and the aforementioned Superman – all became part of the culture. Of course the dirty little secret of these comics is that they've always been as popular with adults as with children. The grown-ups have even turned vintage comics into savvy investment items. The original Spider-Man comic, valued at just a few hundred US dollars a couple of decades ago, is now approaching $100,000 in price. See also *Batman* (The TV Show).

Supermarket Sweep

Contestants on this heart-pounding test of shopping proficiency could walk away with hard cash and Dale Winton's phone number if they played their carts right. Even so, the term 'game show' only loosely applies to this low-rent quiz in which frenzied shoppers crashed their way through a built-in-the-studio supermarket, filling their baskets with all the turkeys, disposable nappies and loaves of bread that the laws of physics would allow. Strip away the mystery envelopes, rhyming couplet clues, and all of Dale's unstoppable enthusiasm for life, and the show was nothing more than physical comedy at its finest, as excitable contestants dressed in matching sweatshirts scrambled down the aisles in goofy desperation that maybe, just maybe, humiliating themselves on television might be the lift they were looking for in their lives. A TV gem as deliciously cheesy as those giant rounds of Gruyère in the deli section. Definitely more Kwik Save than Waitrose. See also *Price is Right, The*; **Winton, Dale**.

Supermarkets (Eating Food From Before You Leave the Car Park)

Popping a few items into your weekly shop that you can eat before you get home is a great way of (literally) having your cake and eating it. You can ostensibly stay on your partner-imposed diet but still feast your face with jam doughnuts, cheese and ham croissants and a packet of fruit gums. Just remember to remove tell-tale wrappers from the glove compartment and to dispose of the receipt.

Supermarkets (Eating Food From Before You Reach the Checkout)

The installation of all those security cameras is surely designed to catch people secreting food about their person for illegal removal from the premises, and not to deal with the petty crime of secreting food *within* your person. Surely the big three supermarkets aren't going to miss the odd grape munched surreptitiously in aisle 5, the sun-dried tomatoes that don't quite reach the 'medium' salad box container, or the couple of sausage rolls that are munched between the deli counter and the exit? Industry sources tell us that supermarkets lose up to five per cent of their turnover through what they describe elegantly as 'shrinkage'. But you can bet your bottom dollar that this five per cent is added back onto their prices so we are, really, paying for it all anyway.

Supermodels

There's no clinical definition for what separates a supermodel from a plain old ordinary run-of-the-runway model. But like legal definitions of pornography, you know a supermodel when you see one. She's the one named Cindy or Claudia or Kate. She's the one who sells magazines just by appearing on the cover and who stretches reporters' skills to breaking point by forcing them to have to write stories about her. While a handful of these glorified coat hangers had previously burst into the national consciousness (e.g., Twiggy), the era of the supermodel essentially lasted through the Eighties to the late Nineties, roughly from the point where we started saying 'Hey, that's Cindy Crawford' to the point when *Vogue* labelled a Naomi Campbell story 'The Last Supermodel'. See also **Masturbation**.

Surgery (Televised)

You could watch some cut-up in *Casualty* or *Holby City*, or you could click over to a documentary on plastic surgery and actually watch someone get cut up. Thanks to the magic of patients and their families signing waivers, voyeuristic viewers can now tune in for a doctor's-eye view of an open head, a peeled-back face, or the delicate details of a nose job. The appeal is difficult to explain to someone not of the surgery-enjoying persuasion. Yet watching doctors do what they do under life-and-death (except for the nose job) circumstances can be more compelling than the real-life-ish activities of *ER* or lesser medical dramas. It is, however, lousy dinner hour viewing. See also **Autopsies (Television)**.

Susann, Jacqueline

Jacqueline Susann single-handedly created the market for thick paperbacks filled with celebrities, millionaires, family strife, and, of course, sex, sex, sex. Her second book was her real tour de force. *Valley of the Dolls* told the story of three vaguely disguised starlets trying to make it in Hollywood and having plenty of sex and drugs along the way. It spent more than twenty weeks at No. 1 on the *New York Times* best-seller list and (according to most sources) remains the top-selling novel of all time.

Other formulaic, X-rated blockbusters followed until Susann's death in 1974. Her fame proved as fleeting as the careers of the starlets she wrote about. But though her books are ancient history, a flock of Susann wannabes, from Jackie Collins to Judith Krantz, pay her homage with every second-rate pot-boiler doorstop they write. See also **Cartland, Barbara**; **Collins, Jackie**.

Sweepstakes

We may have already won? Yeah, right. You can afford to give away millions as a way to promote selling magazine subscriptions? Sure. Yet even though we can't figure out how *Reader's Digest* and other sweepstakes manage to balance their books, we still catch ourselves searching, licking and sticking our way through packet after packet, imagining that prize patrol showing up on our doorstep. See also **Lottery Scratchcards**.

'Sweet Caroline' See Diamond, Neil; Status Quo.

Sybil

It seems a bit silly now, but at the time of its release in 1976, this TV film scared the wits out of many a strong man and woman. It told the mostly true story of a girl named Sybil (played by Sally Field) who manifested sixteen different personalities, and the psychiatrist (Joanne Woodward) who tried to figure out why. Hint: Sybil's mother wouldn't win any Parent of the Year awards. The movie won an Emmy for Field, and blazed the path, for better or worse, for a zillion other 'socially relevant' small-screen flicks exploring every medical/psychological problem from bulimia to narcolepsy. See also **Mentally Impaired (Films Whose Stars Pretend to Be)**.

T

T.G.I. Friday's
Much-mocked for its retro uniforms, brass bar railings and cluttered wall hangings, T.G.I. Friday's was once, believe it or not, a trendsetting New York restaurant. These days, however, any breath of originality in the a-little-bit-of-over-there-over-here chain has long since fled. Still, there's something irresistible about a place with a novella-length menu, perky waiters and Jack Daniel's-enhanced entrées.

Tabloids See *Sunday Sport, Weekly World News.*

Take Hart (Sending Pictures to)
We're not very good at art. Which is a shame, because we always wanted to get our picture on 'The Gallery' and for Tony Hart to wax lyrical about our drawing skills. Thankfully, even if you weren't a budding Michelangelo, artistic success was still possible thanks to harnessing your creativity in a slightly different area: your age. What was a frankly appalling and unfocused effort by 'Tom, aged fifteen' was an inspirational work of great promise by 'Tom, aged five'. It's not really cheating, it's more 'playing' with the 'medium'. And let's be honest, it's what everyone else was doing.

Takeaways (Over-Ordering)
It's Friday night, you've had a long week at work and don't fancy cooking. Fair enough. But whenever you enter your takeaway

choice, be it Indian, Chinese or any other delicious variety, all sense of taste and portion control goes out of the window. Why order sufficient for you and your partner, when the Maharajah's Banquet Special is beckoning or the Emperor's Platter is on special? Oh yes, and we'd better have some poppadoms/nan bread/prawn crackers and fortune cookies as a little extra. Then, when you don't get through it all, you end up filling the fridge with those handy foil containers. These are then thrown out untouched seven days later.

Talking Animals (Films About)

Except for a few members of the parrot family, animals cannot talk. Except in Hollywood, that is, where chatting creatures are often more articulate than Arnold Schwarzenegger, Sylvester Stallone and Vin Diesel combined. Back in the 1950s Disney cornered the market in animated anthropomorphic animals. In the past twenty years, however, membership in this freakily popular category has swelled to include everything from a stock-market-savvy horse in *Hot to Trot* to Danny DeVito- and Diane Keaton-voiced dogs in *Look Who's Talking Now*, to a dog with marginal language skills in *Scooby-Doo*, to entire menageries of babbling beasts in *Babe*, *Dr Dolittle*, *Stuart Little* and their sequels. Which all begs the question: If animals could really talk, wouldn't we be terrified of what they had to say? See also **Talking Animals Who Die (Films About)**; *Scooby-Doo*.

Talking Animals Who Die (Films About)

What's more embarrassing than enjoying a film featuring a talking animal? How about crying at a film featuring a talking animal? From Bambi's weeping for his plugged mamma to the eponymous spider buying the farm in *Charlotte's Web* to the Lion King senior getting trampled, many a guilty tear has been shed for beasts that not only don't exist but *could not* exist. See also **Talking Animals (Films About)**; **Tearjerker Films (for Men)**.

Tambourines

Children who are given tambourines in music lessons at school know exactly what it means: they can't sing or are too cack-handed to handle a real instrument. It's a sad legacy for a device that was played in ancient China, India, and Egypt. When Miriam celebrated the Israelites' escape from Egypt, she did so by banging on her tambourine. In the nineteenth century, composers such as Berlioz even wrote parts for it in some of their works. The instrument has truly come down in the world since the birth of rock and roll, when tambourines were given to singers so they could look busy during instrumental bridges.

Tattoos

Who would willingly volunteer to have a needle stuck in their arm 3,000 times each minute, for minutes on end, without any sort of painkiller to take the edge off? Well, there are over 700 tattoo parlours in the UK, so you do the 'math'. Made by injecting pigment under the skin, tattoos probably pre-date human civilization. Yet like getting pregnant at school or partying too hard at uni and dropping out, getting tattooed is one of those youthful lapses in judgement that can follow you for the rest of your life. Today's modern primitives use them as a way to record their feelings. The problem, of course, is that our feelings change over time (art celebrating an ex-wife no longer feels quite right; celtic tribal patterns no longer tally with a thirty-something bank manager's worldview) – which is why another big business is tattoo removal.

Taxis

They are nice and shiny and take you wherever you want to go, so what is there to feel guilty about? Perhaps it's the fact that in most city gridlocks it is actually cheaper to fly to Nice by easyJet than to get from the pub to a cashpoint to a kebab shop and home? But that said, you are never going to get a cabbie to take you to Nice – 'not South of the River' – not at this time of night

Tearjerker Films (for Men)

Hollywood expends a great deal of effort getting women to cry tears of either sadness or joy. What's more difficult is getting men to cry. Men prefer to get angry during films and then see someone take revenge. At least, that's what they say. But the truth is, men like to cry, too – only on their own terms. A few things can get them to well up, including tales of self-less heroism and friendship (*Saving Private Ryan*), explorations of the father/son relationship (*Field of Dreams*), and, first and foremost, stories in which dogs are in danger. If you'd like to test this theory, tell a man that you've rented a copy of *Old Yeller* and ask if he'll watch it with you. When he refuses, offer him £20. When he refuses again, offer him £50. Chances are he still won't do it, even if you offer him a hundred. See also **Chick Flicks (In Which Someone Dies)**; **Talking Animals Who Die (Films About)**.

Tears For Fears

The original sort of pop psychology, Tears For Fears are Bath duo Roland Orzabal and Curt Smith, who saw fit to marry their knowledge of mind matters with shiny melodic hooks. Yes, they took themselves ever so slightly seriously. Yes, they hated each other's guts. Yes, they were never cool. But you can't deny their ear for a song – as Gary Jules' number one cover of 'Mad World' showed. *Songs From the Big Chair* was their *X&Y*, and the world was similarly theirs in 1985. They then blew it by spending five years recording the follow-up, lapsing into Beatle-ology a good five years before Oasis ended up doing the same thing. *Smash Hits* had a long running joke about Roland Orzabal and a kangaroo, which we never quite understood.

Teenage Boys Losing Their Virginity (Films About)

During the early-to-mid 1980s it seemed as if there were almost as many teenage boys-trying-to-lose-their-virginity films as there were actual teenage boys trying to lose their virginity. The line-up includes *Porky's* (where the objects of lust include a young Kim Cattrall), *Class* (Andrew McCarthy scoring with his best friend's mum), *Revenge of the Nerds* (with a pre-*E.R.* Anthony Edwards), *Private Lessons* (Sylvia 'Emmanuelle' Kristel's stab at legitimacy), *Homework* (Joan Collins gets it on with her daughter's boyfriend), and *Losin' It* (based on the extremely unlikely premise that Tom Cruise was struggling to get any). And that's just for starters. Far from being a creation of the

Eighties, the genre goes back to such respectable films as 1971's *The Summer of '42* (which includes the mother of all condom-buying scenes) and 1969's *Last Summer* (in which Richard 'John-Boy Walton' Thomas and *X-Men* senator Bruce Davison are all worked up about Barbara Hershey). Today the action continues most famously (and most graphically) in the *American Pie* series. Apparently the desire to watch incompetent, horny teenagers experience first-time sexual encounters even more embarrassing than yours is timeless. See also **Collins, Joan**; **Emmanuelle (Films Featuring the Character of)**; *Waltons, The*.

Teletubbies

There's nothing wrong with watching this programme if you're part of its target audience: one-year-olds. There's something *very* wrong with watching it if you're a teenager, student, or, even worse, a fully-fledged adult. Either a) at some point during your childhood you spent a great deal of time unconscious at the bottom of a swimming pool; or b) you smoke far too much weed. And since you have to be home in the middle of the day (as opposed to at school or working) to be an adult Teletubbies fan, we're guessing b). See also **Marijuana**.

Televised US Court Cases

Court cases in the UK come with their own covering of dust, a man doing very bad crayon sketches in the corner, and a judge who has been asleep since 1874, only waking up to enquire what a gazza is, and whether flogging is still on the statute book. In America however, justice rocks. To those that argue that bringing cameras in would reduce the legal system to a branch of showbiz, we say Judge Judy wants to see you in her chambers.

Tequila

Derived from the spiny agave plant, tequila, unlike its snobbier distilled cousins, is used primarily for just one thing: messing people up. If you're planning a really ugly stag party, or just a quiet evening of getting wasted on the sofa, we've got the drink for you.

Terry and June

How revisionist do we get when it comes to our classic comedies? Ronnie Barker is a comic legend, but when he died and the plaudits rolled in, where was the dissenting voice, saying, 'Hang on, wasn't *Open All Hours* a pile of old toss?' In our opinion, *Terry and June* was no worse and yet continues to remain held down as the nadir of all sitcoms. We say, yes it was middle class, mid-life, middle England to its cushiony core, but Terry Scott and June Whitfield did sterling comedy service in getting 10 million people to tune in every week. We'd never admit it, of course, but we can't have been the only people watching it.

Test Driving Cars You Can't Possibly Afford

The perfect weekend pursuit. Dress smartly, park your clapped-out old banger round the corner from the glistening Porsche showroom, buy a *Financial Times* en route and then saunter in whilst talking loudly on your mobile phone about the FTSE, the TECHMARK and the fact that you are meeting Julian and Guy later in Cannes. Wander over to the car of your choice – we're thinking maybe the Carrera GT or the Boxster – and bend down to look critically at some feature or other. Hang up your call and click your fingers – enjoy the sight of the salesmen racing towards you – and then ask a few questions guaranteed to get their financial juices flowing. 'If I buy in bulk, what discount could you do me?' usually does the trick. Ask for a test drive, get into the car and turn the top-of-the-range stereo up to full volume (to drown out any sales patter) and then go off for a leisurely hour-long drive, putting the car through its paces, jumping the odd red light and being pretty cavalier about such technicalities as speed limits, before skidding back into the forecourt. Step out, brush yourself down and hand the keys back to the expectant-looking dealer, who is already calculating his bonus and imagining himself holding the trophy for Dealer Of the Month; look him in the eyes and say, 'Sorry old boy – I just don't like the colour.' Next week select the Lamborghini showroom and start again.

The War of the Worlds (Jeff Wayne's Musical Version of)

In the twilight of the progressive rock era, when Rick Wakeman had inflated the concept album to ridiculous heights with his 'King Arthur on ice' venture (really!), Jeff Wayne somehow managed to get a deal for his epic musical version of the original 'alien invasion' story *The War of the Worlds*. Astonishingly, it's something of a masterpiece; unlike many masterpieces it was loved in its time. The almost interminable disco symphony of 'The Eve of the War' was a huge hit, followed into the Top 10 by 'Forever Autumn'. None of this would elevate it above the ordinary however, if it were not for the gravelly gravitas of Richard Burton's inimitable narration. At the time we may have all been pinching our mum's safety pins to give our blazers that authentic Sex Pistols look, but secretly we loved *The War of the Worlds*, and many copies endured the quasi-Stalinist purges of record collections that took place all over Britain.

Theme Parks (Not Owned by Disney)

During a visit to an old-school theme park, Walt Disney (the man, not the corporation) allegedly looked around in disgust and decided he could build something better – a place that was clean, safe, and full of life-affirming fun. Thanks, Walt. But while the 'It's a Small World' ride is neat and all, a part of us pines for places that are just slightly less clean and calculating, and perhaps a touch more spontaneous, quirky, and (dare we say it?) scary. Welcome to the British theme park experience: Blackpool Pleasure Beach doesn't have year-round shirtsleeves weather, but it does have The Big One, which feels suspiciously like the Big Mistake as you ratchet your way to the top; Alton Towers has its classic corkscrew, perfect for cub scouts and their packed lunches. Chessington World of Adventures, Thorpe Park, Lightwater Valley . . . if you hadn't whined at your parents to take you as a child, only to get there and discover you were too short to go on any of the rides, you've missed out. See also **Parton, Dolly**; **Roller coasters (Enormous)**.

Theme Restaurants

Why simply have dinner when you can have dinner in a rainforest? Or on board a submarine? Or surrounded by

Hollywood props? Written off by epicureans as pathetically proletarian – understandable when the gift shop is often bigger than the kitchen – such eateries are a magnet for tourists and for people who get a guilty kick out of pretending to be a tourist. Of course, the chance of actually seeing Arnold Schwarzenegger eating at a Planet Hollywood or Keith Richards devouring a burger at the Hard Rock Café is about as likely as spotting a drumstick-chomping Henry VIII at Medieval Times.

Thomas, Terry
I say!

Thongs
The bum-floss revolution began in 1981 when Frederick Mellinger mass-marketed his 'scanty panty', now known simply as the thong. Formerly worn only by prostitutes and exotic dancers, his creations are now crammed up the cracks of chavs, Yummy Mummies and socialites alike, making these tiny T-shaped knickers the fastest-growing segment of the world's $2 US billion-a-year women's underwear business. So why have women tossed aside their traditional undies for these skimpy skivvies? If you'd ever spent a day at the office (or a night on the town) trying to nonchalantly dig a pair of cheek-creepers out of your derrière, you'd know. See also **Cotton Knickers (Enormous)**.

Thousand Island Dressing
This tangy condiment with the distinctive coral hue dates back to the early 1900s, when the wife of a fishing guide in the Thousand Island region of upstate New York introduced it as a dinner staple. Over the years, the enigmatic sauce has expanded its culinary horizons. Variations of the original recipe – mayonnaise and chilli sauce studded with finely chopped pickles, onions, olives, and hard-boiled egg – have graced the buns of fast food hamburgers, sealed the deal on Pizza Hut side-salads, and provided the dip for a million pre-dinner party snacks. The beauty of Thousand Island dressing, it seems, lies not so much in its own salty/sweet, creamy/crunchy mélange as it does in its ability to bring out the best

in other foods – though at a price. One serving equals about seventy calories.

3am Girls

The Happy Shopper Popbitch, 3am Girls stories consist of 'wicked whispers' that you saw on Ananova yesterday, and vicarious party hi-jinks with such luminaries as Dean Gaffney and that rubber-looking Geordie bloke off *Big Brother*. Somehow though, at 8 a.m. when you're nursing a nuclear-powered hangover on a lurching commuter train, leaning over someone else's paper to squint at the 3am Girls' frothy blend of harmless gossip and shameless Elton-worship is exactly what you need. See also **Popbitch**.

Three Tenors, The

What do you do if you'd like to be an opera fan but simply can't stomach actual opera? You join the masses who, following Italia 90, either went to live concerts or bought the CDs of that dreamed-up-in-marketing-heaven opera star triumvirate, Luciano Pavarotti, José Carreras, and Plácido Domingo. Thanks to their collaboration, arena audiences and television viewers can experience opera without having to face the fat lady.

Thriller

Don't bother denying that you owned this album. Or that you watched the videos it inspired or danced to the title track, or 'Beat It', or 'Billie Jean', or 'PYT' or . . . After all, this best-selling record has moved an incredible 45 million units since its 1982 release. That's enough to provide one for every citizen of Canada, with Cuba thrown in. But more to the point, it's enough for everyone who happened to be in their teens or early twenties during the early 1980s.

Perhaps inevitably, the album's overwhelming success cast a pall on Jackson's future work. After all, when you sell 45 million of *anything*, whatever comes next is bound to be a letdown. The Gloved One's record sales inevitably fell, and his image and music became appallingly dated. In no time those

Thriller albums were relegated to the back of the wardrobe, right next to all those red leather jackets. See also **Jackson Family, The; Jackson, Michael; 'Members Only' Jackets**.

Time-Life Books

These mammoth, multi-volume book sets, which explored everything from the Second World War to the occult, first hit the market in 1961. Ordering them was like buying a magazine – albeit one that kept harping on the same subject and that you never threw away. In most cases a new volume would arrive each month, sometimes for years on end. Buying them wasn't exactly a sign of intellectual prowess. In fact, displaying a shelf-snapping set in public was akin to framing a swimming certificate. See also **Box Sets**.

Tipping (Not)

'That'll be £13, mate,' says the cabbie as you hand over three crisp fivers. He counts out the change and holds the two pound coins in a way that already suggests ownership. There is a discernible moment – your eyes meet and you are about to say 'Keep the change,' when your mind rewinds through your short half-hour relationship. You remember his convenient deafness when you asked for help with your cases, the distinct sucking of teeth when you asked for your destination, the lurching round corners and the barely contained road rage and you hear yourself saying 'Thanks mate – can I have a receipt please?' as you pocket the change and smile inwardly.

Titmuss, Abi

Abi's attractiveness to Britain's menfolk is rooted not so much in her pleasingly curvy figure, nor the slightly wonky eye that gives her the air of having someone's little chap bobbing a few inches in front of her. In fact Ms Titmuss owes her appeal principally to the video downloaded by every red-blooded Internet user which demonstrates very clearly what an absolute *sport* she is. It's notable that the video in question began its journey from inbox to inbox under the name JOHN_LESLIE.AVI but rapidly became ABI.WMV when people realized who the *real* star of the show was. Since the dawn of the *Carry On* era, the

British public has always loved a dirty nurse, and Abi is – we are pleased to say – the dirtiest nurse available today. See also **Leslie, John**; *Celebrity Love Island*.

Today With Des and Mel

Des O'Connor has never been Michael Parkinson. But his *Des O'Connor Tonight* programme saw him manfully prop up the ITV schedule for decades. Then came the switch to daytime and one of the most bizarre couplings ever to feature on television. Mel, best known for appearing on those adverts for Boddington's, is undoubtedly an attractive woman. Des, let's be fair, is a consummate host and an old hand at keeping things going. But never has there been a double act that is so much less than the sum of their parts. Yet strangely, in one of those inverse law things, it is their utter lack of chemistry that makes the show so watchable.

Tomb Raider See **Croft, Lara**.

Top Gear

Auto-eroticism for the mullet-wearing generation, *Top Gear* is presented by people you actually want to run over – Jeremy 'Roger Mellie' Clarkson cavorts around looking like a toffee-apple in denim, Richard 'panda eyes' Hammond (who gets smaller every week) hangs on his every word like some stalker fan and James May is surely only employed to make the other two look good? The studio audience are on the verge of orgasm at every *bon mot* or 'totally spontaneous' argument between the guys, and a character called The Stig gets to help celebrities terrify their insurers on a test track. Our favourite highlights include the guys racing each other to Switzerland – JC in a Ferrari and RH/JM by plane, train and automobile; JC being chased round a racetrack in his Lotus by an Apache attack helicopter trying to get 'missile lock' on him and a race between Hammond in a bobsleigh and a rally driver down the side of a mountain in Sweden. Unmissable even if you have never driven a car.

Top Gun

This formulaic 1986 film allegedly concerns a lone wolf fighter pilot who learns about teamwork while attending the Navy's

Fighter Weapons (Top Gun) School. In truth, it was one of the Eighties' slicker salutes to cinema's dynamic duo, sex and violence. Blokes enjoyed the aerial dogfights and ogling Kelly McGillis. Women savoured the famous volleyball scene and the shots of Val Kilmer and Tom Cruise lounging, post-mission, in towels in the locker room. Interestingly, there aren't any shower facilities for pilots at the real Top Gun school. See also *Cocktail*.

Top of the Pops

TOTP has been the BBC's flagship, and indeed often only, popular music show for forty years. Regular viewers have been treated to at least two golden ages of *The Pops* – coinciding roughly with the two great eras of dressing up in pop. In the early days of colour television the glam rock era gave rise to some distinctly temerarious wardrobe choices, with naturals like David Bowie draping an ambiguous arm round his guitarist's shoulders and making us all confused, or journeymen like the Sweet draping an ill-advised boa round their thickset bodies and making us feel like becoming a transvestite bricklayer was a valid career path. Interspersed between these alarming sights were periods of relative sartorial normalcy, if you can call Jimmy Savile's tracksuit choices, DLT's beard decision, or Noel Edmonds' inexplicable Robin Hood hat normal. A decade later the New Romantic era once more celebrated the notion of dressing up like a pranny to make music, and the screen was once more alive with lamé and mullets. This time the interstitial shouting was undertaken by the likes of John Peel (avuncular), Janice Long (sororal), or Kid 'Kid' Jensen (kid). The venerable pop warhorse has recently been put out to grass but rumours of its demise are premature and in truth it's merely lying dormant waiting to blossom in yet another great epoch of big girls' blouses in Pop.

Tours (Guided)

Travel scribes make a big deal about the difference between travelling and touring. The clear implication being that travelling – making it up yourself – is much preferable to touring – following a guide's predetermined plan. Yet sometimes you don't want to blaze new trails, take risks with untested eateries, and have to strike up acquaintances on your own. And you don't want to keep flipping through tour books to explain why the church you just passed is of historical significance. Guided tours eliminate those risks, making sure your trip is close to exactly that of everyone else's. When you finish, you really will have been there, done that, bought the T-shirt – because chances are the T-shirt is part of the package. See also **T-shirts (Souvenir)**.

Tracksuit Bottoms

It is a testament to the staying power of cotton blend fabric and stretchy waistbands that trackie bottoms have managed to survive several public relations nightmares, ranging from a general association with obesity (Russell Athletic, a leading manufacturer of slouchwear, offers sizes up to 4XL) to an out-and-out mockery on an episode of *Seinfeld* – the one in which Jerry told a dressed-down George, 'You know the message you're sending out to the world with these sweatpants? You're telling the world, "I give up".' Maybe so. But when it comes to watching videos, sleeping in, or eating ice cream directly from the tub, no other garment will do.

Trisha

As boxing is a theatrical version of a pub brawl, so the Trisha show is a formalized series of family disagreements that should by rights have been aired in the aisles of the nearest Lidl. No lessons are learned from the endless hours of fishwife caterwauling, and no one ever comes across in a flattering light. There are no heroes, and few victims; just an interminable parade of emotionally incontinent, marginally literate dupes who seem to genuinely believe that exhibiting the tawdry details of their inconsequential love lives will lend them a temporary glamour. Of course it won't, but boy oh boy, it's funny!

Trivial Pursuit (Winning at)

Okay, smarty-pants, so what if you were the most intimidating Trivial Pursuit player in your circle of friends/sixth-form/family?

It's not like it got you into a better university or helped you land a better job. After all, it's not called Useful Knowledge Pursuit. But that didn't stop you from feeling really, really good when you nailed a question, especially a History one. See also **Pictionary**.

Trolley Food

One of the delights of travelling by train is the Man With The Trolley. This mystical figure starts off at the opposite end of the train to whichever end you're sitting at, so by the time he reaches you, you're salivating for everything he has to offer. He'll sell you a can of cider at eight in the morning. Or maybe just a cup of tea. Oh, and we'll have a packet of Jaffa Cakes as well.

T-Shirts (Souvenir)

In visiting just about any destination, whether it's a Caribbean island or the nearest Hard Rock Café, it's common practice to pick up a (usually overpriced) souvenir T-shirt. Yet, rarely do we consider why we make such an extraneous purchase. Surely we have enough torso coverings at home. And the experience is unlikely to have been so great that we just *have* to spend additional money to commemorate it. Perhaps we get them because buying and wearing such a garment is a public announcement that you are a worldly person. And buying one for a friend or family member who didn't make the journey – especially one that offers some variation of 'My Grandma Went to Tenerife and All I Got Was This Crap T-Shirt' – is a sign that you really *didn't* want to buy a souvenir but felt the nasty pull of obligation. See also **Theme Restaurants**.

Turner Prize, The

We don't know much about art, but we know that we love the annual debate generated by the Turner Prize. The tabloids invariably go for the 'My five-year-old could have done better' angle, the broadsheets for the 'This is important and maybe you aren't intelligent enough to "get it"' message – and somewhere in the middle we suspect the artistic community is cracking the tiniest of smiles. Much as we hate to indulge them, they MUST have been having a laugh when, in 2001, Madonna handed £20k to Martin Creed for his work 'The Lights Going On and Off', an empty room in which the lights, erm . . . went on and off. The judges admired his Turner Prize piece for its 'strength, rigour, wit and sensitivity to the site'. Whatever next? A pile of bricks?

TV Catchphrases (Quoting)

We all have mental filters to strain out useless stimuli, but they aren't foolproof. For instance, sometimes, often without realizing it, we lift dialogue straight out of TV shows and use it in day-to-day conversation. Painful as it is to admit, rare is the person who has never replaced their standard discourse with such tube-ified nuggets of wisdom as 'Suits you, sir' (*The Fast Show*), 'How *you* doin'?' (*Friends*), 'Am I bovvered?' (*Catherine Tate*), 'Lovely Jubbly' (*Only Fools and Horses*), 'Yeah but, no but' (*Little Britain*), 'Survey says' (*Family Fortunes*), 'Nice to see you . . . to see you? NICE!' (*Play Your Cards Right*). See also **Advert Catchphrases (Quoting of)**; **Alan Partridge Quoting**.

TV Mums (Lusting After)

Lonely is the TV watcher ashamed and confused by the odd stirring caused by Kathy Beale, Alexis Colby or Carmela Soprano. Needing serious help, however, is the one who has those same feelings for Madge Bishop, Dot Cotton or Marge Simpson.

TV Programmes Featuring Animal Protagonists

The plot of every episode of *Gentle Ben*, *Flipper* and *Lassie* (especially *Lassie*) was pretty much the same: stupid humans get into trouble; smart animal bails them out. Why did these shows hold such fascination? Perhaps because we knew there were damn few people we could rely on as completely as these folks did their pets. Let's face it: a dog doesn't count how many drunks you're up against in a pub fight before deciding whether to admit he knows you. What's that, Skippy? This plot line is a pile of pants? See also *Lassie*.

TV Theme Tunes (Instrumental)

TV themes that lack vocal accompaniment are slightly (but only slightly) less infectious than the ones with words. For some reason, though there is no scientific evidence to support it, they usually seem to start rattling through our brains as we drive. Who among us, while sweating out a red light or tooling down the open road, hasn't felt the *Miami Vice* theme tickling their cerebellum, or unconsciously hummed the 'Theme From *The A-Team*'? See also **TV Theme Tunes (Vocal)**.

TV Theme Tunes (Vocal)

They welcome us into our favourite sitcoms or TV dramas. Some, such as 'I'll Be There For You' (the theme to *Friends*) and 'Neighbours' (the theme to, well, *Neighbours*) even become hit singles. Of course, when they are played on the radio there's always that awkward moment when, in an effort to stretch the song to a radio-acceptable length (no station would play a thirty-second song), the vocalist chimes in with a second, previously unheard chorus – or a guitar bridge from nowhere. But think about it this way: at least they keep Chas and Dave from the streets.

Twenty-Four-Hour Flu Bug, The

The 24 hour flu bug, or Workus Skivus to give it its Latin name, is a vicious disease that can strike unsuspecting individuals down the morning after a long night down the pub. Symptoms include tiredness and a banging headache, and speaking in a blatantly put on croaky voice when talking on the phone to your boss. Although the condition may at first appear critical, a sustained dose of daytime television and copious buckets of coffee normally sees the sufferer through, allowing them to return to work bright-eyed and bushy tailed the following morning.

Twilight Zone, The

Want to see people make extremely ill-advised bargains with Satan? Or travel back in time to change history for the better, only to bugger things up even worse? How about extraterrestrial encounters in which the 'aliens' turn out to be cannibals, microscopic in size, a thousand feet tall, or – most mind-blowing of all – us? Well then, this is the show for you. Though the *Zone* long ago devolved from cutting-edge television into a cultural cliché, it's still fun to look for all the soon-to-be-celebrities who appeared there. Omigod, is that Robert Duvall in love with a miniature doll? Is that William Shatner getting spooked by a fortune-telling machine? And look, here comes Burt Reynolds! See also **Reynolds, Burt**; **Shatner, William**; *Star Trek*; *Star Wars*.

Twister

Created by Milton Bradley in 1966, it was called 'sex in a box' by detractors. Consisting of a plastic sheet dotted with rows of coloured circles, Twister's rules call for contestants to follow the directions of a spinner and place a hand or foot on appropriate spots. In no time at all participants get tied up in entertaining and (if you're with the right person) suggestive knots. American TV host Johnny Carson and Eva Gabor demonstrated the erotic potential of the game, and sent sales soaring, when they played a round (or played around, depending on your perspective) on *The Tonight Show*. Overnight, Twister became (and remains) a favourite with drunk students everywhere. See also **Games, Party**.

Txt msgN

Yes we do lov sendg a txt Nstead of tlkN OTP or btr stil face 2 face. NI bt we snd millions a yr n r txt lyfs av nvr bn btr.

U-V

UFOs (Books and TV Documentaries About)

It's a great big universe out there, so it's not such a stretch to believe that our lonely little planet may not be the only one supporting intelligent life. It is a stretch, however, to believe that creatures from some  other world are anally probing backwoods folk and creating elaborate designs in cornfields. Yet television specials such as *UFOs: Best Evidence Ever Caught on Tape* and *Alien Autopsy: Fact or Fiction* (which Fox TV in the States ultimately admitted was a hoax), and books including *Chariots of the Gods* continue to find audiences. Why? Because beyond the hardcore believe-anything yokel, there's a large group of people who may not admit it publicly, but privately wish for a world as interesting as the ones in science-fiction novels and films. Plus there are a few people who like the idea of surprise anal probes. See also **Autopsies (Television)**; *Weekly World News*.

UK Gold

What, exactly, happens to old episodes of *The Bill*? The answer is, they end up on UK Gold, a cable and satellite station that shows a heaving list of old 'classics' from dusk to dawn. These days the schedule might include everything from *EastEnders* to *Minder* to *Eldorado*. OK, maybe not the last one. The question is, what does it say about people who tune in to catch episodes of shows that weren't worth watching the *first* time around?

Unauthorized Biographies

Apart from a handful of shameless stars (step forward Mötley Crüe), few autobiographers reveal as much dirt as we really want from a life-of-the-rich-and/or-famous story. For that, we have to turn to unauthorized biographers such as Kitty Kelley, who slung the mud on Frank Sinatra, Jackie Onassis, and the British Royal Family. How much of what she said was true? Do you really care? See also **Royal Family, The**.

Unbelievable Sporting Comebacks (Films About)

This hoary cinematic genre is the Y-chromosome version of the chick flick. First take the typical romantic tearjerker plot: boy pursues girl; boy almost loses girl; boy finally wins girl. Now substitute the word 'championship' for 'girl' and you've got the rationale for everything from *Knute Rockne, All American* to *The Fish That Saved Pittsburgh*. The story is of course formulaic, but the male response to either a lone warrior battling for respect (*Rocky*) or a group of blokes working hard to become a team (*Mean Machine*, *The Longest Yard*) is so Pavlovian that it's almost impossible to screw up. Done right, a good sporting comeback film makes even the most sedentary male want to hit the gym for a few sets of bench presses – even if the heaviest thing he's ever lifted is a can of beer. See also *Escape to Victory*, **Rocky Movies**; **Stallone, Sylvester**; **Tearjerker Films (For Men)**

Unlicensed Minicabs

We know we shouldn't use them. We know we should go to the taxi rank and queue up with everyone else. But really. It's two in the morning, we've left the club, it's freezing cold, and this nice man is offering me a warm seat in his car for a tenner. So what if it appears he can't actually drive? So what if his understanding of the English language is so rudimentary he can't actually read the road signs (you think this is an exaggeration? I once got a minicab to Heathrow and the driver got there by following the pictures of the planes). And OK, so maybe there's the chance of being mugged or buggered or God knows what, but think of this added frisson as a way of staying awake, allowing you to share such cultural knowledge as how the red circle with a white line in the middle means 'No Entry'.

Upstairs, Downstairs

Monstrously popular, especially in the States, more than twenty years after it was first broadcast, *Upstairs, Downstairs* was perhaps the first great Sunday night TV series. Existing somewhere between a costume drama and a soap, it followed the fortunes of a prosperous London family from the early years of the twentieth century through to the Wall Street Crash, taking in the sinking of the *Titanic*, World War One and the loss of a good many valuable brooches. Even now, with the more critical modern eye detecting wobbly sets and self-contradictory scripts, it has that special Sunday night power which has us calling for a curry rather than stepping into the kitchen for fear of missing something. Although ostensibly aimed at a female market there was enough eye-candy in the forms of the porcelain-skinned Nicola Paget and the endearingly cherubic Pauline Collins to retain the interest of the male viewer.

Urban Myths

Urban myths are nothing new. The compulsion to pass fictional weird/scary/funny tales off as factual is as old as the human race. Remember the one about the fisherman who lost his ring at the beach, then found it years later while cleaning a fish he caught? Check the work of the Greek historian Thucydides and you'll find almost the exact same tale attributed to Croesus, king of Lydia, in roughly 550 B.C. And Thucydides, just like the bloke at work who told you about the family who adopted a chihuahua that turned out to be a rat, swore it was true. Such whoppers never go away; they just get updated. For instance, the lead character in the story of the tall black man in the elevator who says, 'Sit, Lady' to his dog, only to terrify an elderly white woman in front of him, has morphed over the years from Reggie Jackson to Eddie Murphy to P Diddy.

How do you spot an urban myth? If you hear slightly different versions of the story from several people, if the teller can't say exactly where it happened or who it happened to, or, most importantly, if the tale sounds like the plot of a *Twilight Zone* episode, you're probably hearing a whopper. Not that this makes them any less fun. See also **Almond, Marc**; **Gere, Richard**; **Michael, George**; **Nicks, Stevie**; *Twilight Zone, The*.

Vampire Novels

When Bram Stoker's novel *Dracula* was first published in 1897, it became a huge hit by broaching (albeit obliquely) topics that Victorians didn't usually talk about: sex, rape, homoerotica, women's liberation and so on. Today's vampire novels, though not as groundbreaking as *Dracula*, lurk in that same psycho-sexual netherworld. Want homoerotica? Anne Rice's 'vampire chronicles' will oblige. There are even sub-genres of lesbian vampire novels, action/adventure vampire books, and 'romantic' neck-biter novels. Perhaps it's the fact that, unlike Frankenstein's monster, a mummy, or a werewolf, the reader can imagine him or herself hanging out (or at least holding a conversation) with one of these suave gentlemen. Or perhaps it's just the sex thing that makes blood suckers by far the most popular literary monsters. Try to name another semi-mainstream book category with so many penetration scenes and (usually one-way) exchanges of bodily fluids. See also **Rice, Anne**.

Van Damme, Jean-Claude

Belgium's answer to Chuck Norris once said 'I am the Fred Astaire of karate'. Unfortunately, he's also the Action Man of acting. See also **Kung Fu Films**; **Norris, Chuck**.

Velcro (The Sound of Ripping it Open)

Whether you are wearing fetish handcuffs or sat in a space shuttle taking off your space boots, the pleasure and power we feel when we rip apart Velcro surely comes primarily from that distinctive noise – though whether it sounds like a hundred tiny balloons being sequentially popped in an echo-chamber or like a jar of marbles being dropped onto a tin roof during a rainstorm is probably best left to be decided by a high-level debate, probably hosted by Melvyn Bragg on Radio 4. Whatever it sounds like, no one can deny that sense of anticipation when you grasp the two constituent parts (the furry bit and the hooky bit) and the moment is upon you. The connection with dogs and Switzerland may not be immediately obvious but in the summer of 1948 Swiss amateur mountaineer and inventor George de Mestral took his dog for a walk. The eureka moment occurred when he returned home and noted, with some annoyance, that both he and his furry friend were covered in burrs from plants they had brushed past. Checking out his trousers under a microscope, he saw that the small hooks on the little burrs had anchored themselves to the fabric of his clothing. Obviously the idea to create a product that would rival the zip was greeted with bemusement and, one imagines, laughter, but by 1955, Velcro™ hit the ground running and astronauts and fetishists have never looked back. Rippppp.

Velour
There are certain risks associated with wearing clothing made out of a fabric so soft and plush you can't resist running your hands up and down its soothing nap, sometimes at inopportune moments. If this ever happens, simply explain to the people staring at you that it's not your fault a velour track suit feels like an irresistible cross between satin sheets and kitten fur.

Vending Machines
It might appear at first glance that vending machines exist to provide food and drink for thirsty and hungry people. In reality, of course, they are there to provide light relief for the rest of us, an opportunity to mock the afflicted few who have yet to realize that however much money they put in, they're not going to get anything out. If a vending machine is feeling helpful, it might still offer some form of pricing guide. Usually, however, it is a case of sliding in a selection of coins and hoping for the best. What are the chances of the machine not having run out of the can of fizzy drink you actually want? We'll tell you: not big. You can then either select the apple flavoured Soya milk concoction that no one else wanted either, or have your two pound coin returned. In five pence pieces.

Ventriloquists

Occupying a rung on the ladder of entertainment respectability somewhere between celebrity impersonators and magicians, ventriloquists spend their careers feeding straight lines to dummies. Yet while most people aren't willing to admit it, there's a reason why acts as varied as Keith Harris (and Orville), Bob Carolgees (and Spit) and Lord Charles all had their days in the variety show sun. A good ventriloquist delivers the laughs of a comedy act combined with the awe inspired by an expert juggling team. Who can honestly say that at some time in their childhood they haven't put their hand in a sock and tried to order a 'gottle of geer' in front of the mirror. See also **Celebrity Impersonators**; **Variety Shows**.

Very Hungry Caterpillar, The

Yes, we know it's a children's book, but is it only us to whom this Eric Carle tale still brings a warm glow? It's a proper story to start with, with a beginning, a middle and an end: a caterpillar that turns into a beautiful butterfly – now that's what we call character development. But it's also all that food he makes his furry way through as he fattens himself up: each picture with a caterpiller sized hole through the middle of it. After one particularly heavy pig out, he wakes up the following morning feeling a bit poorly. But then he has a green leaf and feels a lot better. There's a message for us all there. No doubt the children of today would far rather be read some story with guns and computers and wizards and shit in. We say, tough: we're the one who can read, and it's caterpillars for you, junior.

Vettriano, Jack

In order to be taken seriously as an artist these days, you have to put your unmade bed on display, or make a tent covered with the names of everyone you've shagged. And for those of us mortals who aren't Charles Saatchi, putting up a shark in formaldehyde in our sitting room just isn't an option. Enter Jack Vettriano. He is (cover your ears Tracy and Damien) a painter. One part traditionalist to two parts Athena poster, you might not have heard of Jack, and you certainly won't have been to his retrospective, but he is by far the most successful artist in this country. Indeed, you probably know more Vettriano than you think: that picture of the couple dancing on the beach with the butler and the umbrella, the one you take down when your arty friends come round? That's him. And many more besides.

VH1's *Behind the Music*
Let magazines from *Rolling Stone* to the *NME* report on the band of the moment. Since 1997, VH1's *Behind the Music* series has been the place to turn to for career-spanning post-mortems of yesterday's hit-makers. The musical equivalent of *This is Your Life*, it's a programme as addictive as the illegal drugs that wrecked the careers of many of the show's subjects. The more the band is a guilty pleasure in and of itself – M.C. Hammer, Meat Loaf, Milli Vanilli, Styx – the better the *Behind the Music* report. That's because the clips and interviews remind us that we actually took these acts seriously once upon a time. See also **Meat Loaf (The Singer)**.

Vibrators
There's a really good reason why your Bel Ami Lukas uncut with removable foreskin, your reflective gel veined eighteen-inch Double Dong, your Chasey Lane Slimline G and your Rhythm Master Bouncing Cannon are kept hidden in your underwear drawer. 'Nuff said.

Village People, The
It's a measure of our collective naïvety that when this group (conceived by record producer Jacques Morali as a spoof of homosexual stereotypes) became famous in 1978 with 'Y.M.C.A.' and 'In the Navy', many in the mainstream didn't realize the songs were about *having gay sex* at the Y.M.C.A and in the navy. Indeed, the U.S. Navy was so clueless that it lent the group a destroyer to use in a video. And it wasn't as if they were trying to keep it a secret. The People danced around dressed as construction workers, cowboys, and pretty much every other gay archetype you'd care to name, short of Judy Garland. See also **Garland, Judy**.

Viz

Although even the creators of this British institution can't remember exactly when they started selling their freewheeling mixture of schoolboy humour and scatological offensiveness, all major authorities agree that it was something like twenty-five years ago. The formula has varied very little in all that time: loose parodies of characters from the *Beano* or *Topper*, strips based unapologetically on one joke, demented letters and top tips, with the occasional wicked parody of Franklin Mint advertisements. Somehow the same joke just keeps on getting funnier. Somehow we manage not to care about the constantly escalating cover price, or those sniffy looks we get from less-juvenile commuters on the train home from work. Characters like flatulent everyman Johnny Fartpants, or inept TV presenter Roger Mellie have become part of British culture – perhaps in part because they're a little bit more like the people we see in our everyday lives than the idealized scamps of the comics that inspired *Viz*; or more probably, because they're just so damned funny.

Vomit (Fake)

In the world of prepackaged practical jokes – the fart powder, the impossible-to-open sugar packet, the insect in the ice cube – fake sick reigns supreme. Why? Because it actually does what it is designed to do. Just drop it on the floor and an unsuspecting victim may well gasp with the sudden belief that someone blew chunks. The best models (including Whoops, Vomit, and Vomit Oops!) are crafted with the understanding that the right mix of carrots/sweetcorn/peas and liquid-like areas makes all the difference. See also **Practical Jokes**; **Whoopee Cushions**; **Dog Pooh (Fake)**.

Wade's Whimsies

The Wade family pottery business started up in around 1810, but it wasn't until 1953 – when then owner Sir George Wade came up with the notion of a range of small sculptures called 'Whimsies' to keep his factory busy during the postwar economic slowdown – that the company became a household nome. No one's pretending that these little figurines are great art or anything, but the lovable little china puppies, leprechauns riding snails, circus pie-throwing clowns and other assorted livestock can command astounding sums on eBay, and the idea that a ceramic ornament that we've had knocking around since our childhood might be *worth* something makes us feel clever. Like we're *investors* or something.

Walt Disney World

Since its 1971 opening, this mother of all theme parks has served as the default holiday choice for people who want to take an exotic trip without actually taking an exotic trip. Encompassing forty-seven square miles of central Florida real estate (that's twice the size of Manhattan), the 'World' features everything from a sanitized slice of Africa (Disney's Animal Kingdom) to a sex-free Hollywood (Disney-MGM Studios) to the original Magic Kingdom, home of such famous rides-turned-into-movies as Pirates of the Caribbean and the Haunted Mansion. But though it will never be fashionable, this hermetically sealed, *Truman*

Show-like complex does offer certain advantages. Parents can, if so inclined, shove their progeny out the hotel door first thing in the morning, then go shopping or relax by the pool while Sarah and Harry exhaust themselves waiting in interminable queues.

Waltons, The

Begun in 1971 as a tear-jerking Christmas made-for-TV film this story of a Depression-era American family made millions of viewers jealous for the good old days of abject poverty. With a folksy opening theme, a multi-generational cast and messages of love and tolerance, *The Waltons* kept us entranced for the best part of a decade. Well, except when one of the sister's husbands who was supposed to have died at Pearl Harbor turned up in Florida. *Then* we were just annoyed. The programme, Energizer-bunny-like, kept going and going despite a stroke suffered by Ellen Corby (Grandma Walton), the death of Grandpa Will Geer, the 1977 departure (and subsequent career disappearance) of Richard Thomas (John-Boy) and Michael Learned (his mother, Olivia), and the replacement of Richard Thomas – the one with the mole – with a different John-Boy (Robert Wightman). See also **Planet of the Apes Movies**; **Twilight Zone, The**.

Waltzer, The See Outdated Fair Rides.

War Films

The problem with war films is that to enjoy them you have to be somewhat blasé about seeing other people get shot. And not just a few people, but thousands. The other problem with war films is that most glorify (some intentionally, some unintentionally) what is without argument the most vile situation in which human beings could ever find themselves. The *other* other problem is that even 'realistic' films such as *Saving Private Ryan* don't come close to authenticity. OK, so the THX-enhanced flying lead sounds real and the torn bodies bleed in a very lifelike (deathlike?) manner, but everyone in the cinema knows he or she is going to walk away from the experience with life and limbs intact. Which is, needless to say, not the case on an actual battlefield.

Viewers who feel bad about getting off on the mayhem have several options. They can avail themselves of politically correct, mostly Vietnam-era films such as *The Deer Hunter* and *Platoon*; or they can watch daft, cartoonish efforts like the Rambo trilogy, but recognize them for what they are: entertainment that's about as realistic as a computer game. See also **Rambo Films**; **Tearjerker Films (For Men)**.

Wartime Singalongs

Very few of us endured the horrors and privations of the Home Front. Nevertheless, whenever we hear Max Bygraves or Roy Hudd (and it's generally one of those two) leading a chorus of 'We'll Meet Again' the lyrics somehow appear, unbidden, in our minds and we savour the mysterious pleasure of communal singing. It's hard to imagine people living in (say) 2040 linking arms to sing a Debbie Gibson or Johnny Hates Jazz classic.

Watching Television at the Gym

When spending time down at the local Fat Farm glistening like a putative Kelly Holmes or Matthew Pinsent on a state-of-the-art Cybex treadmill, the only things that makes all the hard work bearable are the multi-channel huge plasma screens facing you. The real joy is that you can be plugged in and pretend to be improving your mind with the brain-food of BBC *News at One* but actually be watching additive-rich VH-1 or junk-food MTV Bass on one of the other screens. And nobody need ever know . . . See also *Loose Women*; *People's Court (UK)*.

Watching W.A.S.Ps Trying to Get Down with the Kids

It's all about attitude and a sense of time and place. Much as we enjoy watching a white Anglo-Saxon Essex boy trying to live life to the full on a Friday night, when he starts dropping phrases like 'Wassupp – how's it hangin'?' when talking to his similarly white anglo-saxon 'bro' Gary from Accounts, discussing a recent upgrade to his vehicular transport in terms of having 'pimped his ride' and suggesting they relocate to a local hostelry combining drinking and dancing in search of some female company as 'cutting loose and sniffing out some honey-chicks at the 'hood jive-bar' then we will struggle not to giggle into our lagers. Honestly, this won't wash with us – the English language is sacrosanct so slip me some skin and I'll catch you later . . . er . . . dude.

Water Beds

Once used as a treatment for ulcers, water beds are said to be more therapeutic than a standard mattress. But even Charles Hall, the man credited with perfecting the concept while still a student at San Francisco State University in 1968, knew that such benefits weren't the water bed's main selling point. Why else would he have initially called them 'pleasure pits'? He made millions of dollars out of this sex-toy-pretending-to-be-furniture. Waterbeds reached their 1987 zenith when one trade group said that they accounted for more than a fifth of the American mattress industry. Alas, the business sprung a leak. These days, having a water bed is about as cool as having a designated sex room.

Waters, John

Now an icon of the independent film world, director John Waters was once just a dirty-minded cult filmmaker out to make cinema audiences vomit in their popcorn. He came close to achieving that with 1972's *Pink Flamingos*, in which a 'who's the most disgusting' competition climaxed with the on-camera consumption of dog pooh. Now that's entertainment! Yet the notoriety of that film led to more commerical efforts, including the scratch-and-sniff-enhanced *Polyester*, the surprisingly joyful *Hairspray*, and such films as *Serial Mom* and *Cecil B. DeMented*, which featured respectable actors such as Kathleen Turner and Melanie Griffith (though admittedly, both had already exceeded their sell-by dates). See also **Gimmicks, Film**; **Jokes, Sick**.

Wayne, John

Hollywood's prototypical action hero (born Marion Morrison) built his career playing the sort of men psychologists might call repressed: quiet, self-assured, more comfortable with horses and firearms than women. Of course, today's male knows how important it is to express himself, open up to the ladies in his life, get in touch with his feminine side, blah, blah, blah. And yet, when he watches *Rio Bravo*, *The Searchers*, *True Grit*, or pretty much anything else from the John Wayne cinematic canon, he can't help wishing *he* could be that tough under pressure. Because let's face it, when the shit hits the fan, very few people, male or female, find themselves desperately thinking, 'God, I wish Alan Alda were here.' See also **Rambo Films**; **Rocky Films**; **Schwarzenegger, Arnold**; **Stallone, Sylvester**.

Weather Channel, The

Meteorology at school used to be all about measuring rainfall in a plastic tube outside the Chemistry lab and seeing which way the weather vane was pointing. When you grew up, the weather became ubiquitous conversational foreplay with the likes of Michael Fish and Rob McElwee being viewed with a slightly bemused respect. But that has all changed. All of a sudden, those little magnetic clouds and Velcroed lightning strikes just went and grew up and got sexy. www.theweather-channel.com is pure hardcore weather with 24/7 updates on weather anywhere, anytime, anyplace. Suddenly, the ground temperature in Santa Barbara over a ten-hour period compared to the air pressure in Glasgow, complete with moving satellite images and digital barometric readings, has become danger-ously interesting. The Weather Channel even has a download-able screensaver featuring everything from hurricanes to heatwaves . . . apparently.

Weathermen (Fat and/or Jolly)

'I had a call from a woman saying there might be a hurricane tonight,' Michael Fish famously said in 1987. 'Well don't worry, there isn't.' Proving conclusively that weathermen always get things right (ahem) Michael Fish was the greatest of that dying breed: the eccentric weatherman. Together with Bill Giles and John Kettley, Fish brought what can only be described as a Peter Snow with a swingometer approach to forecasting. Sian Lloyd and computerized graphics just aren't the same, somehow.

Webber, Andrew Lloyd

Go on. Say you hated *Cats* and feel all superior. Even among much-mocked musicals buffs, it's safe to trash it. But just remember that *someone* kept the feline follies running for decades. And *Cats* is only the most obvious target of Andrew Lloyd Webber-bashing. The prolific composer has been taking flak ever since he offered up a high-pitched *Jesus Christ Superstar* to audiences in 1971 – a show once labelled sacrilegious and now treated like a fifth gospel. Since then, his music has graced (or disgraced, depending on your bent), such long-running West End and/or Broadway hits as *Evita*, *Starlight Express*, and *The Phantom of the Opera*. A lot of it is overblown. A lot of it is daft. But some of it is, admit it, rather catchy. See also *Cats*.

Weekly World News

You're waiting to pay at the supermarket when a tabloid catches your eye. The usual lurid headlines span the black-and-white cover, but everything, from the 'news' stories ('Feminists Want Robots to Replace Men!' 'Miracle Carp Says the End Is Near!') to the self-help pieces ('How You Can Tell If Your Neighbour Is a Time Traveller!' 'Improve Your Sex Life Tonight – The Amish Way!') seems too weird even for a supermarket rag. Congratulations, you've just entered the twisted alternate universe of the *Weekly World News*. Published by American Media (the same people responsible for the veracity-free zone *National Enquirer*), *WWN* peddles UFO and conspiracy theory-laced hokum so bizarre it would make Barnum blush. While morons may take it as gospel, the intelligentsia (there are many among the rag's roughly 1 million readers) laugh appreciatively at (what they perceive to be) ironic, self-referential humour of the highest order. Perhaps, so that no one misunderstands your motives, you should loudly state, 'I love this magazine for its naïve yet sophisticated, almost dadaist take on modern culture.' Or you could just toss it face-down on the conveyor belt and try not to make eye contact with the cashier.

Weighing Machines (at the Chemist's)

Yes, you've got some scales at home, but if you're feeling particularly svelte at the moment it's a waste of a punishing diet to weigh yourself in private. Rarer these days they may be, but for the true avoirdupois exhibitionist, very much worth seeking out are those scales that actually announce your weight to everyone in a five yard radius. It's the only way of making all those rice cakes worthwhile. See also **Blood Pressure Machines (At the Chemist's)**.

Weird Science
It had to happen eventually – a film that revolves around teenage boys who, thanks to those newfangled things called *computers*, create the perfect woman. Sort of a cross between *Bride of Frankenstein* and *Porky's*, this John Hughes film – who are we kidding, it really was a Kelly LeBrock film – could be the reason why armies of geeks turned from Dungeons and Dragons to the Internet. Many remember LeBrock's over-the-top, seventeen-year-old's-idea-of-va-va-voom entrance. Fewer remember that her character ends up behaving more like the boys' mum (okay, maybe a fit aunt) and less like a sex toy. See also *Breakfast Club, The*; **Teenage Boys Losing Their Virginity (Films About)**.

Werbeniuk, Bill
Big Bill was not your average sportsman. He wasn't even your average snooker player, but a one-man drinking machine who would down forty pints of alcohol during a playing session, on medical grounds. The booze, apparently, steadied his nerves. Our nerves would be steady too, on the grounds of lying unconscious on the floor, but somehow Bill played on. Some sportsmen try to put their opponents off through a mixture of posturing and sledging. Bill would lean over the table and let rip a fat one. Thank the Lord his trousers never scored a maximum break.

West End Musicals
Best viewed at a matinee with a maiden aunt in tow and leaving any sense of irony, realism or the ridiculous behind, the escapism-fest that is the West End musical is a curious artform. In the business that is show we have clapped, cheered and given standing ovations to an extraordinary collection of productions – shows

about talking, singing, dancing animals (*The Lion King*, *Cats*), things on wheels (*Starlight Express*), places (*Oklahoma!*, *Chicago*) and murderers (*Sweeney Todd*, *Les Misérables*, *The Woman In White*). Nothing beats a warm choc-ice, a £4 gin and tonic and the chance to watch two people tap-dancing their way through the Depression chased by a large cat on roller-skates whilst two hundred chorus girls rise up through the stage dressed as French peasants.

Westworld See **Crichton, Michael**; **Pre-*Star Wars* 1970s Sci-Fi Films**.

What Not To Wear

Rangy principal boy Trinny Woodall and callipygian toff Susannah Constantine have been mocking the style-deficient on our behalf for some years now. Initially, the show featured Beadlesque surprise attacks on unsuspecting scarecrows who were having their breasts assessed for firmness and consistency before they had fully apprehended how much trouble they were in. In more recent series our two protagonists begin by being badgered by an inchoate riot of chumps who are apparently willing to endure any amount of ridicule and bosom palpation if it means they can 'get on the telly'. Theoretically this development should have attenuated the *schadenfreude* of the viewing experience but it paradoxically ups the ante by a factor of ten to know that the saggy-bottomed wannabe contestants – who invariably look as if they've just been coated in Araldite and rolled through Primark – are foolish enough to *willingly* submit to an experience that has reduced every previous victim to a blubbering wreck within seconds of entering the 360° mirror. The fact that most of us are watching the show while seated on our sofas clad in pizza-flecked comfy trousers adds a smidgeon of guilt to the otherwise unalloyed pleasure.

When Harry Met Sally . . .

Of all the world's chick flicks, this one is the easiest for men to bear – not that they'd ever admit it. Although the formula is standard romantic-comedy pap (two people dance interminably around the issue of getting together), it does have several important things going for it. For one, Meg Ryan has never looked finer. And for another, director Rob Reiner imparts a refreshing male sensibility to the proceedings. This is the movie to suggest when your wife or girlfriend wants to get a DVD out. You'll score sensitivity points, and you won't be constantly tempted to hit the fast-forward button on the remote control. Just don't get suckered into the rest of the Meg Ryan oeuvre. See also **Pictionary**.

'Where Are They Now?' Features
In a world where fame can dry up quicker than a slug on a sun-baked patio (just try naming the winner of the second season of *Big Brother*), it's no wonder that newspapers, magazines and television shows can guarantee an audience when they promise to tell us what happened to yesterday's familiar faces. While we couldn't have cared less about, say, Chesney Hawkes or Michelle Gayle while they were making regular appearances on our living room TV, if a *Heat* article or *I Love 1989* show offers a retrospective, we're there.

Where's Wally?
These accursed volumes, laboriously painted by Martin Handford (it takes him years to create enough for a single book) are a bane to adults' self-image. The object is to locate a stripe-shirted fellow named Wally, who hides in plain sight in huge pictures jammed with hundreds of other figures. They're designed for children aged five and up, which makes it particularly embarrassing for adults who stare at the pages for fifteen minutes and *still can't find the skinny bastard*. During the early Nineties Wally books were all the rage, though a cartoon based on the character flopped. Perhaps no one could figure out which channel it was on.

Whipped Cream in a Can, Squirtable
Equally at home on a delicate plate of strawberries or as a prop in an episode of *Red Shoe Diaries*, whipped-cream-in-a-can products take a great taste and make it as convenient as (and much more palatable than) foam insulation. Credited with being the first aerosol foodstuff, it taught a generation of not terribly

creative drop-outs how to 'do whippets' by sucking the propellant out of unused cans. It's also useful at a pinch as shaving cream. See also *Red Shoe Diaries*.

Whiteley, Richard

The extraordinary and much-lamented Richard Whiteley was the first face ever seen on cutting-edge Channel 4 when they decided to launch with the extraordinary high-concept anagrams+sums *Countdown*. As host of the Queen's favourite TV programme Whiteley was said in fact to be the all-time most-seen face on British TV after Carole Hersee (the testcard girl) and at one point owned over 600 ties and 200 jackets – many sent to him by viewers who were, we hazard at a guess, all living in middle England and looking like Hyacinth Bucket. He was like a jolly uncle and slightly patrician house master and you got the feeling that, along with sidekick Carol 'one from the bottom' Vorderman, that they were kinda proud of the vibe they had going – it was a bit dull, but with a naughty twinkle, and alas things aren't the same now Des Lynam has taken over.

Whoopee Cushions

Even after outgrowing the fake puke, the handshake buzzer, and putting salt in the sugar bowl, there's still pleasure to be had when amateur, unimaginative practical jokers successfully surprise a victim with a fictional fart. See also **Practical Jokes**; **Vomit, Fake**.

Wife Swap

There are few televisual formulas more reliable or more satisfying than smug-o-vision: shows designed to make you feel better about your life by giving you an insight into the worlds of people even more clueless and maladjusted than yourself. The original and best of this style of entertainment is *Wife Swap*. From a pool of applicants, who have either never seen the programme or are desperate to be humiliated, the two most incompatible are selected. The obsessive-compulsive childless woman is transplanted into the home of the reproductively incontinent slattern and *vice* is of course *versa*. We are then encouraged to 'sit back and watch the sparks fly' – which of course we do, but only as an occasional respite from commenting to our partners that we would never be so solipsistically naïve as to take part in such a farrago and of course adumbrating the participants' myriad shortcomings. Once the half-hour is up, every reasonable viewer will then of course offer his or her partner a nice cup of tea and muse briefly on what kind of couple they might be paired with. For female musers, this generally takes the form of a reverie about being twinned with a family of millionaires with a complete home spa, while for the gentleman *Wife Swap* enthusiast thoughts tend to stray more in the direction of a curvy sexual wildcat who can rustle up a decent fried breakfast.

Wild Things See Richards, Denise.

Williams, Robbie

It may seem odd to include a pop star who can happily sell out Knebworth three nights running in a book about guilty pleasures, but Williams is a man who splits music fans down the middle. Pretty much on gender lines, if we're being honest. Ask any man why they're at a Robbie Williams show and they'll give you an answer along the lines of 'My girlfriend/wife/daughter/dog wanted to go'. Ask any man after a Robbie Williams show why they enjoyed it, and they'll give you an answer along the lines of 'He's a great entertainer', which sounds like a compliment but is a back-handed dig at his musical credentials. Well we say, what's wrong with being a great entertainer? So was Freddie Mercury. And we also say, great entertainer or not, you don't stay at the top for that long unless you write a decent tune now and again.

Wimpy Bars

Despite being bought by Burger King, there remain pockets of this great country where Wimpy Bars have not gone BK, but remain as bad and as British as ever. Maybe the problem with them was that in terms of fast food, they just weren't fast enough. I mean, on a proper plate? Perhaps the nail in the coffin was that the only response to the Big Mac would have been the Big Wimp. Or perhaps it is because, even now, you can go in there, to childish sniggers all round, and order yourself a Big Bender In a Bun.

Wine (The Ridiculous Charade of Tasting It in a Restaurant)

You are indulging in post-ordering but pre-prandial restaurant chat when you are aware of a man standing at your shoulder, holding your chosen bottle of wine at arm's length with a reverence usually reserved for religious icons. You check the label with forensic care and then give a deferential nod before he uncorks it and moves slowly but surely towards stage two of this courtship ritual. Un soupçon of your chosen Chateau de Whaddever is poured lovingly into a sparkling wineglass and as the liquid settles a hush descends on the assembled company. You look to the waiter, back to the glass, pick it up, admire your reflection, carry out the all-important 'swish to release the molecules' and lift the vessel to your nostrils to smell the bouquet. You cast an inscrutable glance at the now nervous looking waiter before lifting the glass to your lips and allowing your taste buds a tantalizingly brief sampling. The wine waiter leans closer, awaiting your pronouncement. Enjoying the moment, you keep him waiting before granting him an imperious nod – resisting the temptation to laugh out loud, grab the bottle and order some lager chasers.

Wine in a Box and Chicken in a Basket

What is it with the English obsession for serving comestibles in inappropriate containers? Whatever people say, chicken is not at its best when served in a plastic 'basket' in a self-styled 'gastro pub' accompanied by a few soggy chips and some condiments served in plastic tear-proof condom-style packets. And likewise you are never going to see Jancis Robinson, Oz Clarke or Jilly 'the nose' Goulden waxing lyrical over Blue Nun in a Tetrapak or Liebfraumilch in a plastic lining with integral 'as hard to find as a clitoris' dispenser tap. But that said, when the atmosphere is right, whether it be on a rainy day on a weekend break in Margate or at a 'bring a bottle' student party in Harlesden, these two items cannot be beaten. Yum.

Winton, Dale

Perma-tanned, blazer-clad, white-toothed and as camp as a row of tents. Housewives' choice Dale has lit up our television screens in a glittering array of programmes designed to showcase his unique versatility and breadth for the last decade or so. After an early career in regional and hospital radio he fronted the innovative game show *Supermarket Sweep* in 1993, followed by the mould-breaking game show *Pets Win Prizes*, the game show *Winton's Wonderland*, the game show *The National Lottery* and even *Dale's Wedding* (not a game show) in which he 'married' Nell McAndrew. In fact he has been the default presenter for anything lightweight and Auntie-friendly – from the *BBC Hall Of Fame: Barbara Windsor* to *Why Shoulderpads Ruled the World* to the *Fortieth Anniversary Celebration* of *Coronation Street*. Look – you are never going to tune in to see Dale presenting *Newsnight* or the *Election Special* but likewise can you imagine Paxman stepping up to the mike to front *Celebrity Fit Club* or *EastEnders – Fighting Fit*?

Wonderbra, The

An engineering feat often called the eighth architectural wonder of the world (especially if you were a B cup with aspirations), this suspension bridge for bosoms not only lifted and supported the bustline, it also gave good cleavage. Created in 1964 by Canadian designer Louise Poirier, it accomplished this by using fifty-four separate design elements, including a three-part cup, underwires, a precision-angled back, rigid straps, and removable pads called 'cookies'. When the Wonderbra Push-Up Plunge Bra first appeared in American shops, it sold at the rate of one every 15 seconds, inflating to first year sales of approximately $120 million.

These days the Wonderbra comes in 'Three Degrees of Wonder' – a trio of designs ranging from the 1st Degree (slightly lined), to the 2nd Degree (a padded or 'add-a-size' model), and the 3rd Degree (a complete push-up bra). Though this cleavage-enhancing creation remains wildly popular, the shame its wearers feel isn't all that different from the days when they stuffed their training bras with Kleenex. Because no matter how perfect the illusion, the truth will come out (in the most literal sense) as soon as your date for the night gets to first base. And once you wear a Wonderbra, it's all you can *ever* wear, lest you risk noticeable cup-jumping (going from a shapely C down to an abysmal B) from one day to the next, in front of colleagues, friends and neighbours. See also **Freemans Catalogue (Lingerie Section)**.

Word Search Puzzles

Why do people play Word Search puzzles? Probably for the same reason they while away hours on noughts and crosses: it's easy.

World's Strongest Man Competitions

It's not really a sport. It's more like a *Guinness Book of World Records* freak show.

www.imdb.com

Once you have tasted the forbidden pleasure of imdb, it's almost impossible to resist going back for more. Every time you watch a film on TV, discussions that begin with the words 'Wasn't he in . . . ?' can be settled by that ultimate arbiter of cinema knowledge. Combined with a wireless laptop for state-of-the-art sofa surfing, imdb is scientifically proven to increase the time-wasting power of television by 76 per cent.

X-Y-Z

Xanadu

This 1980 cinematic epic was like a Viking funeral pyre, upon which the last shreds of disco (along with Olivia Newton-John's acting career) were incinerated. The story, such as it was, revolved around a muse (Newton-John) sent to help two guys open a roller disco. Seriously. The cast includes veteran hoofer Gene Kelly, who tries to lend some dignity to the proceedings (a task roughly analogous to putting a dress on a pig). Ironically, the movie soundtrack spawned several hit songs ('Xanadu' and 'Magic' among them), and in its video afterlife the film has become a cult favorite of sorts. See also **Newton-John, Olivia**.

Xena: Warrior Princess

This surprise TV hit offered lots of illicit thrills: non-stop fighting, wisecracking dialogue, and, of course, the lesbian subtext between Xena and her sidekick, the blonde waif Gabrielle. All the eye candy made it possible to overlook the fact that, when it comes to historical accuracy, the typical *Xena* episode makes a Cecil B. DeMille Bible epic look like a documentary by Simon Schama. Xena is supposed to live in classical Greece, but in her travels she encounters refugees from Troy (circa 1000 B.C.); Xerxes, king of Persia (circa 500 B.C.); and even Julius Caesar, dictator of

Rome (around 50 B.C.). There was even a 'Christmas' episode, which is impressive for a programme dealing with strictly 'B.C.' events. Still, there are worse ways to kill a slow Saturday afternoon. Did we mention the lesbian subtext? See also **Biblical Epics**; **Lesbians (Film Scenes Featuring)**.

X Factor

It isn't about the music any more. It isn't about the acts. It's about the 'judges'. They spend so much time having water fights or shouting and poking each other in the ribs, it's easy to forget that the contestants are there. The only substantial difference between *X Factor* and other classic three-hander TV comedies like *The Goodies* or *Last of the Summer Wine* is that with *X*, at least one burger flipper from Sunderland will get a short-lived pop career and write a (very short) autobiography. At the end of the day, that's what it's (not) all about.

XXX Films See **Films (Pornographic)**.

Yankovic, Weird Al

Everyone's heard Yankovic's music, but almost no one will confess to owning one of his albums. Which isn't surprising. Possessing the work of the man who brought us such parody classics as 'My Bologna' (based on the Knack's 'My Sharona') and 'Eat It' (a take on Michael Jackson's 'Beat It') can earn you Permanent Resident status in Sadville.

YMCA See **Village People, The**.

You Are What You Eat

A programme about poo presented by a nannyish Scottish doctor? How many British obsessions does this combine in one show? It's hardly revolutionary, of course – a wizened old crone tells fat people to change their diets and they do (because they have already told their friends they are going to be on the telly) and they lose weight . . . Genius! Whatever next? A show in which wet people are taught how to use a towel?

You've Been Framed

Cute kittens jumping on sleeping people's heads; babies falling over in paddling pools; dogs pulling curtains down; BMX bikers speeding over hills and landing in lakes; brides and grooms falling head-first into wedding cakes; fat men falling off stages and rabbits impersonating Bruce Forsyth – all human life is here, backed with jolly sub *Carry-On* music and ironic voiceovers from Harry Hill. Of course most of the clips look rather staged and you can't help but wonder whether some parents are actually pleased when their child has a nasty-looking encounter with a Rottweiler, safe in the knowledge that those nice people at Granada will slip them two hundred and fifty notes for it but . . . oh look . . . it's that one with the monkey and that man's wig. We love that. See also *Jackass*; **Kicked in the Nuts (Watching Someone Get)**.

Your Boyfriend's Razor (Using)

When he is downstairs playing on his Xbox or snoring in front of *Ibiza Uncovered*, nothing beats 'borrowing' his Gillette Mach 3 Turbo, snaffling a brand new blade and lying back to shave your legs whilst fantasizing that David Beckham is there to sit on the edge of the bath and rub your back.

Zardoz

Enjoyably barmy Seventies science fiction film that starred Sean Connery as a barbarian battling against the ruling elite, represented by a giant floating head. It may be a subtle allegory on Connery's support for Scottish independence, but the residing image of the film is the glorified nappy the former Bond wears throughout. A rubbish film on all levels, it is still well worth watching whenever it turns up, usually late at night on Channel 5.

Acknowledgements

Michael Moran lives in London or Kent and works on the fringes of the magazine caper. His guiltiest pleasure is pretending to work on this book when he was in fact playing *Halo*, and he would like to thank his lovely wife Cassie and his adorable daughter Leah for pretending to fall for this charade.

Tom Bromley is a writer and editor and lives in Salisbury. He particularly enjoys straightening the cheese and getting the last seat on trains. He would like to thank Joanna for not taking his Tears for Fears records to Oxfam. Oxfam would also like to thank Joanna for this.

Simon Trewin lives in London where he works in publishing. This week he mostly feels guilty about Bathroom Cabinets (Looking in Other People's), Blackberry (Checking Email Constantly On) and Namedropping. He would like to thank ADH, JackT, Claire, Leo and Mr Tumnus.

The authors would like to thank their urbane guilt-free agent James Gill at PFD, their wonderful publisher Ed Faulkner and his splendid colleagues Anya Serota, Ellie Birne, James Spackman and all at John Murray (Publishers), Jon Howells for *Zardoz* and, of course, the Pope, who inspired the whole project.

Tom Bromley, Michael Moran and Simon Trewin are also the authors of *Rock and Pop Elevens* (O'Mara Books).

'To the makers of Zocor, the cholesterol-busting drug that allows me to indulge in my favourite artery-clogging guilty pleasures without keeling over – so far.' — Sam Stall

'This one's dedicated to my brother George, who still believes that E.L.O rocks.' — Lou Harry

'To Mom and Dad for their biggie-size hearts. They never doubted me – at least not to my face.' — Julie Spalding